POLITICAL THINKERS

POLITICAL THINKERS

Edited by David Muschamp

St. Martin's Press
New York

ISBN 0-312-62558-8

Contents

Notes on Contributors

Douglas Adeney, M.A. (Monash), Ph.D. (St Andrews), has taught at both Monash University and the University of St Andrews. He now lectures in philosophy at Melbourne College of Advanced Education.

Max Charlesworth, M.A. (Melbourne), Ph.D. (Louvain), formerly Reader in Philosophy, University of Melbourne, Dean of Humanities and now Professor of Philosophy, Deakin University. Author of *Philosophy and Linguistic Analysis* (1963), *St Anselm's Proslogion* (1965), *Philosophy of Religion: the Historic Approaches* (1972), *Church, State and Conscience* (1972), *The Existentialists and Jean-Paul Sartre* (1975), *Religion in Aboriginal Australia* (1984).

C.A.J. Coady, B.A. (Sydney), B. Phil. (Oxon.), M.A. (Cantab. and Melbourne), is a Reader in Philosophy at the University of Melbourne. He has held appointments at Oxford and Cambridge and in the USA. Mr Coady has published on a variety of philosophical topics in a number of prominent journals.

Brian Costar, B.A., Ph.D. (Queensland) has taught Politics at the University of Queensland and Queensland Institute of Technology. He is co-editor of *Labor to Office* (1983), and *Country to National* (1985). He is a Senior Lecturer in Political Studies at Chisholm Institute of Technology.

W.V. Doniela, M.A. (Sydney), Dr. Phil. (Freiburg). He has published in various journals including *Politics*, *Hegel-Jahrbuch* and the *Australian Journal of Philosophy*, is a member of the International Hegel Society and of The Hegel Association (West Germany) and is currently Associate Professor of Philosophy at the University of Newcastle.

Eugene Kamenka, B.A. (Sydney), Ph.D. (ANU), Professor of the History of Ideas in the Research School of Social Sciences at the Australian National University. He has worked in the UK, the USA, the USSR, Singapore and Germany and lectured in most countries of Asia. His books include *The Ethical Foundation of Marxism* (1962), *Marxism and Ethics* (1969) and *The Philosophy of Ludwig Feuerbach* (1970). He has edited, among other books, *Nationalism* (1974), *Feudalism, Capitalism and Beyond* (with R.S. Neale, 1975), *Human Rights* (with Alice Erh-Soon Tay, 1978), *Intellectuals and Revolution: Socialism and the Experience of 1848* (with F.B. Smith, 1980) and *Community as a Social Idea* (1982).

Bruce Langtry, B.A., Ph.D. (Sydney), is a Senior Lecturer in Philosophy at the University of Melbourne. He has also held appointments at the University of Sydney and the University of Tasmania. He has published on a wide range of philosophical topics, including epistemology, metaphysics and ethics.

G.D. Marshall, M.A. (N.Z.), Ph.D. (Melbourne), is a Reader in Philosophy at the University of Melbourne. He has taught at the University of Western Australia and at King's College, University of London and has published philosophical articles in the areas of philosophy of religion and of philosophical psychology.

Norma Marshall, M.A. (Melbourne) has taught Politics at La Trobe University, Swinburne Institute of Technology and at Chisholm Institute of Technology. She has published articles in various journals and in edited collections.

H.J. McCloskey, M.A., Ph.D., Litt.D. (Melbourne) is a Professor of Philosophy at La Trobe University. He is a Fellow of the Australian Academy of the Humanities and is author of many articles in learned journals and of *Meta-Ethics and Normative Ethics* (1969), *John Stuart Mill: A Critical Study* (1971), *God and Evil* (1974), *Derechos Y Sociedad En La Filosofia Analitica* translated by F. Quintana (1976), and *Ecological Ethics and Politics* (1983).

D.H. Monro, M.A. (New Zealand) became the foundation professor of Philosophy at Monash University after teaching in the Philosophy Departments of Otago and Sydney Universities. He has held visiting fellowships at Oxford and Cambridge and in Canada. He is a Fellow of the Australian Academy of the Humanities and of the Academy of the Social Sciences in Australia. His publications include *Argument of Laughter* (1951), *Godwin's Moral Philosophy* (1953), *Empiricism and Ethics* (1967), *The Ambivalence of Bernard Mandeville* (1975), *Ethics and the Environment* (1980), and *The Sonneteer's History of Philosophy* (1981).

David Muschamp, M.A. (West. Australia) has taught philosophy at the University of Western Australia, Monash University and Trinity College, University of Melbourne where he was resident senior tutor. He is currently a Senior Lecturer in Political Studies at Chisholm Institute of Technology.

Michael Stocker, B.A. (Columbia), M.A. and Ph.D. (Harvard), is a Reader in Philosophy at La Trobe University. He has held appointments at the University of Chicago, Cornell, Macquarie, Sydney, Australian National University, and the University of Utah. He has published on a variety of philosophical topics, specializing in ethics and moral psychology.

C.L. Ten, B.A. (Malaya), M.A. (London), is a Reader in Philosophy at Monash University. Before joining Monash University in 1970, he was Lecturer in Philosophy at the former University of Singapore (now the National University of Singapore). He is the author of *Mill on Liberty* (Oxford, 1980) and of papers in journals and anthologies of philosophy, law, politics, and the history of ideas.

F.C. White, M.A. (Cantab.), Ph.D. (Tasmania), read classics and moral sciences at the University of Cambridge. His works include a book on Plato, *Plato's Theory of Particulars* (New York, 1981), a book on relativism, *Knowledge and Relativism* (Assen, 1983), and papers in various journals. He is at present Reader in Philosophy at the University of Tasmania.

Robert Young, B.Ec., B.A. (Sydney), Ph.D. (Flinders) has taught at Flinders University, the University of Wales and La Trobe University where he is currently a Reader in Philosophy. He is author of *Freedom, Responsibility and God* (1975) and *Personal Autonomy: Beyond Negative and Positive Liberty* (1985).

Preface

We are all much affected by the political world which is itself very largely fashioned by political beliefs. This book is a discussion of the principal political beliefs of some of the greatest and most influential political thinkers.

The substantive volume begins with an essay on Plato (427–347 BC) and finishes with a dialogue on modern political ideas. Many of the issues raised and discussed by Plato were re-examined and rejected by his pupil Aristotle. The rediscovery of the writings of these two gave shape and energy to the Renaissance and thus to the modern world.

All the chapters were written especially for this book, which was designed principally for undergraduates. The volume should also be useful to people who, although not enrolled as tertiary students, desire to know more about the big political questions and the sorts and the strengths of the answers given to them. Readers should all expect to have to read carefully and thoughtfully, which will usually require them to re-read the text carefully and thoughtfully.

The Introduction sketches the political realm and its principal subjects, and gives an account of the elements of sound argument construction and appraisal. The essays may, of course, be read in any order, though there is much to be said for beginning with the chapter on Plato and then going either to the modern political ideas dialogue or to the chapter on the theorist of one's choice or fancy.

One of the reasons for reading this book is that, as Bertrand Russell once said, it is interesting to find out what the great thinkers thought. Another reason is that, by increasing one's understanding of the perennial political problems, one can develop a sensible and better informed rational judgement about immediate as well as recurrent political problems. The sixteen authors would hope that readers will be satisfied in both respects.

Introduction

The Political Realm and its Principal Subjects

Political predicaments began shortly after God created Adam and they have multiplied ever since. They caused Theseus to know the labyrinth, Israel to flee from Egypt, Arthur to round his table, Joan to be burned at Rouen. Bright swords and ballot boxes, concentration camps and courts of justice, gold coin and silver speeches, high roads and low incomes: all these are at once signs and products of the political worlds which people inhabit.

While many problems, activities, relationships and institutions are usefully said to be political, some things are not political. Attempts to distinguish the realm of the political – in which realm the thinkers discussed in this book spent at least a good deal of their time and which they explored, mapped, altered and disputed – fall into three main types.

One way of making the 'political'/'non-political' distinction is by pointing to something or other – ostensive definition. It is said that a great and well-loved Cambridge philosopher sometimes preferred this way. Answering the question 'What is philosophy?' Professor Moore gestured to his bookshelves and replied, 'It is what all these are about'. This, while probably true, was only rather helpful since it contains at least a trace of circularity.

The second way is by verbal definition, in which one attempts to capture the essential characteristics of the one which are not possessed by the other. Thus: 'politics (and not astronomy, botany or philately) is whatever concerns the state,' 'politics (and not astrophysics or numismatics or zoology) is the study of power relations between people', and the like. Among the many things to say here, is this: a person has to know a good deal about the thing being defined to know which of the competing definitions is best, so while verbal definitions may provide a good beginning they are rarely decisive in instructing one who knows little about either the elements in the definition or the closeness of the definition to the concept.

The third main way of acquiring the distinction is by examining the ways words such as 'politics', 'political' and 'politician' are used. We say such things as 'Politics is a dirty business', 'I left the tennis club because it became too political', 'Professor Aardvark was a great zoologist but a hopeless politician', 'Morality (or sport, or art, or religion) and politics don't mix', 'Humans are political animals', 'I'm glad I live in a country where some things are not political'. In understanding these statements we use 'politics', 'political' and 'politician' in different but, of course, related ways. Some com-bination of these three ways of finding out more about what 'political' encapsulates and thus what political thinkers would think about may produce some richer view than one had had, although on this as on many similar matters, the observation of St Augustine may commend itself to readers: 'When you ask me, I do not know, but when you do not ask me, then I know.' We can say, certainly and vaguely, that the terms 'politics', 'political' and 'politician' cover such a large area of the unknownly deep continent which is human activity, that political thought must be said to be reflection upon a very extensive range of human behaviour and arrangements.

'Politics' is also widely used as the name of a broad area of academic study whose purpose is to assist us to understand the sorts of things said in the previous paragraph. Perhaps the term 'Political Studies' is more apt because it is more clear – it shows that we are examining political matters rather than engaging directly in some form of primary political behaviour such as standing for election, making a speech, deciding who will pay more taxes and the like. Political Studies shares the characteristic of standing aside from and reflecting upon human activities with such other academic disci-plines as Psychology, Sociology, History and Language Studies. These academic studies are often said to be the first-order disciplines in the great family the Humanities. First-order disciplines in the Physical Sciences, such as Physics and Chemistry, have in common with the Humanities and with the Biological Sciences such as Botany, Zoology and Genetics, the primary aim of increasing human knowledge. Philosophy is a second-order discipline whose task is to classify and analyze the terms, statements and arguments of the first-order disciplines. Both logic and mathematics are tools for engaging in the first and second-order disciplines and each is the subject of intellectual inquiry in its own right.

This crude and bald account of discipline areas is very different from the picture which would have been given to undergraduates at universities at their origins in the High Middle Ages and it is rather different from the picture most orthodox educated Europeans had even well after the Enlightenment. During all this time, indeed even before Plato's school in the grove of Academus, people's beliefs about the world largely determined in what ways they studied it. If the world was seen as being like a machine, such and such a way of investigating it would be best; if like an organism, some other would be better; (if like a god, perhaps it should be left alone). Furthermore, people's study of the world often transformed their picture of it, their *weltanschauung*. It often still does.

Disputes about what things should be studied and how they should be studied have occurred and do occur within particular discipline areas. Indeed, disputes about directions and emphases, methods and methodologies, and truth and significance have often been more energetic inside most disciplines than they have been between them. This is certainly true of Political Studies.

Fairly recently, from about the 1880s until about the middle of the 1950s, the generally received view about Political Studies, or at least what was conceived to be the important part of it which was called Political Science, was that its task was to produce descriptive or factual accounts of political institutions, activities and relationships. The mass of information so obtained was then, usually by the application of theories about the functions of the institutions, activities and relationships, used to produce general principles which were supposed to account for the operations of the political systems studied. All of this, it was often argued, could and should be 'value-free', that is neutral with regard to judgements about the moral worth of the functionings and ideal ends to which the political institutions should be tailored. Such stuff about values was often labelled ideology and when this term was used by those positivists who reduced moral judgements to statements about mere and perhaps whimsical or idiosyncratic or socially induced feelings, it seemed to many that the funeral of classical political thinking which discussed moral as well as descriptive statements, would soon take place. Political Science was thus often said to be purely empirical and not at all judgemental, a view which required that the distinction be sustained permanently. This distinction between empirical political phenomena (the subject of rational inquiry) on the one hand and wishy-washy talk about ideals in politics on the other hand, had been attacked, principally by philosophers, for some time and by the 1960s it had been dropped by almost everyone.

We can mention here only two of the many causes of this collapse of the distinction between the Purely Descriptive and the Merely Prescriptive. The first was the recognition of what austere empiricists had blinkered themselves from seeing, that rational discussions about the merits of competing ideals do take place and not only in

Figure 1. A contemporary map of the Political Studies continent

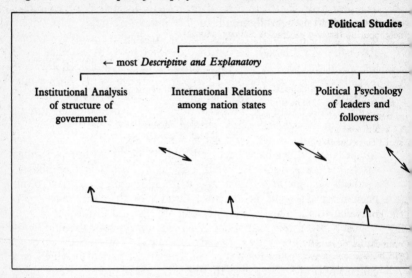

the shadows of monstrous massacres and barbarous brutalities but also in the more decently human activities such as the formation of public policy about the distribution of valuables such as health, educational and transport services. Since these discussions do arise, they will best be examined openly and sensibly.

The second major cause of the abandonment of the harsh good fact/bad value distinction was the acceptance of the observation and argument that there are moral strands and fibres in most language concerning matters about human activities.

Consequently Political Studies is in most places seen as being composed of a number of connected areas of investigation, discussion and theorizing. A contemporary map of the Political Studies continent would be such as shown in Figure 1.

The political thinkers discussed in this book span a considerable period, and between them they have argued about all of the areas shown in the diagram. Some, Plato and Aristotle supremely, raised for the first time the questions they answered; others, Machiavelli, Locke and Mill supremely, gave a new sharpness to old questions. Most of them attempted to show why what was so was so; that is, they tried to produce explanatory theories. Yet, and more than this, they attempted to weave these theories into theories about what should be the case; that is, they tried to produce justificatory theories in answer to broad and fundamental questions. The most important political questions, which between them the great political thinkers discussed in this book raised and answered, are or can be found in aspects of the following:

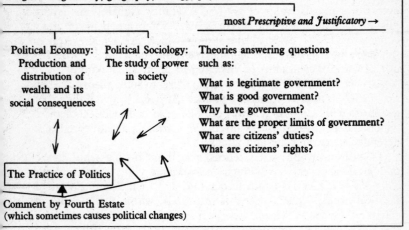

relates to and draws upon resources of
neighbouring history, geography, biology, physics

most *Prescriptive and Justificatory* →

Political Economy:
Production and
distribution of
wealth and its
social consequences

Political Sociology:
The study of power
in society

Theories answering questions
such as:

What is legitimate government?
What is good government?
Why have government?
What are the proper limits of government?
What are citizens' duties?
What are citizens' rights?

The Practice of Politics

Comment by Fourth Estate
(which sometimes causes political changes)

(1) What sort of beings are people?
(2) What is government?
(3) What, if anything, constitutes a legitimate government?
(4) What is a good government?
(5) What are the proper limits of government?
(6) Have citizens any duties to their governments, and if so, what and when?
(7) Have any citizens any rights, and if so, what are these and which have they, when?

The first two of these questions are usually answered as if they are standard enough (which is not to say simple enough) requests for clarification of an idea, notion or concept. 'What is?' questions of this type ('What is a weed, a slave, an ICBM, a government, a person?') are partially answered when important characteristics are pointed to in reply and are completely answered when intelligible, logically equivalent terms are given. Sometimes one may be deceived in either item, that is, one may suppose that the terms are intelligible when they are not or one may suppose that the terms are equivalent when they are not. Thus 'a weed is a plant out of place', 'a slave is anyone who has to work in order to survive', 'an ICBM is an essential consequence of technological capitalism', 'government is the most efficient means of the rich exploiting the poor', 'a person is any being entitled to own property' replaces the term to be accounted for by an idea which is not its logical equivalent. In these and millions of other instances, someone is trying to sell not a descriptive definition but a stipulative or persuasive definition. While many of these are illuminating and even witty ('a house is a machine for living in', 'a cynic is one who knows the price of everything and the value of nothing', 'tyranny is merely monarchy misliked') others are not worth much. Some are bankruptingly expensive at any price. Determining which are which requires sensible and informed rational judgement the acquisition of which is one of the principal aims of engaging in political thinking.

Answers to 'what is?' questions may lead to some theory or they may be left as isolated items of language. Answers to any of the seven questions will be or will readily become the sorts of political theories which the political thinkers discussed in this book advanced and defended or denounced and attacked.

Theories in the physical sciences (and, if one distinguishes, in the biological sciences) have much in common with theories about elections and theories about leadership, all of which are aspects of Political Studies: their success is measured, within the confines of clarity of concepts, internal consistency and external coherence by their explanatory and predictive powers, and their utility. The success of theories about at least the last five of our seven fundamental political questions is measured not only or even principally by the

Figure 2. A Legitimacy Map

Question: What, if anything, transforms political power into political authority?			
Answer: Nothing	Tradition¨	God¨	Supremacy of Power¨
Anarchists e.g. Wat Tyler?	A large number of	Pharaohs, 'Divine'	Thrasymachus ('Who has
Proudhon	societies	Caesars,	the gold
Kropotkin	including	Dalai Lama,	makes the
Bakunin	Australian	Ayatollahs	rules')
Marx	Aborigines	————	but doesn't
(differs	(*vide* Weber)	Divine	address the
from e.g.		Right of	question
Proudhon)		Kings	
Tolstoy?		(e.g. James I)	
R.P. Wolff		Filmer;	
		attacked by	
		Locke in	
		First	
		Treatise	

¨   these theories justify loss of liberty
\#   these theories are Social Contract theories
+   these theories say you can obey and be free.
@   see-able as necessary but not sufficient conditions

sorts of related empirical generalizations which form the chief part of the other types of theories (about the behaviour of genetic tissue or gases or unsupported objects or stags in the rutting or voters or wages or power elites or leaders); they are not principally explanatory or predictive, they possess a large slice of the justificatory. That is, they account for things not only in the links and chains of empirical causal occurrences, but also in terms of argued values. Thus, where physicists have as central concepts 'particle', 'mass', 'velocity', 'temperature' and so on, our political thinkers use 'justice', 'equality', 'liberty', 'dignity', 'destiny', 'progress', 'the state', 'power', 'happiness', 'rights' and the like as their central conceptual tools. In all of these there is at least a strong strand of the moral, the judgemental, the gerundive. A great deal of political language, like moral language, its sibling, is used to denounce, to commend, to claim and to command: it is the language of the advocate, the judge, the prophet and the seer, the huckster, the charlatan and the saint.

Something of this is shown when we look at sets of competing answers to any of the fundamental political questions and especially any of the last five of them. Let us take the first of the considerably justificatory questions, 'What, if anything, constitutes a legitimate government?' as an example of and a pattern for the questions which followed it on our list. As always, the first thing to do is to clarify the

Historical Evolution"	Contracted Sovereign"#	Consent of the Ruled #+	The General Will #+	Good Consequences @
Burke	Hobbes	American	Rousseau	e.g. the
Hegel?		Settlers	some	production
Spencer		Locke	Fascists	of
Marxists?		Jefferson, etc.	many	Justice
Spengler		Rawls (hypo-	dictators	Security
Oakeshott		thetical)		Liberty
		Nozick		Happiness
		(invisible)		Dignity
				etc.,

terms used, if possible by providing intelligible, logically equivalent terms. If we say – as we don't have to but as we reasonably might – that a legitimate government is the proper repository of supreme political power, we have made a beginning. If we say – what is difficult to resist – that political power consists in the ability to make decisions and to enforce them, then we have proceeded down the track. What we now want is a transformation theory, that is a theory which distinguishes political power from political authority. The first might be obeyed solely because one had to, the second could be obeyed because one believed one ought to obey. Political authority is proper political power: the question of legitimacy is the question 'what, if anything, transforms a political power into a political authority, whose commands one ought (defeasibly) to obey?'

The map[1] shown in Figure 2, a rich thing and not my own, helps to locate the theories of some important political thinkers on political legitimacy.

All of the great political thinkers discussed in this book held some position about power and authority, as do the people represented in the last chapter, Professor Monro's 'Modern Political Ideas'. Most of them have positions on the other questions as well, that is they would claim to have a general theory about these matters of political facts and values. Often their positions and theories are their response to the positions and theories of other people which they find unsatisfactory.

Any of us may find other people's political positions and theories inadequate; indeed, we sometimes reflect upon our own beliefs and find them unsatisfactory. Such a finding is either the product of rational analysis (whose results may take us by surprise) or they are the expression of moral and political intuitions which arise in our passive breast. Either way, old doubts and new positions must be put to the test of rational appraisal if we are to suppose that the opinions are worth holding and acting upon. Let us, therefore, consider what are the constituents of good argument.

Thinking

Like thinkers in other areas, political thinkers do not merely assert, they argue. Unless one supposes that all arguments are of equal rational worth and that this worth is zero (a view which one couldn't

---

[1] Eric D'Arcy and John Price devised something like this when they worked together in the Philosophy Department of the University of Melbourne. I am grateful to Mr Price, who later taught with me at Chisholm, for his permission to reproduce what I remember of it, and to Dr D'Arcy, who is now the Roman Catholic Bishop of Sale, for his imprimatur.

sensibly argue for) one has to say that some arguments are better than others. The general theory of what makes arguments good or bad is logic, about which only little can be said here.

To begin, here is some essential terminology:

An *argument* is a contention supported by reasons: thus 'this is better because it is stronger' is an argument. The process of passing from the reasons (or premises or considerations) to the contention (or conclusion or result) is called *inference*.

Statement, *proposition* and *assertion* all mean roughly the same as each other (though some logicians distinguish between them). They all refer to any remark which could be said to be true or false: thus 'he is jubilant' is a statement, but 'is he jubilant?' or 'is he jubilant!' and other questions and exclamations as well as commands and exhortations are not propositions. The premises and the conclusion of an argument must be propositions.

All propositions are said to have *quantity*, either universal ('all') or particular ('some') and a *quality*, either affirmative or negative. Thus 'some political thinkers are foolish' is particular affirmative, 'no political thinkers are stupid' is universal negative, and so on.

Logicians generally recognize two great types of good arguments, *deductive* and *inductive*.

In all logically correct deductive arguments, the conclusion must follow logically from the premises. When this is the case, the form or structure of the argument is *valid*, that is, in accordance with justifiable rules. Only one type of deductive reasoning can be mentioned here, the *syllogism* which, in standard form is an argument containing two premises and a conclusion. Thus: (premises) 'All A's are B's. All B's are C's. Therefore (conclusion) all A's are C's.'.

Syllogisms are engagingly impartial. Our approval or disapproval of the conclusion is irrelevant, as is our opinion of the person who advanced the argument. If a syllogism is structured in accordance with the following six rules it is valid, and it is bootless to gainsay.

Rule 1. Every syllogism must contain exactly three terms, all of which must be used in the same sense throughout the argument.

Rule 2. The term which does not appear in the conclusion (the 'middle term', B in the above example,) must be quantified by a universal ('distributed') in at least one premise.

Rule 3. No term can be distributed in the conclusion if it is not distributed in the premise.

Rule 4. No syllogism can have two negative premises.

Rule 5. If either premise is negative, the conclusion must be negative.

Rule 6. When the conclusion is particular, one of the premises must be particular.

Of course, simply from the fact that a syllogism is valid (that is, does not break one of the six rules) one cannot properly infer that its conclusion is true. Thus: 'All great political thinkers were tee-totallers. Plato and Aristotle were great political thinkers. Therefore Plato and Aristotle were teetotallers'. The first premise is false so the argument is unsound. Again, the premises and the conclusion may be true yet, because the form of the argument is invalid, the argument is fatally flawed. Thus: 'Some great political thinkers were Christians. Augustine, Aquinas, Luther, Hobbes, Locke and Burke were Christians. Therefore Augustine, Aquinas, Luther, Hobbes, Locke and Burke were great political thinkers'. What is certain is that when an argument's form is valid and when both its premises are true, the conclusion is rationally irresistible and the argument is impeccable.

Inductive argument differs from deductive argument in this respect: that where the inductive method is used there is always some theoretical possibility that the premises are true yet the conclusion is false. Inductive theory coincides with probability theory since it discusses the question 'what are the chances of the premises being true but the conclusion being false?' Thus: 'there has never been general agreement about what is the best theory of justice, therefore there never will be general agreement about what is the best theory of justice' is an inductive argument, as is 'no-one has ever made 1,000 runs and taken 20 wickets in the same Test match so no-one ever will'. Conan Doyle's master detective Sherlock Holmes was no doubt right in many of his inferences concerning tobacco and red hair and silent dogs but he was wrong in calling his thinking process deduction. Holmes played empirical probabilities not logical certainties.

While we can be simply delighted to discover that all our arguments are either deductive or inductive, in the manner of Molière's M. Jourdain when he discovered that he had been speaking prose all his life, it is also possible to gain real benefit from the discovery. One can of course talk in prose (or even in poetry) without knowing rules of grammar but knowing rules of grammar is likely to help us avoid grammatical mistakes. Moreover, if we disagree about the correctness of a sentence and we want to settle our dispute we must appeal to the rules of grammar. Similarly with logic. Logicians may make mistakes and people innocent of learning may argue well but we can only know this by appeal to the rules of logic. Moreover, training in examining arguments does develop our ability to make good arguments of our own and it does sharpen our capacity to detect flaws in, and thus to protect ourselves from, the arguments of other people as well as the arguments we ourselves construct. Irving M. Copi says this better than I just have and he says much more besides in the Preface to the Fourth Edition of his *Introduction to Logic*.

> There are obvious benefits to be gained from the study of logic: heightened ability to express ideas clearly and concisely; increased skill in defining one's terms; enlarged capacity to formulate arguments rigorously and to scrutinize them critically. But the greatest benefit, in my judgment, is the recognition that reason can be applied in every aspect of human affairs.
>
> Democratic institutions are under attack today from all directions. They can best be defended by being made to work. And this can be accomplished only by each citizen thinking for himself, discussing issues freely with his fellows, deliberating, weighing evidence, and acknowledging that with effort we can tell the difference between good and bad arguments. If we are to govern ourselves well and responsibly, we must be reasonable. The study of logic can give us not only practice in reasoning but respect for reason.[2]

One way of increasing both our respect for reason and our skill in reasoning is to look at some types of correct argument, as we have done with the syllogism. Another way is to look at some types of incorrect argument.

There are very many types or patterns of incorrect argument, called fallacies, and we can here mention only the most common and the most seductive.

Most authorities speak of two species of fallacies, formal and informal. The first includes those deductive arguments which are defective because they break any of the six rules of the syllogism. The most commonly breached is Rule 2 which requires that the middle term be distributed in at least one of the premises. Here is an example of a syllogism with an undistributed middle:

All students are intelligent and industrious.
Charlie is intelligent and industrious.
Therefore Charlie is a student.

A subspecies of the undistributed middle fallacy is the guilt by association fallacy, much employed in armchair pursuit and detection of heretics, traitors, witches and other unworthies. Thus:

(All)   Nazis wore boots.
        Biggles wore boots.
        Therefore Biggles was a Nazi.

This type of fallacy is also useful in producing unjustifiable claims of

---

[2]   Irving M. Copi, *Introduction to Logic*, New York, 1972.

unjustified merit and it might be called the virtue by membership fallacy. Thus:

(All)   Saintly people ate food.
        Marmaduke ate food.
        Therefore Marmaduke was saintly.

Two other common formal fallacies occur in mixed hypothetical syllogisms, whose first premise is such as:

If Charlie has a highly paid job Charlie is clever.

One is affirming the consequent: Charlie is clever, therefore Charlie has a highly paid job.

The other is denying the antecedent: Charlie is not clever therefore Charlie has not got a highly paid job.

Variations on these formal fallacies are sources of useful and harmless fun and there are many companion logic text books to enhance it.

Most authorities, whom we will again follow, divide informal fallacies into two groups, fallacies of ambiguity and fallacies of relevance.

We all have our favourites of each and this is not the place lavishly to discuss and exemplify them but rather to list a few in the hope that the reader will recognize instances of them and will profit by reflecting upon them.

Copi lists five fallacies of ambiguity:

(1)   *Equivocation:* same word but different meanings, e.g. 'bank', 'pen', 'brother'; and see Rule 1 of the valid syllogism.

(2)   *Amphiboly:* whole statement is so unclear that it might be true on one interpretation and false on another, e.g. 'Mary and Joseph and the Babe lying in the manger'. The inexact use of negative signs, especially 'not', is a rich source of confusion, e.g. 'everybody won't get the same pay', 'all that blisters is not gold'!

(3)   *Accent:* where emphasis on a word or some words alters the meaning, e.g. 'he seems to be a very kind person'.

(4)   *Composition:* where what is true of the parts is wrongly alleged to be therefore true of the whole, e.g. 'every part of the aeroplane costs less than $1,000, therefore the whole aeroplane costs less than $1,000'.

(5)   *Division:* the reverse of the fallacy of composition, that is, that what is true of the whole must be true of the parts, e.g. 'the aeroplane costs $180 million, therefore every part costs $180 million'.

Fallacies of relevance might well be thought of as fallacies of irrelevance because of the irrelevance of the considerations or supports to their contentions or conclusions. Appeals to force ('if you don't agree I'll hurt you') abuse of opponent ('he's got a shifty face') or of types of opponents ('he's a typical trade-union grizzle grouper') arguments from ignorance ('we don't know she's innocent so she must be guilty') appeals to pity ('he can't be guilty because he is an orphaned unemployed sincere agnostic') and their cousins, appeals to flattery ('a clever person like you') the traveller's fallacy ('I've been to South Africa so I know about apartheid') and the untravelled fallacy ('you've never been to South Africa so you know nothing about apartheid'), appeals to authority ('Professor Muller says this chocolate is nutritious so it must be') false cause – especially post hoc, propter hoc ('the rain began after the plane flew through the cloud, therefore the flight of the plane caused the rain'), accident, where exceptional circumstances render a useful rule inapplicable ('you shouldn't ever help any person because some might resent help') begging the question ('he must have committed the crime because I'm sure he's guilty') are part of a longer list of engaging and recurrent fallacies. The great political thinkers had not been inoculated against ever committing a fallacy: it is comforting as well as cautionary to see instances of their errors and to be reminded of the fallibility of us all.

Companion Reference Books
Roger Scruton's *A Dictionary of Political Thought*, London, 1983, is a peerless and invaluable compilation of political thought and political practices. Equally splendid in a related area is A.G.N. Flew (ed.) *A Dictionary of Philosophy*, London, 1983.

Chapter One

Plato and the Good of the Whole

F.C. White

Plato, almost certainly the greatest philosopher of the West, was born at Athens in 427 B.C., and died there in 347, at the age of eighty. Thus the years of his childhood and early manhood were spent during the Peloponnesian War, a conflict which ended in the defeat and collapse of his native city, in 404 B.C.

As we might have expected, Plato's political beliefs were greatly influenced by these events and their consequences; but this, while important to the historian and to the sociologist, is of little significance to the student of political philosophy. The interest of the latter, at any rate in the view of those who side with the non-historical, non-sociological tradition initiated by Plato himself, lies not in accounting for the origin and shaping of political ideas, but in analyzing them and in assessing their worth. Accordingly, no further biographical references will be made in this chapter.

Plato's best known and most challenging political thoughts were set down in his central dialogue, the *Republic*, and consequently this is the work now to be looked at – a composition of lasting fame and importance due to three of its characteristics. The first of these is that it displays an attractively bold method of doing political philosophy: a method harshly rejected in past decades, but now restored to favour through the works of Rawls and Nozick. It consists of a systematic, sustained treatment of issues – for example, the issues of the just society, the state and the individual – without reference to passing historical circumstances. Instead, it appeals to timeless principles. The second characteristic ensuring its lasting fame is that the *Republic* reaches bold and novel conclusions of major interest in their own right: that is, independently of the merits of the theory and arguments used to support them. Third, the *Republic* provides epistemological and metaphysical foundations for its political theory, and attempts in addition to integrate this theory with

Plato's views on aesthetics, theology, psychology and education. Finally, these many tasks are undertaken with a literary style as yet unrivalled.

The quickest way to achieve an understanding of the *Republic's* political philosophy is through an examination of its fundamental tenets or principles. There are three of these.

Principle 1

> *A political society constitutes a natural whole, with its own kind of excellence and well-being.*

This claim contrasts with atomistic views, according to which a political society is a mere aggregate of individuals existing side by side – either inertly, like the grains in a heap of sand, or in active and natural hostility. But at the same time it does not entail that a political society constitutes a unique sort of item, existing over and above its individual parts and in possession of an independent destiny or set of goals. What Plato holds is something in between. He says nothing which could be seen to favour later theories of the 'organic state'; yet plainly he views society as more of a unity than many liberals would allow, and makes this clear in several ways. To begin with, he claims to find many close likenesses between society and the individual. He spends about one third of the *Republic* [368–444],[1] for example, arguing that a society and an individual are so similar that each has a proper and analogous set of virtues. A society, he asserts, is capable of being wise, just, courageous and temperate; and in saying this he is not referring to the obvious fact that a society may contain wise, just, courageous and temperate people. He means that a society is so tight a whole that it can itself be just, courageous and the rest. Moreover, he holds that the virtues of a society are easier to discern than those of an individual; owing to which they can help our understanding of the latter.

In addition to these points, there are less intricate parallels that Plato draws. For example, he likens society as a whole to a statue, the proper unity of which ought not to be destroyed by an ill-judged distribution of colour [420]. Elsewhere he likens society's populace to a great beast [493], and to the crew of a ship [488].

More important yet, Plato expounds the thesis that the character, opinions and attitudes of individuals are the products of society, and that an individual, therefore, in his or her most important aspects,

---

[1]   The figures in square brackets (referring to the pages of the 1578 edition of Plato by Stephanus) are those usually given in the margins of translations.

has no existence without society [491–3]. It follows plainly that society is more than an aggregate of atomic, pre-existing and self-made particulars.

Plato's commitment to the first principle may further be seen from the way in which he describes the origins and functions of a society. In the second book of the *Republic*, where he sets out to show what he means by justice (in society), he proceeds as follows. A society, he argues, is founded upon those needs which are common to men, and which the latter can satisfy efficiently only if they co-operate by dividing their labour. Some individuals are gifted, say, with the skills of the shoemaker, others with those of the farmer. If these individuals work on the land while the former concentrate on shoes, all will more successfully satisfy their wants than if each party were to engage in both forms of labour. And so on, *mutatis mutandis*, for other skills. Having explained this, Plato goes on to trace the inevitable development of society from these logical beginnings up to the stage where soldiers and finally rulers are needed. And now he makes the important point that the task of these rulers – emerging naturally and in keeping with the principle of the division of labour – is to care uniquely for that co-operative whole which constitutes society. They are 'to look upon society as their special concern', to be 'full of zeal to do whatever they believe is for the good of society, and never willingly to act against its interests' [412]. But above all they are to possess that kind of knowledge which takes thought 'not for some particular interest, but for the best possible conduct of the *society as a whole*, both in its internal and in its external relations' [428].

Finally, the principle that society is a whole with a common good is supported in the brilliant pages where Plato describes different corrupt societies. All of these turn out to be of the kind in which sight is lost of the common good, and in which sectional interests prevail [544–69].

In the light of his views on the nature of society, one would expect Plato to underline the importance of unity, and to stress that divisions are destructive. He does. An excellent society, he tells us, is one in which there is agreement on all sides: about who should rule, who should fight, who should farm, and so on. It is, further, one in which there is the sort of harmony which results when individuals contribute to society the best which nature and education together make possible. It is not surprising, then, that when Plato comes to ask explicitly in what sort of society justice is to be found, he answers: in the kind of society which is so constituted that its well-being as a whole is secured, not that of any particular group [420].

It is important to be clear about what Plato means here, and even more what he does not mean, by the 'well-being of society as a whole', since subsequent philosophers have made use of the same phrase. He does not mean the simple criterion that the utilitarian philosopher applies: the greatest amount of happiness for the greatest number of individuals. Nor does he mean the sort of well-being that might follow from the application of Rawls' difference principle[2] – the principle that the plight of the worst-off members of society is to be considered first. In Plato's view, the well-being of the whole is attained when the interest of no group in society predominates – whether that group comprise the wealthy, the powerful, the ambitious, or simply the majority.[3] Much of the *Republic* in fact constitutes a head-on attempt to refute the opposing claim, advanced by the sophist Thrasymachus, that what is right is what furthers the interests of a particular group: namely, that which happens to be the strongest in society [338].

One final point on the *Republic's* first principle. Plato's concern with the well-being of society does not mean that he is not interested in the individual. It is doubtful if any philosopher has shown a more persistent concern for the individual's well-being. In many dialogues he gives the impression that he cares for nothing else; and even here in the *Republic* – for all its politics – he is concerned chiefly to defend the thesis that justice *in the individual* is better than injustice. It is important to bear this in mind, since the second principle may appear to deny it.

Principle 2

> *A political society should look to its well-being as a whole as an overriding aim: that is, as an aim which, in cases of conflict, takes precedence over others.*

This principle is very much opposed to the liberal assertion that individuals, in what concerns their well-being, are endowed with natural, sovereign and inalienable rights – antecedently to society. It is not opposed, however, to the weaker claim that individuals have rights consequent upon society – that is, derived from it and partially constitutive of its well-being. An example will bring out what is at issue here. Two philosophers may with equal conviction hold that men have the right to possess property; but while one of them sees this as a claim which is so independent that it may, if necessary, be

---

[2]   In addition Rawls has a prior principle, protecting the individual's basic liberties. See *A Theory of Justice*, (Oxford 1972), pp. 60ff.

[3]   Although the notion of well-being is expressed negatively here, Plato always has the positive good of society in view: its happiness, the satisfaction of needs, wants and so on. That no group be favoured is a necessary condition, but not sufficient, of society's well-being.

adduced against society, the other interprets it as having force only because it is guaranteed by society and necessary to its well-being.

Plato's commitment to this second principle is evident in many places; as, for example, where he discusses the education of the future rulers of his ideal society. He does not see this education as a fundamental right of his rulers *qua* individuals; nor does he see it as something to be justified on the grounds of its intrinsic worth. Rather, he sees it simply as a preparation for his future rulers *qua rulers* [376–412]. From childhood onwards, up to the age of thirty-five, they are to be prepared exclusively for dedicated service to society, and everything is to be subordinated to this end. Thus, whatever literature is put before them during their early, character-forming years, is to come under the scrutiny of the censor, and such things as disedifying stories about the gods, or unnerving accounts of the after-life, are to be banned. This is not because these stories are false – or not only because they are false – but because they are likely to have a bad effect on the future rulers, and through them on society [377–92].

Plato asserts later on – to the surprise of his own contemporaries and still to some of ours – that women are to be recognized as equal to men in being candidates for selection to rule. Plato is not uniformly appreciative in this way of the claims of women [388, 455], but he finds no difficulty in making his unexpected assertion; for if the well-being of society requires that women be rulers, he thinks there is nothing further to be said [451–7].

To take another example, Plato argues that none but those educated to rule are to take part in the government of his ideally just society. Indeed he holds that the essential feature of an unjust society is precisely the interference in government by those without the required character and education. But, however special the rulers are, and although they usually 'breed true', Plato does not fall into thinking of them as members of an hereditary class. Rather, he lays down that a child born of rulers, but lacking the right qualities, is to be excluded from becoming a ruler; while a child of other parents, but possessing the right qualities, is to be advanced [415]. As in other cases, Plato makes this stipulation – much against the grain of his aristocratic upbringing – because it accords with the sovereignty of the common good.

So far it has been shown that the well-being of society is important in Plato's eyes, but not that it is overriding. There is no doubt, however, that he does consider it overriding, since on all issues (among those mentioned) where liberal philosophers ascribe fundamental rights to individuals, Plato gives precedence to society. For example, liberal philosophers for the most part accord men and women the following rights: to marry; to have children if and as they judge fit (instead of being used as selected sires and dams); to own property; to be told the truth on important political matters – or at least not to be told lies; to live where they wish; to have a say in how society should be run. According to Plato, by contrast, in the interests of society his rulers are to be prevented from marrying [457]; they are not to be allowed money or property [416]; they are to live and train in common barracks [416, 458]; they are to breed as and with whom their elders design [458–60]; they are not to know who their children are [457]; they are to take part willy-nilly in the ruling of society [519, 539–40]. These measures are intuitively disturbing; and Adeimantus, who in the *Republic* is discussing the matter with Plato's mouthpiece, Socrates, says so. The answer which Socrates gives him is worth quoting:

> . . . our aim in founding the commonwealth was not to make any one class specially happy, but to secure the greatest possible happiness for the community as a *whole*. We thought we should have the best chance of finding justice in a state so constituted, just as we should find injustice where the constitution was of the worst possible type; we could then decide the question which has been before us all this time. For the moment, we are constructing, as we believe, the state which will be happy as a *whole*, not trying to secure the well-being of a select few; we shall study a state of the opposite kind presently [420].

The same point is made later on:

> You have forgotten again, my friend, that the law is not concerned to make any one class specially happy, but to ensure the welfare of the commonwealth as a whole. By persuasion or constraint it will unite the citizens in harmony, making them share whatever benefits each class can contribute to the common good; and its purpose in forming men of that spirit was not that each should be left to go his own way, but that they should be instrumental in binding the community into one [519–20].

Those who are not rulers or future rulers lead a much freer life; but they too are without many of the rights that most liberals would grant them. They have no vote or any other formal means of influencing the running of society [427–34]; they can be moved, and even separated from their families at the rulers' will [540–1]; they can be lied to [414–5]; they are not even allowed to make money as they please – since the rulers will take care to abolish extremes of wealth and poverty [421–3].

It will be obvious that on these points Plato is in stark opposition to those who would argue that in establishing what constitutes a good and just society we should look solely to the rights of individuals, and should allow governments to play no more than the role of night-watchmen – protecting individuals but not otherwise interfering.

Principle 3

What constitutes the well-being of society is a matter of objective fact, discoverable by those who have the relevant ability and specialized training.

On this principle, what is politically good and right is as much a matter of fact as that the earth turns on its axis or orbits about the sun; for Plato, moral and political claims are not questions of decision, convention or prescription. *A fortiori* they are not arbitrary, and consequently the rulers of any society have moral and political facts to measure up to: they have no better grounds for judging at whim in politics than mathematicians have in mathematics.

Plato does not simply assume this principle and then go on to make use of it. He attempts to back it up with an epistemological theory, a simplified interpretation of which is as follows. First, in all cases in which a statement is true, this is because it corresponds to the way the world is – in other words, to certain features of reality. Second, there are two kinds of statement. There are those which are contingent: that is, those whose truth-values could have been different from what in fact they are. (The statement that Tom, my cat, is on the mat is true; but it could have been false.) And there are those which are necessary: those whose truth-values could not have been different. (It is true, for example, that the angles of an equilateral triangle are equal; and this statement could not have been false.) Third, the reason for the contingency of statements of the former kind is that the sorts of things they are about are themselves contingent: that is, they do not have to be as they are, and as a matter of fact are constantly changing. (Tom does not have to be on the mat: he could well have been on the roof.) Correspondingly, the necessity of the truth-values of statements of the other kind is rooted in the fact that these are about things which could not be, or have been, other than as they are, and consequently are unchanging. (Equilateral triangles could not be, or have been, other than equi-angular.) In brief then: if a sentence is true, it is true because it corresponds to the relevant features of reality; if it is only contingently true, this is because it corresponds to features which themselves are contingent; if it is necessarily true, it corresponds to features which themselves are necessary. In Plato's terminology, these necessary, unalterable items or features of reality are said to be 'Forms'. Numbers, for example, are Forms, and so are the shapes and solids dealt with in geometry books: their properties never alter. But so too, according to Plato, are such things as Justice, Beauty and Goodness. These are as unchangeable in their properties as numbers and geometrical shapes; and consequently they too are capable of constituting the subject-matter of unalterable, necessary truths.

Finally, Plato believes that the apprehension of these Forms, and a systematic grasp of the truths related to them (through what he calls 'knowledge'), is the proper task of the philosopher, and of the philosopher only.

To apply all this to political theory, what Plato holds is the following. The task of the future rulers is first and foremost to become philosophers – in the sense of 'philosophers' just described. They are to acquire knowledge of such Forms as Justice, Courage, Temperance and, above all, Goodness. Then, having a firm, expert grasp of these Forms, as the result of fifteen years or so of specialized training, and looking to them as one looks to a pattern, they are to rule in society justly and well. It is true that societies and human affairs change; but that does not matter. The philosopher will be able to apply to this changeable world his knowledge of that other world which is immutable – the Forms. In this he resembles the mathematician; for the latter is able usefully to apply unalterable formulae – truths about the Circle, Square and the rest – to the changeable and imperfect figures to be found here in the physical world. The philosopher, analogously, will be able successfully to apply unalterable moral and political formulae – truths concerning Justice and Goodness – to the changeable and imperfect affairs of men.

Only the philosopher has this capacity: only the philosopher must rule.

What are we to make of Plato's political philosophy as embodied in the above fundamental principles? No doubt most readers will feel unhappy with it, but it is important to grasp that Plato's theory cannot with propriety be rejected out of hand: each of its principles must be looked at.

The first principle – the one concerning the nature of society and its having a well-being of its own – is likely to be rejected only by the more extreme among political atomists. In point of fact, provided that we bear in mind that it does not ascribe a special ontological status to societies, it is hard to see this principle as excessive. For while men do not resemble the several organs of a body to the extent of being altogether without aims and purposes of their own, they just as certainly are not detached items, like the grains in a heap of sand. Rather, men are by nature interacting, communicating and co-operating beings – social animals. They evolved and have survived successfully only because they possess these social characteristics. But in any event, whatever their biological background, reason itself demands that men form societies; for most human aims, even those which can plausibly be thought of as atomic, can be fulfilled with ease, if at all, only through co-operation. Plato makes this point by stressing – perhaps overstressing – the importance of the division of labour.

What requires much more discussion is the *Republic's* second principle – that a society's well-being should constitute its overriding aim. Almost all philosophers, other than extreme atomists, hold that in some sense the well-being of a society is a thing to be pursued, at least as one among several goals. What usually prompts this view is that the interests of individuals not only clash, but clash in such a way that it is impossible to satisfy them all; so that a moral principle is needed to lessen the conflict in a manner which is intuitively fair. The utilitarian's answer to this problem, as was mentioned earlier, is that a consideration of the greatest amount of happiness for the greatest number of individuals should constitute the required guiding principle. This proposal, however, has a much-canvassed weakness. It countenances what most men would judge to be obvious injustices. To cite the usual example, on the assumption that the torture and killing of a few innocent people will lead to the greatest happiness, the utilitarian seems committed to saying that it is thereby justified; and this has persuaded the majority of philosophers to reject the entire solution. Plato's proposal, by contrast, is not obviously at odds with most people's moral intuitions. For it is simply that society's affairs should not be arranged to the advantage of a particular group: that the interests of all must be considered. It is therefore a proposal which is less sharply defined than the utilitarian's, and more difficult to apply. But not impossible. It enjoins the kind of consideration that parents usually bring to bear in looking to the well-being of their family. They are concerned not with the greatest happiness of the greatest number of their children, but on the one hand with ensuring that none is unduly favoured, and on the other with providing a balanced distribution of goods among them.

Even so, in the light of the exceedingly severe conditions imposed on the rulers – the denial of their right to marry, to own property, and so on – it might appear that for Plato there are no limits of any kind to what might be done in securing the well-being of society. What, then, would he have said to the suggested torture and killing of the innocent for the benefit of society? There are no signs anywhere that he would have accepted such actions as justified: indeed all the evidence is to the contrary [344, 443, 543–76]. But the philosophical question remains whether or not, in spite of himself, his theoretical beliefs would have committed him to endorsing these deeds.

Plato certainly is in trouble here. Having gone so far in stripping the rulers of their basic rights, on what credible grounds can he now hold back? There is only one obvious way open to him: to assert that *built into his notion of a society's well-being* are certain fundamental components, one of which is the rule that innocent men and women are not to be tortured and killed. But there is something *ad hoc* about this; worse, it is disquietingly close to a covert introduction of natural rights. (On the other hand it might be argued that while there is no difference here in practice from asserting that innocent people have a natural right to freedom from torture and death, there is a great difference in theory. In the one case the conclusion is drawn from considering the individual: in the other from considering society.)

This last point may serve to remind us that the doctrine of individual rights is the sharpest theoretical challenge yet to the claim that society is overridingly sovereign. In the assessment of Plato's principle, therefore, it might seem that much needs to be said of it. But in one sense there is very little that can be said of it. For when the liberal philosopher talks, say, of natural rights to marriage, property, voting and so on, what he says is scarcely a criticism of Plato's view: instead it is a radical substitution. In other words, what the liberal puts forward is a counter-proposal, not a refutation. And, in the outcome, it is a counter-proposal beset with difficulties. Its proponents disagree on the correct analysis of rights, on the epistemological status of these, and even on which claims may count as rights and which may not. Consequently, the liberal's doctrine is embraced by strange bedfellows. Some, upholding the rights to liberty of person and property, but no more, are staunchly conservative; others, pleading the rights of individuals to material well-being, employment and so on, are radically reformative.

The point of raising issues like these is not to defend Plato; even less to urge the sovereignty of society in its own right. It is simply to bring out that, at any rate in this second principle, Plato is not inconsistent, or in any other way conspicuously wrong.

What then of his third principle – the declaration that morals and politics are questions of objective, expert knowledge?

In most discussions on fundamental political and moral issues, philosophers and laymen alike use the language of objective assertion, as if speaking of matters of plain fact: matters over which men can be mistaken, properly argue, and make discoveries. They assume, that is, that there are objective answers to be had. What is more, they cannot do otherwise; since without that assumption there is no discussion: only rhetoric and professions of faith.

When it comes to complex issues – for example, abortion or nuclear warfare – the added assumption is made that, in order to arrive at answers, ability and expertise are required; straight-off intuition and native wit are not enough. Men and women need to be informed, but also they need to be educated in analyzing problems, in seeing ramifications, in grasping principles and in assessing consequences.

If these common assumptions are justified, Plato has a good *prima facie* case for holding that morals and politics are matters of objective fact, and (in principle at least) matters also of complete expertise. But Plato does not rest there. He adds a corollary, asserting that moral and political experts, and they alone, are to rule society.

Many of the objections raised to this assertion concern Plato's theory of Forms and knowledge; and these may be waived, on the grounds that the assertion makes sense independently of its metaphysics and epistemology. By contrast, what cannot be waived is the more widespread objection that what Plato says is not democratic.

In discussing the virtues of democracy in relation to Plato, we need to distinguish two sets of arguments: those supporting democracy in the absence of Platonic philosophers, and those supporting it absolutely – whether such philosophers are to be had or not.

There are many good though disputed reasons for concluding that Western, constitutional and representative democracies are, in the absence of Platonic philosophers, the best political societies devised so far; and Plato himself could have allowed this, accepting that they come closer than others to securing the well-being of their wholes. But at the most he would have conceded this on balance; pointing out that the conduct of democracies, whatever their sort, is unlikely to be uniformly just. It was a democracy, he might have reminded us, which put Socrates to death for insisting on open discussion, and the same democracy which, not long before, had killed or enslaved a whole people for not wishing to be a confederate of Athens. He could have gone on to predict fairly that, owing to similar weaknesses, modern democracies would be equally capable of oppressing their minorities, and of enslaving others. For these and like reasons, Plato would have argued that modern democracies at best could be placed poor seconds to his ideal society.

According to some recent philosophers, on this point Plato is at his most wrongheaded. The case for democracy, they say, is absolute and indefensible, resting on the ultimate and sovereign worth of the human person. The dignity of man, they argue, demands that all persons have a say in how and by whom they are governed; without such participation they would lack fulfilment as adults, resembling children or slaves. To this argument, however, Plato might with justice reply that he had not sought to belittle the human person; but that while the modern democrat sees the dignity of man in the fulfilment of self, he had always seen it in the surrender of self, in service to the common good. He might add that if a society were to be ruled by philosophers, possessing total political expertise, it would be as childish to argue that all individuals should play a part in its government as to argue that non-mathematicians should provide the calculations for building its bridges.

These replies would not silence the democrat, because he has a greater worry yet. Even if *ex hypothesi* the rulers of a Platonic society possessed the sort of expertise attributed to them in the *Republic*, they might still become corrupt and oppressive, and so favour sectional interests after all.

Plato in fact shared this worry; but he believed that education could go most of the way to making his rulers govern fairly, showing neither favour nor prejudice. If the democrat is not satisfied with this answer to his worry, there is little more that can be said to him. Except perhaps to point out that democracies too rely on education for functioning as just societies, governed and governing without favour or prejudice.

Further Reading

Crossman, R.H.S., *Plato Today*, London, 1937.
Hall, R.W., *Plato*, London, 1981.
Levinson, R., *In Defense of Plato*, Cambridge Mass., 1953.
Popper, K.R., *The Open Society and its Enemies*, vol. 1, *The Spell of Plato*, London, 5th ed., 1966.
Thorson, T.L., *Plato: Totalitarian or Democrat?* N.J., 1963.
Wild, J.D., *Plato's Modern Enemies and the Theory of Natural Law*, Chicago, 1953.

Chapter Two
Aristotle and Polity
Michael Stocker and Bruce Langtry

Ethical Considerations

Aristotle's *Politics* is at once intensely empirical and also intensely moral. It is a vast fund of factual information about different political arrangements throughout the ancient world known to Greeks. Aristotle assembled this information to guide action. Political science, as he conceived it, is concerned with characterizing and giving people a good life – politics is concerned with how one should act. These moral views are developed in the *Politics*, but they also rely on Aristotle's more explicitly ethical works, such as the *Nicomachean Ethics*.

Aristotle held that moral matters can be known, even if not with the precision of mathematics or the physical and biological sciences. He argued that well-being, living a good life, is what is good for people, and that such a life consists in the exercise of fully developed human capacities. Put very briefly, this requires one to act and feel in a way constitutive of a whole-hearted commitment to a well-ordered life, which life is aimed at what is truly important, truly human. Such living well was called *eudaimonia*, slightly misleadingly translated by 'happiness'. 'Well-being' and similar words are often more accurate. The aim of ethics and also politics is to show people how to achieve *eudaimonia*.

For our purposes, the important source of eudaimonia is practical life – a life lived in a society and concerned with that society. People who are living such a life and doing this well are active, spirited, believe in what they are doing, have due self-esteem and proper love for themselves and others.

The elements needed for a good practical life include courage, temperance, justice, liberality and friendliness. Each of these elements is called an *arêtai*, most often translated as 'virtue'. Here, a virtue must be understood as any characteristic of something which allows it to do its job well or be a good exemplar of its kind – for example, one virtue of gas for home heating is that it highly calorific. The human virtues Aristotle singled out concern both what is good for the agent and also what is good for others affected by the agent.

Having these virtues is only necessary, not sufficient for a good life. He recognized that a good person may lose the good life – for example, through a physical disaster. But, he claimed, only a good person can live the good life, and only a person with these virtues can be a good person. Thus, the notion of being too good for one's own good finds no place in Aristotle's thought.

The good life consists in whole-heartedly feeling and acting in truly human ways. But many people are unable to act and feel as they should, or can do so only with difficulty and pain. Aristotle's explanation for this difference between people is found in his account of moral development. He saw young children as being moved largely by instincts and by pleasure and pain. Only by being raised and trained in certain ways do they come to act upon reason and to develop various adult traits such as courage or cowardice, justice or injustice. They can be trained not to give in to just every fear or just every bodily desire, and to be able to do this whole-heartedly so that the proper things just come easily and naturally. Such a life, then, is a harmony of reason and desire. Education, in Aristotle's view, is intended to develop both proper reason and proper desire and their harmony. [VIII][1]

If people have such a harmony, then, barring misfortune, they will live well. They will lead good and fulfilling lives without having to be compelled by laws. For reasons to be considered later, they will still need laws but not as compulsions. If the laws are good laws, these people will not have difficulty in obeying them. However, those without such harmony or those who are inclined to do what is bad will need compulsion through laws. And, of course, they will also find obedience difficult.

Most people, on Aristotle's assessment, do not find it natural to do what is good either for themselves or others. Lacking virtue, they need compulsion through law. The other side of this is that, as he claims in Book X of the *Nicomachean Ethics*, people do not resent being told what to do by law, although they would resent being told this by other people.

---

[1] Here, as elsewhere, the capital roman numeral is the book number, the arabic numeral the chapter number. There is some controversy over the exact order of the books since the *Politics* was almost certainly not written as one book. We follow what is now the standard, which has the Bekker page numbers in order. All passages from the *Politics* are translated by B. Jowett.

Laws, then, are seen by Aristotle as doing what reason does in regard to wrong desires. Indeed, in the *Politics*, Aristotle characterized law as reason unaffected by desire. [III, 16]

In these last claims about law, we are introduced to various important themes in Aristotle's politics: the need for law, its concern with getting people to do what is good, and the psychology of those addressed by law.

The Community

The basic concern of the *Politics* is centred on the notion of community. Once we understand how the state is a community, we will understand how it should be ruled. We will also understand what sort of being a person is and why people need the sort of community given by and only by a state.

First, let us consider the word 'state'. Aristotle talks mainly about the word that gives us our word 'political', *polis*. A polis is a city state, for example, Athens and Sparta, but not a nation, such as Persia and Egypt.

Aristotle had principled reasons for restricting his attention to city states: smaller groupings than this were too small to be self-sufficient for well-being, larger groupings were too large for well-being. Further, the *Politics* is addressed to Greeks, perhaps mainly Athenians, whose political context and arena of political action was the polis. Thus, to apply his claims to our situation, we may have to make significant modifications. To help make it clear that the polis is not our state, we will use both 'polis' and 'state' interchangeably.

What makes a polis a *good* polis? This question, we might note, is rejected or not even considered by many contemporary political theorists who see their task as describing, explaining, predicting, and the like – but assuredly not evaluating.

For Aristotle, the questions 'What makes a polis good?' and 'What is a polis?' were close to being identical. This is based on the foundational claim that to find out what an X is, one should examine good Xs – ones that have all the characteristics, the virtues, that make something an X. We classify this way, too, for example, when we describe plants and animals in terms of the features of healthy and fully developed specimens rather than sick or stunted ones.

This identification of being a polis and being a good polis helps us understand how Aristotle can start the *Politics* by saying that every state is a community, every community aims at some good, and 'that the state which is the highest of all, and which embraces all other communities, aims at good in a higher degree than any other, and at the highest good'. We must understand this as a claim about good states and in that way about states in general.

But even so understood, how can it be justified? 1. Why is a state said to aim at any good at all? 2. Why is that good said to be the highest good?

The answer to 1 is that a state will not be a good state to the extent that it fails to achieve that good. 'Aim' in 1 can be understood as referring again to the connection between being an X and being a good X. To some extent at least, we join Aristotle in thinking that the natural process of developing as an X, for example, as a tree, will, unless thwarted, produce a good X. In this sense, we may say that the natural process aims at or has as its goal or end a good X. This is not to posit a conscious being with X as its goal, nor is it to take X to be an artifact. Rather, it is to talk about natural tendencies and their connections with good specimens. (The Greek language called attention to this connection with the common root of the word for 'goal', '*telos*' and for 'perfect', '*teleos*'.)

But why hold to the question posed in 1? Aristotle's answer, for example, at III, 9, hides many complexities in its simplicity. The standard by which states are judged is the well-being of its subjects. A state is a good state to the extent that its subjects are well-off. It would be better to say that a state is good to the extent that it *makes* it subjects well-off. For the subjects in a good state beset by bad circumstances, (for example, poor land), may be worse off than subjects in a not so good state in ideal circumstances. (Aristotle held that the statesman must, of course, be concerned with non-ideal as well as ideal circumstances.)

Before taking up some of the issues this answer raises, we should note that it provides an answer to question 2. Politics is a practical concern, dealing with what people are to aim at. And Aristotle did not see any good in having people aim at that which is higher than their own good. The state is not seen as something independent of, potentially in conflict with, the good or the interests of its subjects. (This, as Aristotle recognized, leads to problems about risk and sacrifice, for example, in wars.) Rather, it is judged as good or bad simply according to how well it serves its subjects' good.

But how can a state make its subjects live well? And why is it the business of a state to make its subjects live well?

We have already seen one way in which states can play a role in the well-being of subjects: through laws. Aristotle did not hold – as noted, he denied – that if people do what is good through fear of punishment, they are good or are thereby living well. But he did hold that they and those whom they affect will not be so poorly off as they otherwise would be. So, he wrote in the *Politics*: 'For man, when perfected, is the best of all animals, but when separated from law and justice, he is the worst of all ...' [I, 2]

Secondly, good education – which is a vital concern of the state –

will be encouraged by good laws and this may in turn produce good people, who, thus, do not need to be coerced by laws. Further, laws are, themselves, educative. People tend to judge and regulate themselves by the ideals presented in and by laws. Both actions and attitudes are changed by laws. (So, Aristotle held that attitudes can be changed by law and that, even were this not so, there could justifiably be laws to compel correct action.)

This concerns people who are not good. But what about good people? That they are protected from the others by laws is one of the least important claims made by Aristotle. Even good people are made good by a good polis. Only in a polis can people be fully developed people. Only there can they lead a truly human life. Keeping in mind the connection between being an X and being a good X, we can understand his famous claims that 'man is by nature a political animal' and 'the state is a creation of nature'. [I, 2]

Aristotle recognized that people can live outside of a state. In his view, the state arose from villages, which arose from extended families, which arose from families of man, woman, and children. The move from the smaller to the larger grouping was made – and is shown to be worthwhile – by the greater goods the larger has. A family on its own will have to be lucky to produce enough and be secure enough. An extended family allows for some division of labour, a diversity of products, and greater security. A village allows for still more diversity and security. A polis is near enough to being self-sufficient in regard to these goods and services.

But although a polis is important for providing such goods and services, it is far more important for allowing a person to become, finally, a person. A truly and fully developed person is one whose life is caught up in sociality and political concerns. It is through and only through interaction with people in activities that exist only in a polis that people can realize their true and full nature. So for example, it is only in a polis that governance and political co-operation are possible. It is only in a polis that the cultural and social possibilities so essential to a truly human life are possible.

It is in this way that the state is natural for people. It is their habitat – where they can thrive and become truly developed.

Aristotle also pointed out that people talk and have a social instinct. These may show that, in another if related sense, people are by nature social beings. But it goes only part of the way toward showing that by nature people are political beings. For one can talk and exercise sociality in a family or a village.

It is important to note that 'by nature' is used in different senses here: speech and sociality may be natural in the sense of their being inborn in us; a polis is natural in that it is the arena in which we develop, indeed it is the context that develops us. We might here extend the claim made earlier about the formative nature of laws: the polis gives us our particular way of seeing the world and our fellows.

These claims that the polis develops us and gives us our true self are difficult, both to articulate and to defend. But they are, we think, foundational to Aristotle's thought and to that of many other profound philosophers. In so far as they are correct, they help indicate an answer to the question, still pending, of why it is the business of the polis to make its subjects good.

That question is often posed from the standpoint of what might be called the night-watchman view of the state – found most recently in Robert Nozick's *Anarchy, State, and Utopia*. This view has it that the role of the state is simply to make things safe for subjects to get on about their business. It is meddling on the part of the state to provide for the well-being of its subjects (or to do this to any greater degree than that needed for them to be able to take care of themselves).

Aristotle gave a partial answer to this by his claim that were security all that is important then wherever there are protective alliances, either between states, or among villages or tribes, there would thus be a state. But, he said, these are not states.

States, rather, form their subjects in various ways. They create people, i.e., people who now have and can use fully human capacities. Indeed, were they only to provide the goods and services of the smaller groupings, and not also to create such people, states would lack their special philosophical interest and importance. To hold that states are not to be evaluated as good or bad by how well or poorly off they make their subjects, is to hold that they are not to be evaluated in terms of what they are most notable for doing – what is most important about them.[2] (We might ask whether we, too, think well or poorly of a state for making its subjects lives good or bad.)

Sorts of Constitutions

Aristotle differentiated political rule from various sorts of non-political rule, such as the rule of a master over a slave, of a husband over a wife, and of a father over children.

He first defined what he calls *natural* slaves. These are people who have a full enough range of desires and passions, but their reasoning

---

[2]   A parallel argument is given about the function or *ergon* of the psyche in *Nicomachean Ethics* I, 7 to show that eudaimonia has the characteristics Aristotle argued for. See, for example, T.H. Irwin, 'The Metaphysical and Psychological Basis of Aristotle's Ethics' in *Essays in Aristotle's Ethics*, A.O. Rorty (ed.) (Berkeley, 1980.)

capacities are seriously defective. They are incapable of deciding what to do on the basis of rational plans and arguments drawn up by themselves. They are not self-directing, but can only obey orders. As noted above, executive reason is essential to a truly human, good life.

Given their defects, it is no more wrong to rule over natural slaves than over oxen. It is part of the scheme of nature that both be used by us. It is clear enough that Aristotle thought that certain peoples – not just individual defectives – are natural slaves. But it is remarkable that – except for some comments about barbarians, i.e. non-Greeks, which may, but are not clearly intended to, identify natural slaves – he did not identify these peoples. [I, 2, 7, 8; III, 14; VII, 7]

Although he argued in favour of slavery of those without reason, he also argued strongly against enslavement of those taken in war or raids, or those sold, for example, by their families or those who have pledged themselves as surety for a debt, and the like.[3] His argument here is as important, and as contrary to the then prevailing customs, as the previous one might well seem only a rationalization of such practices. For the standard justification then offered for slavery had to do with purchase and legal arrangements, not with lack of reason. His argument against the justification of what he called slavery by law – to distinguish it from natural slavery – was that were the justifications for such slavery good ones, then any Greek, no matter how rich and powerful, no matter how well born and noble, could justifiably be enslaved. And this, he assumed, his readers would find equally repugnant and absurd.

Aristotle's argument that husbands should rule over wives is based on his claim that in women their emotions are not controlled by reason. Without commenting on his views about women, this shows the stress he placed on a being's nature. For even though he said that men (males) are capable of having effective reason, he was at pains to argue that many men are ruled by passion.

The case for rule over children seems far less objectionable. Children are not yet reasonable. They must be shaped and educated, as well as protected, for example, from their own desires.

In these three non-political forms of rule, Aristotle was insistent that ruling is for the benefit of all concerned. The concern the ruler should have for a slave is what he should have for a beast or tool.

Political rule concerns the rule over free people, and people who are capable of reason and self-direction.

To discuss Aristotle's view of political rule, we should first note

---

[3] See M.I. Finley, *Economy and Society in Ancient Greece*, B.D. Shaw and R.P. Saller, (eds), (London, 1981), especially part two, 'Servitude, Slavery and the Economy'.

how he characterized a polis, i.e., what makes something a polis. For reasons similar to those already noted, a polis cannot be identified as what makes trade possible or provides security. Trade alliances or groups of tribes can do this without being a state. Nor can a state be characterized by physical features, such as location. A state can be discontinuously spread over different pieces of land, islands, and the like. And two states can be juxtaposed.

Rather, a state is characterized in terms of having one government or constitution, where this is understood in terms of the principal powers and offices of a state. This, too, is pretty much how we define states – both nation states and states within a nation.

In pure form, there are six sorts of constitution: monarchy, aristocracy, polity, democracy, oligarchy, and tyranny. [III, 7] These form two groups of three, one right and the other perverted. The right ones are right because they are, by definition, rule in the interest of all members of the state. These are monarchy, rule by one person, aristocracy, rule by a small group, and polity, rule by many. The other three are said to be perverted because they are rule for the sake of the rulers. Democracy is rule by the poor, and probably the many, for their sake. Oligarchy is rule by the rich and probably the few, for their sake. Tyranny is the rule of one person for his own sake. (It often looks as if Aristotle kept only loosely to these characterizations.)

Aristotle divided government into various sorts of offices and functions – for example deliberative, judicial, and executive. Each of these parts and their subparts can be of different sorts of these six sorts. Thus, there can be mixed forms of constitution.

We should note, first, that the distinction between the two groups of three is made on moral grounds. Second, the distinction between democracy and oligarchy is put in explicitly economic terms. So too, the conflict between democracy and oligarchy was seen in explicitly, though not exclusively, economic terms, which reflected the dynamic of ancient Greek society.

These six constitutions were presented in order of merit, as seen by Aristotle. But this is merit on the scale of the possible, not on the scale of the practicable. He argued that a monarchy would require the sort of moral giant found nowhere. So too, aristocracy requires goodness among a group of people that is not to be found. Perhaps polity is practicable: we will return to it.

Tyranny is the worst of all forms of constitution. It involves treating men as slaves, unable to direct their own lives. Further, it involves ruling for the sake of only the one ruler. Aristotle had many harsh things to say about both democracy and oligarchy, but on the whole seemed to favour democracy. This, however, is a matter of generality. For in some circumstances a democracy is not the best arrangement, but an oligarchy or even a tyranny might be.

Democracy

We do not have space to examine all the various sorts of constitutions, nor the circumstances in which they are best. So we will here concentrate on Aristotle's view about democracy.

Democracy, which in many modern views is the best and perhaps the only justified political system, did not receive that accolade from Aristotle. He regarded polity as the best of the practicable systems. (The Greek word, transliterated as and translated by 'democracy' is the combination of 'demos', 'people', and 'cratia', 'power' – power to the people.) Explaining this will help distinguish his notion of democracy from ours and also test both his and our evaluations of democracy and polity. We must of course take into account that even today many different systems vie for the title of democracy.

In *Politics* VI, 2, we read the following characterizations of democracy: 'The basis of a democratic state is liberty; which according to the common opinion of man can only be enjoyed in such a state'. 'One principle of liberty is for all to rule and be ruled in turn.' 'Every citizen must have equality.' 'The will of the majority is supreme.' 'A man should live as he likes.'

The reason for the last is that 'not to live as a man likes is the mark of a slave'. Thus, democrats must be opposed to oligarchies and tyrannies, as well. But there is a real conflict between living as one likes and majority rule. So, Aristotle had the democrat holding, still in VI, 2, that men are 'to be ruled by none, or, if this is impossible, to rule and be ruled in turn'. Perhaps ruling and being ruled in turn is not too much of a diminution of being ruled by none. At the least, it is not being ruled by someone claiming superiority. This is to say that liberty and equality are importantly interconnected – which is a profound view, whether or not ultimately defensible.

As Aristotle noted, there are many different sorts of democracy. These are distinguished mainly by which free people are citizens – i.e, are eligible to take part in government. [See *Politics* IV, 6 and VI, 4.]

The best democracies, based on Aristotle's views, are those where only financially independent husbandmen and farmers are citizens. Since they would not have the leisure or interest to meet frequently and take active part in running the state, they would elect others to take care of the day to day, even the month to month, running of the polis. They would retain ultimate control by elections and by periodic inspections of accounts and the like. The worst democracies are those in which all free men take active part in all levels and offices of the deliberative, judicial, and executive branches.

To appreciate Aristotle's evaluations and worries, it must be recognized that the political activity he was concerned with is a frequent, perhaps a daily, affair – on the model of a town meeting, where all or near enough all attend and vote and can have a voice.

Aristotle's worries about democracy centred on the claim that the vast majority of the poor men – the mechanics, the day labourers, the craftsmen – would have neither the education nor the leisure needed for taking part usefully in government. Because of their occupations and habits of thought, they would lack the temperament and judgement needed for wise statecraft. Moreover, they would be poor, which invites bribery by the rich or factions, and involves also not having the free time to devote to governing.

So, if they were to take part in the actual day to day running of government, they would have to receive pay. But without plundering the rich or the state treasury, there would simply not be enough money to support them. Notwithstanding its benefits, administrative work is a cost.

All this leads, Aristotle thought, to several very real dangers. The first is that a demagogue will all too easily gain control. This either is or leads to tyranny. The second is that the people will so outrage the wealthy, by disregard for their interests, that the latter will attempt to overthrow the democracy in favour of an oligarchy. The third is that the people – by taking too absolutely the claim that the will of the majority should rule, perhaps urged on by demagogues – will see it only right and proper to take themselves as the law, not as bound by it.

This last, Aristotle held, is the destruction of a polis. For, as indicated above, law and obedience to law are the foundations of a polis. If the people do not bind themselves to the law – if, that is, they do not rule constitutionally – there is no polis or none worth speaking of.

So, Aristotle said, a principled democrat should not try to maximize democracy by instituting majority rule without constitutional constraints. Rather, there must be a trade-off between such maximization and the maximization of the security and longevity of the democracy, similarly for oligarchies and tyrannies.

This might seem harsh or unrealistic. Isn't the Westminster system one where parliament can change any law? But in Australia and Britain, for example, even if the law cannot force them to feel and act this way, parliamentarians do feel bound to act, to a great degree anyway, in accord with precedent and past law, including overarching constitutional principles. Just consider the outrage when this is or seems to be infringed.

We see here, as Aristotle saw, obedience to the law by the rulers (those with power) is not something that can be enforced. The rulers must simply respect the law, nothing can make them obey it. Thus, again, the need for proper education is reinforced.

Foundations of Rule and Polity

Perhaps we can now see why Aristotle was worried about extreme democracy. But why did he not favour more limited democracies? And what did he favour?

One of Aristotle's main worries about democracy concerned its ultimate principle: that in virtue of being free, people should have equal political power. This is the principle of democratic justice. And, Aristotle held, it makes a fundamental error about justice – i.e., about how the state should be ruled.

To illustrate this point, we must take up Aristotle's account of distributive justice in the *Nicomachean Ethics* V. If people contribute money to an economic undertaking – set up a company, place a bet – then, Aristotle held, the profit should be divided proportionately to the contribution they each made to that undertaking. We saw earlier that the point or the good of a state was the well-being of all subjects. To settle what political arrangement of powers, obligations, and benefits is just we must, therefore, look at the contribution the various people make to the well-being of all and to the preservation of the state.

Certainly, being free is an essential constituent of a good state, that is, a state composed of free men, not just slaves. But wealth, too, is essential to the well-being of all. A financially poor state will not be able to supply the services its subjects need – for example, as in Athens, welfare and food supplements to the needy.

Indeed, this is the point fastened on by oligarchs who claim that oligarchy is the just political arrangement. (Advocates of all political systems claim, according to Aristotle, that their system, and perhaps only their system, is just.) As oligarchs urge, they contribute more financially to the state, so they should have most control. But as Aristotle replied, the state is not – or not simply – an economic venture. Were it only that, oligarchs might be justified. So too for those who would apportion political power in virtue of the necessary role of military power so necessary for protection.

In reply to all of these, Aristotle said that they do have a claim but only a partial claim. And it is partial because the role each of those claimed things plays in regard to well-being is only partial.

When Aristotle said that the political organization should favour people to the extent that they contribute to the good of the polis, he did not extend this to slaves, foreigners, and other non-citizens. He attempted to draw a distinction between those who constitute, and those who merely contribute to, a state. An analogy is the differential role played in universities by students and lecturers compared with the administrators and secretaries.

With this qualification, all legitimate claims of making up and preserving the good of the polis must be given due weight. This would lead, Aristotle suggested, to recognizing the claims of being a free person and a citizen. It would also lead to recognition of the claims of wealth, education, and perhaps above all, political and moral virtue. [See *Politics* III, 10–13.] We will here merely note the controversial implication that sufficient care is given to the well-being of all if they are treated according to this principle of justice. This is a correlation of the controversial identification of justice and the well-being of all.

The claim, then, is that a citizen who has political skills and virtue should be given more power. This might seem anti-democratic and élitist. But then how can one justify giving – for example, by election – more power to those more skilled and more public spirited? This, too, is not complete democracy, but at best only democracy in regard to who votes, not in regard to who receives the votes.

Further, as Aristotle pointed out, if one really believes that all are equal in the relevant respects and thus anybody is as good as anybody else, then one must believe that there is no reason at all to choose one person rather than another for any political office. But then, offices should not be filled by voting, for voting seems a way of registering views about differences in suitability – if it is not a way of maintaining a faction or expressing an irrelevant preference. Rather, offices should be filled by lot. That, after all, is the fair way of choosing among people if there are no good grounds for distinguishing between them.

The ideal state, then, will give due weight to the competing claims. Aristotle was enough of a realist or pessimist to hold that if the rich were very strong, there would be an oligarchy, and if the poor were very strong, there would be a democracy – failing a tyranny, of course. Economic self-interest is very strong. So, it is very unlikely that the various claims will be given due weight.

What would be necessary in a practical sense for this, Aristotle held, is that there be a large and powerful enough group, a middle class, who were neither rich nor poor, but who were public spirited. They must have the balance of power. If they did, then there was some chance of the proper distribution of power. The poor free people would have their powers and rights; the wealthy and noble would have their powers and honours; and the educated and virtuous would have their powers, rights, and honours. There would also be due regard paid to rule by law, not decree.

Even though most current states were polities, not pure democracies, oligarchies, or tyrannies, they were impure polities. The various classes were not accorded their due – thus people felt threatened or insulted – nor was due regard paid to constitution and law. Thus, Aristotle found it entirely natural that these states were in destructive tension and were not good states.

Bibliography

Aristotle, *Politics, Nicomachean Ethics, The Athenian Constitution.*

Further Reading

Discussions (those with asterisk have very useful bibliographies):
J. Barnes, M. Schofield, and R. Sorabji (eds), *Articles on Aristotle: Ethics and Politics*, (London, 1977).✭
E. Barker, *The Political Thought of Plato and Aristotle*, (New York, 1959).
M.I. Finley, *Economy and Society in Ancient Greece*, B.D. Shaw and R.P. Saller, (eds), (London, 1981).✭
G. Glotz, *The Greek City and Its Institutions*, (London, 1969).
R.H. Mulgan, *Aristotle's Political Theory*, (Oxford, 1977).
W.D. Ross, *Aristotle* (London, 1923).
A.O. Rorty (ed.), *Essays on Aristotle's Ethics*, (Berkeley, 1980).
G.H. Sabine, *A History of Political Theory*, (London, 1968).

Original Sources:
Aristotle, *Politics, Nicomachean Ethics, The Athenian Constitution*

Chapter Three

Augustine and Aquinas: Church and State

Max Charlesworth

Christians and the State

The attempt by Christian thinkers in the West to provide an account of the nature of political society draws upon a number of different sources. Christianity was born into a world dominated by Roman institutions, including Roman law, and by Greek philosophical concepts. Roman ideas on the nature of the 'civitas' defined political society as a community under 'the rule of law'; Plato and Aristotle, on the other hand, saw the 'polis' as an agency of moral education and formation since for them it was impossible to live a fully human life outside society. Only beasts and gods, Aristotle said, live outside the 'polis': beasts because they are sub-human and gods because they are superhuman. For the Greeks the civil law must always be in accordance with the moral law, otherwise tyranny ensues. Tyranny is that form of government where the naked will and power of the ruler (be the ruler one or many) prevails – in other words, where might is right.

The Christians of the first three centuries took an ambivalent attitude to the Roman State. Some were convinced that the end of the world and the advent of the kingdom of God were nigh, so that for them it was not a pressing concern to elaborate a Christian theory of the State. Others identified the State with the anti-Christian and 'pagan' Roman State and rejected it completely. For them the Church, the community of believers, was the only true 'society'. Just as the Christian philosophers had no need of pagan wisdom since the Scriptures were sufficient for them, so also Christians had no need of Greek and Roman political concepts and institutions. The 'City of God', the Church, was sufficient for them. Theocracy (the view that the Church is the only authentic political authority) and fideism (the view that faith is the only authentic avenue of knowledge) tend to go hand in hand. Other Christians recognized the role of the State and groped tentatively towards some kind of theory about the relationship that ought to obtain between the Church and the State – the supernatural society and the natural society – just as in the sphere of knowledge certain Christian thinkers attempted to define the relationship between what is known by 'faith' through revelation and what is known by 'natural reason' alone.[1]

St Augustine and *The City of God*

St Augustine of Hippo (354–430) was the first Christian thinker to grapple with these questions about the respective roles of the two 'societies' – Church and State – in an explicit way. It needs to be remembered, however, that St Augustine was not a political philosopher in the way that both Plato and Aristotle were. Augustine was primarily a theologian expounding the content of the Christian faith and his remarks on the nature of political society are in the nature of *obiter dicta*. Thus the *De Civitate Dei (The City of God)* is not a book on political philosophy in the same sense as Plato's *Republic* and Aristotle's *Politics*. *The City of God* is a general apologia or defence of Christianity against the charges of those who attributed the fall and decline of the Roman Empire (Rome was sacked in 410 A.D. by Alaric) to the influence of Christianity, and Augustine's reflections on Church and State are incidental to his apologetic purpose. For all that, it is not difficult to construct from what Augustine says in *The City of God* a theory about political society and the inter-relations between society and the Church.[2]

As we have already remarked, for Augustine the Church is not just a group of people with a common set of religious beliefs and practices; it is a society in the strict sense, that is a community of believers with its own organization and its own laws and its own 'common good'. The very title of his celebrated work, *The City of God*, makes that clear. ('Civitas', it might be remarked, does not mean 'city' in the modern sense: it is rather the body of 'cives' (citizens) and has much the same sense as the Greek 'polis' and our

[1]   See Henry Chadwick, *The Early Church*, (Harmondsworth, 1967). On St Augustine's background and context see Peter Brown, *Augustine of Hippo*, (London, 1967), especially pp. 287–338.
[2]   *The City of God* is available in an English translation by John Healey in the Everyman edition, (London, 1945). See the introduction by Sir Ernest Barker. See also the bibliography in Herbert A. Deane, *The Political and Social Ideas of St Augustine*, (New York, 1963).

'society'.) For the Greeks the 'polis' was the supreme form of society (superior to the family and the clan), but for Augustine political society is subordinated to the higher form of society brought into being with the Christian church. One can see from this how radically different Augustine's perspective is from that of Plato and Aristotle. The supernatural society that is the Church is in effect founded by God and it is sustained by His spiritual help or grace; it is only in this society that people can be 'saved' and made fully happy through union with God; again, this society is based upon the altruistic love of its members for God and for each other.

By way of contrast with this supernatural society, the city of God or the Church, Augustine describes the 'earthly society' (*civitas terrena*), that is the secular society, with its laws and institutions, which exists outside the Church. Augustine's attitude to the 'earthly society' is ambivalent: thus at times he appears to admit that it has its own proper place and role in providing for our non-spiritual welfare and that from this point of view it is good in itself; at other times he appears to suggest that the earthly society only comes into being because of human sinfulness after the Fall, so that if the Fall had not taken place then the State would not have been necessary and the Church would have been sufficient; at other times again, he says quite explicitly that secular society originates in human selfishness or 'self love' and that it is typified by conflict and power. Augustine says:

> These two cities derive from two different loves – the earthly city derives from the love of self which rejects God: the heavenly city derives from the love of God which rejects love of self. The first seeks human glory; the second desires only to bear witness to God, the greatest glory... The first is governed by ambitious tyrants led by the lust for power: the second is one in which all work together in love, both the rulers in ruling and the subjects in obeying.[3]

At times indeed Augustine's view of political society outside the Church seems to be a theological version of Hobbes' theory of the State: that is to say, political society is defined as that form of human society in which there is a locus of absolute power or 'sovereignty'. So in the famous passage in *The City of God*, Augustine writes as follows:

> Without justice are kingdoms anything more than the results of robbery? Robber gangs are in fact little kingdoms for they are under a commander and sworn together in a confederacy, the pillage being shared out among them. And if these gangsters become powerful enough to build forts and conquer cities and neighbouring countries,

---

[3] *The City of God*, Book 14, ch. 28.

then their confederacy is no longer called a gang but is adorned with the high-sounding title of 'kingdom', not because they have ceased to be really gangsters, but because they may now continue to be so with impunity. The pirate's retort to the great Alexander of Macedon was very much to the point: when the King asked him what right he had to lord it over the seas, the pirate replied cheerfully: 'Well what right have *you* to lord it over the whole world? I am called a pirate because I happen only to have a small ship: you are called a King simply because you have a navy behind you'.[4]

Augustine's final position appears to be that in principle the State does have its own proper autonomy and purpose – the preservation of peace and order – and that the Church must respect the independence of the State and not interfere directly in the political order. As he puts it:

> ... The spiritual society, while it is here on earth, is made up out of people from different temporal societies and does not concern itself with the laws made by those societies. It does not go against these laws but rather observes them, so long as they have as their purpose the preservation of the temporal order and do not oppose the worship of the One True God.[5]

However, in practice human beings are so corrupted by the effects of sin that they are incapable of acting altruistically if they are left to their own devices. Unless they are helped by God's grace, mediated through the Church, they will tend to follow their own individualistic self-interest and political society will be very much as Hobbes described it, a mechanism of power and coercion for regulating conflicts between self-interested individuals. From this perspective Augustine's view of the State is a pessimistic one in that he thinks that politics is basically a power-game and that we ought not to expect too much from politics and politicians. In the last resort the State is a necessary evil.

Again, while in *principle* Augustine's view of Church and State is not a theocratic one where the State becomes absorbed into the Church, in *practice* Augustine's position lends itself to a theocratic interpretation. This is in fact what happened in Western Christian thought from the sixth century onwards. Thus Gregory the Great in the late sixth century, under the influence of Augustine, sees the State and the political order as the instrument of the Church; again Isodore of Seville at the end of the seventh century argues that the State is simply the 'secular arm' of the Church employing force to

---

[4]   ibid., Book 4, ch. 4.
[5]   ibid., Book 19, ch. 17.

establish and maintain Christian beliefs and morality. The religious ceremony of the coronation of kings and queens in Western Europe was in fact a symbol of the dependence of the secular political power upon the spiritual power of the Church. In other words, the king or the queen or the emperor held their power from God through the intermediary of the Church.[6] Augustine's influence continued in Calvin's theocracy in Geneva, and in the early Puritan settlements in the United States which were for the most part theocratic in outlook. His position also has echoes in some modern Christian views which claim that the Church can and must interfere directly in politics in order to secure its spiritual and moral ends.

The debate about the relationship that ought to obtain between the Church and the political order continued right through the Middle Ages both at the practical level in the struggles between popes and kings and emperors, and at the theoretical theological level. By the thirteenth century, partly due to the realities of politics and partly due to the introduction of Aristotelian thought into the new universities, a new view began to emerge in which the State – the 'temporal power' – was seen as having complete independence in its own sphere, and the Church – the 'spiritual power' – was likewise seen as a 'perfect society' with its own proper autonomy. Christ's injunction: 'Render to Caesar the things that are Caesar's and to God the things that are God's', was constantly invoked to give Biblical justification for this new dualistic view.

Aquinas on the Two Societies

The introduction of Aristotelian philosophy to the West in the thirteenth century had a revolutionary effect upon Christian theology in that it forced Christian thinkers to acknowledge the autonomy and independence of the 'natural order' and of 'natural reason' (what could be discovered by reason alone without the help of religious revelation). The intrinsic value of the natural world, including political society, was recognized and the provinces of philosophy and the sciences (though these latter were not yet fully defined) were also seen as having their own independence. Christian theology, explicating the body of supra-rational knowledge (gained through religious revelation) of the supernatural order of reality, complemented this natural knowledge and did not contradict or overrule it. The medieval theological dictum, 'grace does not destroy nature but complements and perfects it', expresses this view very nicely.

---

6   See H.X. Arquillière, 'Reflexions sur l'essence de l'augustinisme politique', in *Augustinus Magister*, (Paris, 1954), vol. II, pp. 996–7. See also J.N. Figgis, *The Political Aspects of St. Augustine's 'City of God'*, (London, 1921).

In the area of political society this implies that the State has its own intrinsic value as securing the peace and order necessary for living the good life and in maintaining the basic human 'virtues'. Whether or not a society is a good and just society has therefore nothing to do with the Church since the Church's function – the spiritual and supernatural good of its members – is quite distinct from that of the State. As said before, Church and State are viewed as two distinct societies with diverse but complementary purposes and aims. To paraphrase the dictum mentioned before, the Church does not destroy or overrule the State or make it unnecessary, but presupposes it and complements it.

This new view was given its clearest formulation in the thirteenth century by St Thomas Aquinas (1225–1274), and it is largely Aquinas' position on Church and State that was adopted later by the Catholic Church.

Aquinas' views on political society are developed mainly in 'The Treatise on Law' which is part of the vast work, the *Summa Theologiae*.[7] In the Treatise Aquinas provides a subtle and detailed analysis of what he calls 'natural law' (*ius naturale*), that is the basic moral rules or laws on which political society depends, and positive civil law (*ius civile*), that is the body of law promulgated by the ruler of the State. He also discusses the 'divine positive law', that is the laws or regulations promulgated within the Christian Church and which apply only to members of the Church.

Like his Greek philosophical masters, Aquinas thinks that it is possible to elaborate a detailed set of moral rules by rational reflection on 'human nature'. Whatever fulfils or actualizes the basic potentialities or needs of human beings is morally good in that it makes us more fully human, and whatever frustrates these basic human 'inclinations' is morally bad in that it makes us less human. Aquinas' theory is in fact very similar to that of Aristotle in that for both the morally good person is the one who is fully actualized as a human being.

According to Aquinas the laws of the State ought to be framed in accordance with the moral law: in fact the function of the State is to translate into concrete political practice in particular circumstances those moral rules which are concerned with others. The civil law therefore acts as a moral pedagogue in that its function is to make the citizens more morally virtuous. 'It is evident', Aquinas says, 'that

---

7   The Treatise on Law is available in an English translation by Thomas Gilby in *St. Thomas Aquinas: Summa Theologiae*, vol. 28, (London, 1965). See also *The Political Ideas of St. Thomas Aquinas*, D. Bigongiari, (ed.), (New York, 1963). For background see T. Gilby, *Principality and Polity: Aquinas and the rise of State Theory in the West*, (London, 1958). See also A.P. d'Entrèves, *Natural Law: an introduction to legal philosophy*, (London, 1970).

the proper effect of law is to lead its subjects to their proper virtue: and since virtue is that which makes its subject good, it follows that the proper effect of law is to make those to whom it is given, good, either simply or in some particular respect'.[8] Aquinas recognizes, however, that the law is a crude instrument for inculcating morality and that there are severe limits to what the law can do in making people virtuous. There are many immoral acts which do not directly affect others and the law does not concern itself with these. (Gluttony, for example, is a moral fault but we do not expect there to be a law against gluttony.) Again, in many cases the attempt by the law to control immorality may bring about more harm than good. In these cases the principle of lesser evil enjoins that no law should be enacted and that the immorality in question should be tolerated. For example, prostitution is a moral evil but the attempt to forbid prostitution by laws may bring about more harm than good, so that it is better for the State to tolerate prostitution. As Aquinas says:

> Human law is framed for a number of human beings, the majority of whom are not perfect in virtue. Wherefore human laws do not forbid all vices, from which the virtuous abstain, but only the more grievous ones, from which it is possible for the majority to abstain: and chiefly those that are to the hurt of others, without the prohibition of which human society could not be maintained: thus the human law prohibits murder, theft and suchlike.

And again:

> The purpose of human law is to lead men to virtue, not suddenly, but gradually. Wherefore it does not lay upon the multitude of imperfect men the burdens of those who are already virtuous, viz. that they should abstain from all evil. Otherwise these imperfect ones, being unable to bear such precepts, would break out into yet greater evils...[9]

However, Aquinas insists very firmly that unless the civil law of the State is in accordance with the moral law it does not have the force of law at all. Following Augustine he says that a law which is not just (i.e. not in line with the moral law) 'seems to be no law at all': 'if in any point it deflects from the law of nature (the moral law) it is no longer a law but a perversion of law'.[10] Thus a law may be duly promulgated by the authorities of the State and it may be enforceable in the courts, but if it is contrary to the moral law it has no real force so that a citizen may legitimately refuse to obey it

---

8   *Summa Theologiae*, 1, 11, 92, 1.
9   ibid., 1, 11, 96, 2.
10   ibid., 1, 11, 95, 2.

(though of course the citizen may have to suffer the sanctions imposed by the courts for his disobedience: again the citizen has to take account of the possible effects of his refusal to obey a law). Aquinas' position here, it is clear, is quite contrary to later positivist views of the law proposed by Austin and others according to which a law is simply the command of the legal sovereign.

For the positivist it is nonsensical to say that an unjust law is not really a law since a law is a command that is decreed by the appropriate legislative authority in the State and enforced by the judicial system. But for Aquinas, while a law may be duly promulgated and enforceable, it cannot, if it is unjust, have a claim upon my obedience any more than a bandit who puts a gun to my head and coerces me has a claim upon my obedience. As a latter-day follower of Aquinas, Professor Peter Geach, has robustly put it:

> University people argue mightily about whether laws that violate these principles are laws or (as Aquinas called them) mere violence. Of course it doesn't matter whether you *call* them laws or not: the question is what consequences follow. An unjust piece of legislation exists *de facto*, as an institution: but it is no debt of justice to observe it, though it may be imprudent to ignore it. And though a private person should not lightly judge a law to be unjust, its contrariety to the Law of Nature and the peace and justice of society may be so manifest that such a judgement is assured... I think Old John Brown rightly so judged about the slave-owning U.S. Commonwealths of his time.[11]

Aquinas' position is also contrary (at least in theory) to the views of later political theorists such as John Stuart Mill who distinguish very sharply between the sphere of personal morality and the sphere of law which is solely concerned with preventing 'harm' to others. For Mill the law has no moral function. There is no doubt that for Aquinas, on the other hand, law and morality are inextricably intertwined and the law and State have a moral purpose. In practice, however, Aquinas' ideas can be interpreted in a quasi-Millian sense in that the province of the civil law is restricted to preventing those acts 'without the prohibition of which human society could not be maintained' and has nothing directly to do with acts of private morality. A number of modern Catholic thinkers have developed Aquinas' ideas in this way.[12]

As has been said, for Aquinas the sphere of civil law does not depend for its legitimacy upon the Church. Of course, there is, or

---

[11] *The Virtues*, (Cambridge, 1977), p. 128. See also John Finnis, *Natural Law and Natural Rights*, (Oxford, 1980), pp. 363–6 on 'Lex injusta non est lex'.

[12] See my essay 'Catholics and the Free Society' in Max Charlesworth, *Church, State and Conscience*, (St Lucia, 1973). See also J.E.A. D'Arcy, *Conscience and its Right to Freedom*, (London, 1961).

ought to be, a coincidence between what the Church enjoins upon its members and the moral law and the civil law of the State, but the Church cannot dictate to the State nor interfere directly in the political order.

Since the law of the State is subordinate to the moral law any kind of political absolutism is ruled out for Aquinas. In other words, might is not right and the mere will of the ruler does not have the force of law. But Aquinas goes further than this in holding that political authority and power spring from the community which, so to speak, transfers its political authority and power to the rulers. The political sovereign, Aquinas says, 'has not the power to frame laws except as representing the people'.[13] Aquinas therefore rejects any theocratic idea – political authority and power come from the Church – or any divine right of kings theory – political power is given by God directly to the ruler. The ruler is the representative (*vice gerens*) of the people and his power is legitimate in so far as it furthers their 'common good'. The citizens have no obligation to obey a ruler who flouts the moral law or who does not rule for the good of all the people. At the same time civil disobedience is not to be undertaken lightly since it may foster contempt for the law.

Following Aristotle's *Politics* Aquinas distinguishes three different forms of government or 'régimes': monarchy (government by one), aristocracy (government by the élite few), democracy (government by all the people). Which régime will be chosen will depend upon the circumstances of the people. However, Aquinas argues that a 'mixed régime' is best:

> This is the best form of polity, being partly monarchy, since there is one at the head of all; partly aristocracy, in so far as a number of persons are set in authority; partly democracy, i.e. government by the people, in so far as the rulers can be chosen from the people and the people have a right to choose their rulers.[14]

This, so he says, was the form of government established by Moses for the Jews. One could surmise that something like the constitutional structure of the United States with a President (monarch), Senate and Congress (aristocracy), with all elected by the people as a whole (democracy), would fit Aquinas' description of the 'mixed régime' quite well.

Developments

The big question, which Aquinas leaves unresolved, is who is to interpret the moral law and judge when there is a conflict between it

---

[13] *Summa Theologiae*, 1, 11, 97, 3.
[14] ibid., 1, 11, 105, 1.

and the civil law? In the Middle Ages from time to time the Church
tended to claim to be the interpreter of the moral law and the judge
of any conflicts between it and the law of the State. But there is
nothing in Aquinas' theory which gives the Church this right. The
interpretation of the moral law is the business of 'natural reason' and
the Church authorities have to use the ordinary processes of reason
just like the rest of us. If one were to follow out the logic of Aquinas'
position one would have to say that they have no more competence in
the sphere of 'natural law' than they have in the sphere of the natural
sciences. The Church has special rights only within the area of its
own competence, the spiritual welfare of its members.

Later Catholic thinkers distinguish between the 'direct power' of
the Church over the political order, and what they call the 'indirect
power' of the Church vis-à-vis the State. They reject the first, but
they argue that in pursuit of its proper spiritual and religious
purposes the Church may sometimes run up against a certain law of
the State. Thus for example the Church might, in pursuit of its
religious mission, set up its own educational system; but then it
might come into conflict with a law of the State decreeing that only a
State-controlled education system will be tolerated. In this case the
Church may, in defence of its own proper religious interests,
legitimately protest against the policy of the State.[15] To that extent it
may (indirectly or obliquely) 'play politics'.

Clearly the theory of the 'indirect power' of the Church can be
interpreted in a very permissive way so that the Church is allowed a
good deal of interference in politics. But, by and large, later Catholic
thinkers, including the nineteenth and twentieth century Popes in
their statements on social questions (Leo XIII, Pius XII, John
XXIII), have resisted this temptation and kept fairly closely to the
position established by Aquinas.

Aquinas' ideas have also been developed by certain twentieth
century Catholic thinkers with reference to liberal democratic
'pluralist' societies where the State largely opts out of the realm of
private morality and restricts itself to providing a framework of
peace and order within which people can, as Mill puts it, follow out
their own 'experiments in living'. Catholic political philosophers
such as John Courtney Murray welcome the advent of the liberal
democratic state in that it has no religious (or anti-religious)
commitment. The Church, like any other group, is free to live
within such a society and to fulfil its specific religious task without
being tempted to play politics. In the older 'confessional' societies
(sixteenth and seventeenth century France, nineteenth century
Austro-Hungary) in which the Church had a privileged place, the

---

[15] J. Maritain, *The Things That Are Not Caesar's*, (London, 1939). J. Lecler, *The Two Sovereignties*, (London, 1952).

Church's religious mission was often compromised by its political commitments. In modern liberal democratic societies the Church cannot demand any special or favoured place: it must take its chance in promulgating its views with other groups. But because of this the Church's essential spiritual mission is more clearly manifested.[16]

Conclusion

What point do the ideas of Augustine and Aquinas have for contemporary political theory? No doubt, the medieval debates over the relations between Church and State do not now have much application in modern liberal democratic societies where the Christian churches have for the most part lost their special and favoured position and churchmen no longer wish to 'play politics'. There are, however, still some (like the 'Moral Majority' in the United States) who argue that the State should actively espouse specific religious views, and in Islamic societies such as Iran there is a strong tendency towards theocracy with the religious authorities assuming political power and using the law to enforce Islamic beliefs and precepts. The theory of the two societies elaborated by Augustine and Aquinas obviously has something to say with regard to these theocratic tendencies.

In more general terms, Augustine's political 'realism' has continuing relevance in that it reminds us that in practice in the political order self-interest remains a pervasive factor, and in that it warns us not to expect too much from politics. As it has been put, for Augustine

> the two major defects of fallen man, perversity of will and ignorance
> . . . infect every action that the State takes through its all too human
> agents. Since all those who bear political power – rulers, officials,
> judges, policemen, soldiers – are only men, their judgement is fallible,
> their information is inevitably inadequate and often incorrect, and
> their decisions are frequently biased by passion and self-interest.
> Their actions, even when they are successful, never dispose of the
> problems that they face, whether these be domestic issues or foreign
> relations.[17]

Aquinas' relevance lies in a different direction. As we have seen, Aquinas insists that the main instrument of the State, law, necessarily has a moral basis. Any positivistic theory of law which defines it merely in terms of the will of the 'sovereign' – whatever the

---

[16] John Courtney Murray, *We Hold These Truths*, (New York, 1960).
[17] Herbert A. Deane, op. cit. p. 234.

State decrees through its duly appointed legislative and judicial
bodies – is defective for Aquinas and his followers. Thus it has been
argued that it is only on a natural law basis that a justification can be
provided for human rights (claims by the individual against the
decrees of the State) and for international law (a legal system
which transcends particular State systems). The contemporary
rejuvenation of Aquinas' natural law theory by Finnis[18] and others
shows how much point and meaning it still has even for those who do
not subscribe to Aquinas' Christian world-view.

Further Reading

On St Augustine:
Peter Brown, *Augustine of Hippo*, (London, 1967). The best general
  introduction to St Augustine – man and work.
Herbert A. Deane, *The Political and Social Ideas of St Augustine*, (New
  York, 1963). A good survey of Augustine's political thought.
J.N. Figgis, *The Political Aspects of St Augustine's 'City of God'*, (London,
  1921). An old but still useful commentary.

On St Thomas Aquinas:
A.P. d'Entrèves, *Natural Law: An Introduction to Legal Philosophy*, (London, 1970). A little dated but still valuable as an introduction.
John Finnis, *Natural Law and Natural Rights*, (Oxford, 1980). A sophisticated and up-to-date analysis of Aquinas' natural law theory by an Oxford
  legal philosopher.
T. Gilby, *Principality and Polity: Aquinas and the rise of State theory in the
  West*, (London, 1958). Quirky but illuminating on Aquinas' political
  theory.

General:
Max Charlesworth, *Church, State and Conscience*, (St Lucia, 1973). Essays
  on contemporary aspects of Church–State relations.
J. Lecler, *The Two Sovereignties*, (London, 1952). A scholarly treatment of
  Catholic Church–State relations.
J. Maritain, *The Things That Are Not Caesar's*, (London, 1939). An old but
  still excellent analysis of the theory of 'indirect power'.
John Courtney Murray, *We Hold These Truths*, (New York, 1960). An
  illuminating attempt to reconcile traditional Church–State theory with
  liberal-democratic society by a great American Jesuit thinker.

---

[18] John Finnis, op. cit.

Chapter Four

Machiavelli and Political Morals

Douglas Adeney

It must be said that Niccolo Machiavelli has not had a unanimously good press. Though most of his works were published by Papal authority in 1532, they were reconsidered by Rome and placed on the first Index of Forbidden Books in 1559. To Shakespeare he was 'the murd'rous Machiavel';[1] Frederick the Great called him a 'monster', and his *The Prince* 'one of the most dangerous works that have ever been poured out on the world'.[2] To be sure the book has its admirers, but they include Hitler, who kept it by his bedside, and Mussolini, whose father read it to the family by the fireside. It was once believed that Machiavelli's given name was no coincidence, that here was a manifestation of Old Nick himself; his surname has given us a byword for political ruthlessness and skulduggery. Yet, as we shall see, it is possible to view him in more than one light.

Machiavelli was born in 1469 in Florence, which in a fragmented Italy was one of five major powers in company with Venice, Milan, Naples and the Papacy. In the same year control of Florence was inherited by Lorenzo de' Medici, Lorenzo the Magnificent; he was succeeded in 1492 by his disappointing son Piero, who panicked into ceding valuable territory to the advancing French and was exiled by his angry compatriots in 1494. Under the fanatical and puritanical monk Girolamo Savonarola, 'republican' government was restored, though in fact only some 3,200 of 90,000 inhabitants had any political rights as citizens. In 1498 Savonarola was deposed and

---

[1] *King Henry VI*, III, ii, 193. Note the anachronism.

[2] *L'Antimachiavel*, written in 1739, the year before he became King of Prussia. An extract is included in De L. Jensen, (ed.), *Machiavelli* (Lexington, 1960), pp. 5–8. It is doubtful whether Frederick's subsequent practice was quite as 'antimachiavel' as his preaching.

executed, but the republic survived him, and the young Machiavelli was given the important post of Second Chancellor. He seems to have lacked administrative experience, but thanks to his lawyer father he did have a knowledge of Latin classics, much valued as an education for civil servants in Renaissance Florence; and his appointment may well have been aided by the happy circumstance that his former professor at the University of Florence, Marcello Adriani, had just become First Chancellor.

The duties assigned to Machiavelli included a large amount of diplomatic business with Italian and foreign powers. His often delicate missions took him to the courts of the King of France, the Emperor Maximilian, the Pope, and, in 1502, Pope Alexander VI's alarming son Cesare Borgia in the northern Italian region of the Romagna. In the course of his work Machiavelli made many of the observations which, together with those of ancient Rome via the historian Livy, were to be so characteristic of his political books. In 1512, however, his career came to a sudden stop. Florence, which had supported France against the pugilistic Pope Julius II, was no match for the latter's new ally Spain when it swept the French aside in northern Italy. The republic collapsed, the Medici were restored, and Machiavelli, who had been close to the former head of government Piero Soderini and strongly criticized the Medici in their absence, was first dismissed from the chancery and then on slender evidence imprisoned for conspiracy and tortured. His luck changed in March 1513, when Cardinal Giovanni de' Medici was elected as Pope Leo X; during the celebrations in Florence an amnesty was declared and Machiavelli was set free. He lived in reluctant retirement, writing. In the next few years he completed his two most important political works, *The Prince* and the *Discourses on the First Decade of Livy's History*,[3] and lighter pieces including the celebrated comedy *Mandragola*. In 1516 he dedicated *The Prince* to a new Lorenzo de' Medici, who had just succeeded to power, but his hope of employment went unfulfilled. Not until 1526 did the Medici give him a permanent appointment, and ironically they lost power in May 1527 and Machiavelli was again out of work. He died of a stomach illness a few weeks later.

Now Machiavelli was not a philosopher in the way in which many of those introduced in this book are philosophers. He did not develop a systematic or sophisticated account of the basis and limits of political authority and obligation, nor did he show much interest in the analysis of important political concepts. His concerns were more with the practical principles of statecraft, of gaining and exercising effective power. In advocating his principles he sub-

---

[3]   That is, Books I–X. Of the 142 books only these and XXI–XLV have survived intact.

scribed however to certain ethical views and values; it is on these that I shall concentrate and briefly comment.

The Prince begins innocuously enough, with a classification of types of government. All governments, said Machiavelli, are either republics or princedoms; he would concern himself with princedoms and how they should be 'governed and maintained', and he drew several distinctions among them. They may be acquired hereditarily, or by addition to an inherited dominion, or by an 'absolutely new' prince; in the latter cases their peoples may be used to either princely rule or 'freedom'. In early chapters of the book there is advice as to how princedoms with various combinations of these characteristics should be handled, advice which is sometimes disturbing: the conquering prince should in certain cases wipe out the family of the previous ruler (ch. 3), and in certain others destroy the city or territory itself (ch. 5). But Machiavelli was particularly interested in a further distinction, between ways in which the non-hereditary princedom may be won. One may rely on other people's arms, which is, he suggested, to rely on Fortune; or one may use one's own, which is to exercise the admirable quality of *virtù*.

Fortune is needed, he said in ch. 6, to provide one's opportunity to become a prince. It was thus required even by such men as Moses, Cyrus, Romulus, and Theseus; but they were not obliged to Fortune for anything but the opportunity, and they took care to be armed. Armed prophets prevail; unarmed ones, such as Savonarola, fall.

Machiavelli did not deny however that Fortune may affect the affairs of princes in other ways. Like a terrible river whose flooding may be limited by dykes and embankments, Fortune 'shows her power where there is no organised, vigorous resistance, and consequently directs her attacks where she knows that no dykes or embankments have been built'. Italy, he added ruefully, was a land with no embankments and no dykes to protect it against the 'flood of invasion'. Different times required different strategies, but – though men find it difficult to act against their natures – it is better overall to be bold than cautious. For, said Machiavelli with a startling twist to his metaphor: 'Fortune is a woman and must be mauled and beaten if you want to keep her in subjection'; and 'she prefers young men, because they are less cautious, more ardent, and more daring in their demands' (ch. 25).

If Fortune is a woman, the other great contributor to princely success is an attribute which in English Machiavelli may well have wished to call manliness. His word *virtù* represents a group of specific qualities, prominent among which are strength, self-reliance, courage, resoluteness and practical wisdom. *Virtù* enabled the mercenary soldier Francesco Sforza to become Duke of Milan in 1450, and in Machiavelli's judgement it was also demonstrated by Cesare Borgia, Duke Valentino. Though in gaining his dominion he owed much to Fortune through his helpful father Pope Alexander, he acted thereafter, apart from one mistake, as a new prince should (ch. 7):

> Anyone . . . who wishes to secure himself in a new principality against the attempts of his enemies, and finds it necessary to gain friends, to surmount obstacles by force or by fraud, to make himself beloved and feared by his people and respected and obeyed by his soldiers, to destroy all those who have the will or the power to harm him, to replace old institutions with new ones, to be both severe and beloved, magnanimous and generous, to disband an army that he cannot trust and to raise a new one, to maintain good relations with kings and other princes, so that they are willing to help him or at least reluctant to harm him – such a prince, I say, cannot have a better or more recent model than the actions of the duke.

Some of the exemplary ducal deeds are cited. He won friends from the ranks of rival parties by rewarding them well. He lured his rebellious mercenary commanders to a 'conference' at which they were strangled. He discarded his mercenary forces altogether, and built his own army. He established order in his dominion by giving absolute power to the cruel governor Ramiro de Lorqua, and then, to avoid being generally hated, had Ramiro 'cut in two' and publicly exhibited; 'this fearful spectacle both satisfied and cowed the spirits of the people'. He wiped out all he could of the lords he had dispossessed; few escaped. He set up in his province a civil tribunal, in which every city had its own advocate. And he developed useful relations with France and Spain, who, if not keen to help him, were at least afraid to move against him. On the death of his father in 1503 he made, said Machiavelli, his one error, in failing to use his influence to prevent the election (as Julius II) of the family enemy Cardinal Giuliano della Rovere. 'For men are moved to harm others either by fear or by hatred', and there were cardinals available who had neither motive. Borgia was duly dispossessed by Julius, though Fortune contributed to his downfall by way of malaria.

The main foundations of every state, wrote Machiavelli in ch. 12, 'are good laws and good arms. Now good laws cannot exist without good arms, and where there are good arms there must be good laws; and so I shall here say nothing more about laws, but discuss the question of armed forces.' And indeed he did not in *The Prince* discuss good laws further, neither explaining nor supporting his claims about their connection with good arms. Rather, he returned to the importance of reliance on one's own arms, that is, on forces consisting of one's own subjects or citizens or dependants, rather than on mercenaries or on auxiliaries, who are forces supplied by a foreign power. Experience had shown that mercenaries were lukewarm fighters and brought 'nothing but disaster', while auxiliaries might be effective forces in themselves but 'if they win you become their prisoner' (ch. 13). One's army should be as much as possible one's own. Machiavelli was so convinced of this, and so stung by his diplomatic experience of French derision of Florence for her deserting Gasçon mercenaries and mutinous Swiss auxiliaries, that in 1505 he got authority to recruit a militia from the Florentine territories. It performed however without distinction and crumbled before the Spaniards in 1512.

In ch. 15 Machiavelli turned from the topic of war to that of the prince's conduct towards his subjects and friends. He took 'a very different line' from the usual, thinking it better to ask how things are in the real world than how they should be in an ideal one; and the truth is that anyone who tries to be virtuous on all occasions is 'bound to come to grief' among so many who are not virtuous. To stay in power the prince must learn to be, when necessary, 'other than virtuous'. Everyone will admit, said Machiavelli, that it would be 'most excellent' for a prince to be generous, bountiful, merciful, faithful, bold, courteous, chaste, sincere, affable, serious, pious, and so on; but the real world does not permit him to be such a paragon. He must know the usefulness to him of each quality, and also the value of a *reputation* for each. A reputation for generosity, for example, though useful in gaining power, can be maintained thereafter only by ostentatious extravagance, financed by oppressive taxation which will make him despised and vulnerable. The prince should not mind being called a miser – and in fact, wrote Machiavelli, he will later be recognised as being generous – when it is seen that his parsimony enables him to finance defence and other enterprises without distressing his people (ch. 16).

Similarly, he must not mind a reputation for cruelty, provided that he uses his cruelty for good ends. Borgia was accounted cruel, but his cruelty 'reformed, united and pacified the Romagna, and assured its allegiance to him' (ch. 17). By making a few examples, harming only individuals, the prince will prove 'more merciful in the end' than those whose indulgence allows crimes which harm the whole community. If he cannot be both feared and loved, however, it is better to be feared:

> For it can be said of mankind generally, that they are ungrateful, inconstant, pretenders to virtue and concealers of vice, avoiders of danger and lovers of gain; as long as you help them, they are all yours, and will offer you their blood, their property, their lives, and their children,...provided that the crisis is a long way off; when it comes closer, they soon turn their backs on you... Love is maintained by a bond of obligation which men, out of the depravity of their hearts, will break at the first prompting of self-interest; but fear is maintained by an apprehension of punishment...

Yet, he observed, to fear someone is not necessarily to hate him, and the prince must avoid being hated. He may avoid hatred if he executes people only with 'proper justification', and if he keeps his hands off his subjects' property and their women; but especially their property, 'for men will forget the death of their father more quickly than the loss of their patrimony'.

Chapter 18 begins:

> Everyone knows how praiseworthy it is for a ruler to keep his word, and to live with integrity and not by cunning: nevertheless experience shows that, in our own times, princes who have cared little about good faith, and have used cunning to confuse the minds of men, have achieved great things; so that in the end they have outstripped those who founded themselves on honesty.

Machiavelli explained there are two ways of deciding a contest: by law, which is proper to man, and by force, which is proper to beasts. But law is often ineffective, and so one must resort to force; one must, like the centaur, combine man and beast. And the beasts to take as models are the lion and the fox. The lion can scare off wolves, while it is the fox (though cunning is hardly *force*) who can recognize traps. Those who play only the lion 'do not know what they are about':

> A wise prince ... cannot and should not keep his word when it is disadvantageous to him and when the reasons for his original promise have ceased to exist. If all men were good, this advice would be wrong; but since in fact they are bad and would not keep faith with you, you in your turn do not have to keep faith with them, and a prince will never lack good reasons to colour his bad faith. We could quote countless modern examples of this, and show how often peace has been breached and promises have been broken through the bad faith of princes; and the leader who knew best how to play the fox has often had the better of it. But it is also necessary to know how to disguise this craft...
>   I will give one recent example. Pope Alexander VI never did or thought of doing anything but deceive others; and he always found someone to trust him.

Now in the preceding chapters Machiavelli said that the prince must not mind being blamed for vices or apparent vices which will in fact bring him, and indeed his people, security and prosperity. Thus he should not mind a reputation for parsimony, or even for cruelty; if he acts judiciously these reputations will actually be replaced in due course by contrary ones. In ch. 18, however, he specified five qualities for which the prince should take care to acquire a reputation even while behaving otherwise when it is to his advantage. He must seem to be honest and true to his word, in playing the fox; but he must also appear to be merciful, humane, and religious. Machiavelli did not see a need to reconcile his claim that a reputation for mercy was important with his earlier claim that a reputation for cruelty did not matter. Nevertheless he said here that a reputation for these five qualities was advisable, and especially for religion: this was 'most important of all'.

The value of religion to a ruler was taken up in the *Discourses* (I.11). It was appreciated, said Machiavelli, by Numa Pompilius, whose contribution to the greatness of Rome may thus have surpassed even that of his predecessor Romulus. The respect for religion which Numa established lasted for centuries:

> And anyone who carefully studies the history of Rome will readily see how well its religions promoted discipline in the armies, patriotism among the common people, and in general the encouragement of the virtuous and the disgrace of the wicked...
>
> The strict observance of divine worship always promotes the greatness of a state, just as contempt for religion will cause its ruin.

As Machiavelli was well aware, he was giving us an argument not for the truth of religion but for its utility, its value in promoting social discipline and cohesion. He quite probably lacked religious belief himself, and made no attempt to use claims about divine revelations or intentions to justify any form of government or principle or law; it is this as much as anything which distinguishes him from the mediaeval political theorists. But he certainly saw in religion great practical value, and advised rulers to encourage miracle stories even if they thought them false (*Disc.* I.12). His approval of religion was qualified, however, in two important ways. First, it did not mean approval of the Church of Rome, which in his opinion was doing no service to Italy: for one thing 'the corrupt example of the Roman court has extinguished all sense of religion and piety', but worse, the Church 'has long kept Italy divided', by being too weak to take over the whole of it but strong enough to call in foreign powers to defend its possessions. Secondly, Machiavelli maintained in a later chapter (II.2) that not all religions were of equal value. The pagan religions, he said, venerated great commanders and political leaders; they regarded worldly glory as the supreme good, which made the people bold and fierce in their actions. Christianity, however,

> glorifies the humble, the meek and the contemplative more than men of action. Its supreme good is to be found in humility, submission, and contempt for the things of this world; the supreme good of the pagans lay in greatness of mind, bodily vigour and everything else which makes men strong. If our religion demands strength of us, it is strength in suffering rather than strength in performance. This way of

living seems to have weakened mankind and given them up as a prey to wicked men, who can dispose of them as they please, knowing that most men hope to reach heaven by patiently enduring injuries rather than by avenging them. Thus it seems as if the world has grown effeminate and Heaven has laid aside its arms...

Curiously, he added that the fault lay not in Christianity itself but in its cowardly interpreters; the religion itself 'allows us to defend and exalt our country'. Perhaps he was trying to avoid the suggestion that the ruler in Christian Europe should take on the difficult task of promulgating a non-Christian religion. But he offered no argument against the 'passive' interpretation, and indeed he appeared to revert to it in a biting passage (*Disc*. III.1) in which he said that such men as St Francis and St Dominic, exemplifying and preaching the essential Christian ethic of meekness and submission to our superiors, were encouraging those superiors to 'do all the harm they can'. This disdain for Christianity may be likened to that of Marx, for whom religion of this type was 'the opium of the people' keeping them content to be exploited,[4] and Nietzsche, who scorned it as a sacrifice of all freedom and pride, as enslavement, self-mockery, and self-mutilation.[5] The places of all three in the demonology of Western European culture are no doubt due in part to their opinion of its religion.

To return now to *The Prince* and his list of virtues, Machiavelli said that the remainder may be summed up as follows: that the prince should avoid anything which may make him hated or despised. He will be hated if he robs his subjects of their property or their women, that is, of their property or their honour. He will be despised 'if he is thought to be changeable, frivolous, effeminate, cowardly or irresolute. He must avoid all this like the plague, and ensure that his actions appear full of greatness of heart, courage, gravity and strength' (ch. 19).

Thus acts the prince of *virtù*, who, not relying on capricious Fortune, gives himself the best possible chance of holding power. He is a prince who is able and ready to play both the lion and the fox: to be, as the occasion requires, 'other than virtuous'. And he is a prince whose admirer Machiavelli has been reviled for four centuries as the most wicked of writers, the Devil incarnate, a Real Renaissance Rotter. More specifically, he is condemned as a man whose morality for princes was a quite unscrupulous egoism, endorsing the pursuit and retention of power by whatever means are necessary. Yet this judgement of Machiavelli has not been the only one.

Some have thought that the recommendations in *The Prince* are

---

4   *Towards a Critique of Hegel's 'Philosophy of Right'*, D. McLellan, (ed.), *Karl Marx: Selected Writings*, (Oxford, 1977), p. 64.

5   *Beyond Good and Evil*, R.J. Hollingdale, (tr.), (Harmondsworth, 1973), sect. 46.

too bad to be true – that it is in fact a satire, written to warn us of the ways of tyrants. It is pointed out for a start that the character of Machiavelli's other writings, including the *Discourses*, is decidedly republican. 'Experience shows', he claimed (*Disc.* II.2), 'that no city ever extended its dominions or increased its wealth except at a time when it enjoyed civil liberty'; and liberty he identified with self-government, that is, republican government. The reason for the greater success of republics was, he said, simple enough:

> for it is not a regard for the good of one particular man which makes a city great, but regard for the good of the people as a whole. And there can be no doubt that proper attention to the public good is to be found only in republics: for there every measure which favours the general advantage is carried through; and even if it should turn out to the prejudice of one or more individuals, there are so many who stand to gain by it that they can ensure it will be put into effect...
>
> It is very different under the government of a prince, where it often happens that what is good for him is bad for the state, and what is good for the state is bad for him.

Now Machiavelli may well be right on the last point, but it does not follow, and it is certainly not true, that the interests of the prince and his state *never* coincide so that no prince has ever increased his state's territory or wealth. But despite this extravagance or perhaps because of it, Machiavelli's republicanism is believed to indicate that *The Prince* is satirical. The historian Garrett Mattingly, who takes this view, also raises the issue of Cesare Borgia. He is the major hero of *The Prince*, but in reality, as Mattingly puts it, a 'bloodstained buffoon' who led brutal and undisciplined troops, who had always ridden on his father's shoulders, and who was hated and despised as well as feared even by his father's supporters. He was, says Mattingly, a man whom the Medici (as Machiavelli must have known) could not possibly wish to emulate, and whom Machiavelli himself had judged harshly elsewhere. He also asks whether Machiavelli would really wish to give advice at all to the Medici, who had recently imprisoned and tortured him; and he thinks it significant that there is no evidence that *The Prince* was ever in the library of the younger Lorenzo.[6]

Yet the book simply does not read as a satire. Neither its language nor its structure suggests such an intention. Moreover, in a well-known letter of December 1513 to his friend and former colleague Francesco Vettori, Machiavelli writes in all seriousness of *The Prince*

---

6 'Machiavelli's *Prince*: Political Science or Political Satire?', *The American Scholar*, XXVII, 1958; reprinted in Jensen, op. cit., pp. 98–108. The Machiavellian writings critical of Borgia are certain diplomatic despatches and a historical poem of 1504, the *Decennale Primo*.

and his intention to dedicate it to the Medici so that they might employ him, 'even if they start by setting me to roll stones'; and in another, of January 1515, he tells Vettori that Borgia was a man 'whose actions I would always imitate if I were a new prince'.[7] Finally, for all the republican and libertarian sentiments of the *Discourses*, we are explicitly referred (III.42) to the discussion of promises in *The Prince*.

If the latter is not a satire, what is it? According to Ernst Cassirer:

> *The Prince* is neither a moral nor an immoral book; it is simply a technical book. In a technical book we do not seek rules of ethical conduct, of good and evil. It is enough if we are told what is useful or useless. Every word in *The Prince* must be read and interpreted in this way. The book contains no moral prescripts for the ruler nor does it invite him to commit crimes and villainies.[8]

This, I think, is quite misleading. Machiavelli plainly said that the 'wise prince' in this real world would practise self-interested dishonesty and infidelity, for example, and this is surely an invitation to commit what would commonly be deemed 'crimes and villainies'. And it is not merely a matter of there being no objection. Machiavelli *admired* the prince who combined the lion and the fox.

To appreciate his values we must also consider ch. 26, the famous ending to *The Prince*. Cassirer plays this down as not integral to the book, but Machiavelli did include it. It is a passionate call for the liberation of Italy from the 'barbarians' – for Italy has, as he had put it in ch. 12, 'been traversed from end to end by Charles (VIII of France), despoiled by Louis (XII of France), ravaged by Ferdinand (of Aragon) and put to shame by the Swiss'. He begs God for a deliverer and will eagerly follow his banner. There was 'someone' – Machiavelli was probably thinking of Borgia – who might have been that man, but was deserted by Fortune; now, he said to the Medici to whom he was dedicating the book, his hopes were in 'your illustrious family'. Those who have suffered the barbarians' 'stinking tyranny' would greet their deliverer with love, loyalty, and tears: 'What Italian would refuse him allegiance?' These words have led some to see Machiavelli as above all an Italian patriot, and helped to inspire the nationalistic movement known as the *Risorgimento* as Italy moved towards the liberation and unification of 1870.

But whether it be Italy as a whole or some smaller or for that matter external unit, Machiavelli clearly esteemed a strong and independent state. In a well-known passage near the end of the

---

[7] *The Literary Works of Machiavelli*, J.R. Hale, (ed. and tr.), (Oxford, 1961), pp. 140 and 156.

[8] *The Myth of the State* (New Haven and London, 1946), p. 153; Jensen, op. cit., p. 65.

Discourses (III.41), he maintained indeed that *any* action was justified if that end required it:

> When the safety of our country is at stake, all regard to what is just or unjust, merciful or cruel, praiseworthy or shameful, must be put aside. The policy which will save the country and preserve its liberty must be wholeheartedly followed, regardless of any other consideration.

Earlier in the *Discourses* he gives stark examples of 'extraordinary measures' which he saw as justified by the interest of the country or state – by what is now often called *raison d'état*. For Machiavelli, this was not an interest over and above, or competing with, that of the people; rather, he appealed in utilitarian terms to the 'common good'. In I.9, for instance, he defended Romulus over the killing of his brother Remus. This act was necessary, he said, so that supreme authority in founding the new state should be in one person's hands; this was essential for the success of such a venture and thus for the common good. He believed that this was indeed Romulus' objective, since he soon appointed a senate whose advice he respected, and that in fact it was only in the founding stages that one-man rule was best. Whether these things actually happened, whether they were actually done for the common good, and whether they actually achieved it, need not concern us here. The point is that Machiavelli apparently accepted the doctrine that the common good, the well-being of one's people, provided the sole criterion by which the morality of a political act should be judged. He did not explore the notion of the common good, and ask for example whether it consists in happiness and what that is, but his position here is recognisably and ruthlessly utilitarian. One may have to slay not only one's own brother as did Romulus, but also 'the sons of Brutus': legend has it that Lucius Junius Brutus, one of the founders of the Roman republic in the sixth century BC, condemned his own two sons to death for plotting to restore the Tarquin monarchy. Piero Soderini too, in Machiavelli's Florence, had to contend with those who wanted to restore the previous régime; yet he thought 'that his patience and kindness could overcome his opponents' ill-will', and shrank from using extraordinary powers which would mean breaking the law and risk bringing his office into disrepute. But it can never be right, said Machiavelli, 'to allow weeds to grow among the corn, when they can easily smother it'; and Soderini could have appealed to the common good as well as protecting that good against any abuse of power by his successor. His failure 'led to the loss of his reputation and authority, and of the liberties of his country: and all because he did not know how to follow the example of Brutus' (*Disc.* III.3).

In a couple of passages quoted earlier from *The Prince*, however, there is a quite different line of moral thinking to be found. It proceeds from a premise of the deepest pessimism about human nature. Men, he said in ch. 17, are 'ungrateful, inconstant, pretenders to virtue and concealers of vice'. This pessimism recurs in ch. 23, where he said that men 'will always behave like villains towards you, unless they are under some compulsion to be honest', and early in the *Discourses* (I.3):

All those who have written about civil government lay it down as a principle, which is supported with many examples by all historians, that anyone who wants to found a state and provide it with laws must assume that all men are bad by nature, and that they will not fail to act in accordance with the wickedness of their hearts whenever they have an opportunity. Human wickedness may indeed remain hidden for a certain time, but this is due to some secret reason, which we do not recognise because we have no experience of what is involved; but time, which is sometimes called the father of truth, will bring it to light in the end.

Now it is one thing to believe the assumption of universal human wickedness to be necessary in framing laws, and another to believe that assumption to be true; and even if it were the case (which it is not) that all writers do the former, it does not follow that they all do the latter. But Machiavelli is one who does, and he told us again in the next paragraph: 'men never act well except through necessity'.

So laws are needed to 'make men good'. Machiavelli's universal pessimism as an argument for government has some similarity to that of Hobbes, but while Hobbes thought that in the 'state of nature' there would be 'a war of every man against every man' (*Leviathan*, ch. 13), he saw many of us as joining that war simply through fear. Machiavelli's view of our nature was blacker. And from it he drew another conclusion, as we have seen. If all men were good, that is, honest and faithful and so on, then the prince should be likewise; 'but since in fact they are bad and would not keep faith with you, you in your turn do not have to keep faith with them'. Faithless actions are thus permissible not in so far as they are done for the sake of an all-important end, but because the obligation of fidelity lapses when nobody else is respecting it. Machiavelli does not however pursue, as he might have done, the implications beyond infidelity. To follow him with an example in Italy, I recall seeing my father-in-law being roundly jostled by local women while boarding the ferry from Capri; normally as civil as you or I, he hesitated for a moment and then reciprocated with relish. When there is not just a seat on the boat at stake but a seat of power, and everyone (else) is a villain, what may we not do?

It has often been protested that Machiavelli's pessimism is

excessive. Certainly there are villains who would lightly break their word or even your neck, and others who would do so were it not for the law or perhaps religion, or some unpleasant 'secret reason'; but most people are just not like that, and it is hard to believe that they were like that in Machiavelli's day either. Indeed he does not himself seem thoroughgoing in his pessimism. Later in the *Discourses* he said that men are easily corrupted, conceding that they may be good to begin with (I.42), and that when they are bad it is usually the fault of their rulers (III.29). And of course the very presumption of the argument in *The Prince* is that his audience needs to be persuaded that infidelity is justifiable. But even if our fellow men were all 'bad by nature', and would act accordingly but for coercion or some 'secret reason', should we regard our moral obligations as lapsing? I believe not. For while they may in a sense be wronging us in having some such motive for doing their duty, this does not warrant our wronging them more in return by not doing ours. And Machiavelli would surely not claim that in his society people always or usually failed to do as they should; he would have to admit that most people most of the time did behave well enough, even though he believed that they did so for the wrong reasons and that in ancient Rome, partly because of the influence of less corrupt religious leaders, they behaved better.

I have briefly considered several interpretations of Machiavelli's political morality. When he endorses all those controversial actions, is he an egoist, valuing supremely the individual's ruthless pursuit of power; a satirist, in reality appalled at Borgia and his ilk; a mere political technician, saying what one must do if one wants power; a tough utilitarian, concerned above all for the good of the people; or a moral pessimist, believing that obligations lapse in a world of villains?

It is not easy, from his writings, to settle on any of these as his true position. But the task of identifying a consistent Machiavellian line is made more formidable still, I think, by the fact that in one or two places he appears to baulk at actions he endorsed elsewhere. One of these places is the often overlooked ch. 8 of *The Prince*, where he considered Agathocles of Syracuse and Oliverotto of Fermo. These men became princes not through Fortune or *virtù*, but by 'wicked and infamous means'. Agathocles lived 'a most wicked life' in progressing from abject poverty to military command; in 317 B.C. he made himself king by calling a 'meeting' at which all the senators and richest citizens were suddenly killed by his soldiers. Despite the courage and daring shown by Agathocles during his rise to power and in holding it successfully against Carthage, Machiavelli declared that it cannot be called true *virtù* 'to murder one's fellow-citizens, betray one's friends, and to live without faith, pity or religion. Such methods may gain power, but can never win glory'. Agathocles used his cruelties *well* (if, said Machiavelli, we may speak thus of what is evil in itself) in that they were carried out 'once and for all' at the outset of his rule; where this is done 'their bitterness will last for as short a time as possible and so cause less resentment' than if they continue and grow. And so Agathocles, unlike many other treacherous and cruel rulers, was able to live securely and keep foreign enemies at bay. Nevertheless, 'his atrocious cruelty and inhumanity and his many crimes do not allow him to be numbered among the great'. To this classical example is added a contemporary one, that of Oliverotto, who in 1501 seized power in Fermo by a ruse similar to Agathocles'; his victims included the uncle who had raised him. Despite what the *Discourses* were to say about Romulus and Brutus and the irrelevance of kinship, Oliverotto is here condemned for this murder even though he thereafter 'lived in safety in Fermo' and 'became formidable to all his neighbours'. From Machiavelli's account it is difficult to feel much sympathy for Oliverotto when, the following year, he was among those tricked and slain by Borgia.

In the *Discourses*, too, Machiavelli ruled out certain means to power as unacceptable. He did it, indeed, in a chapter (III.40) immediately preceding a clear statement of his utilitarianism. The former is entitled 'That it is Permissible, and Indeed Glorious, to Make Use of Deceit in War', and he cited clever ploys by Hannibal and a Samnite general against the Romans; but he declared that deceit was 'odious in all other transactions', and moreover that it was not praiseworthy 'when it involves breaking your word or violating a treaty; for though kingdoms and states are sometimes won in this way ... you can never acquire true glory by it'. His distinction between power and glory might suggest that he was really subscribing to the 'enlightened' egoistic view that one should seek self-interest of a particular kind, namely glory in the eyes of others and of history; but I think it is clear that Machiavelli was condemning certain people not for what they had failed to do for themselves, but for what they had done to others. They forfeited posterity's approval, but that is not why they forfeited his.

What then are we to make of Machiavelli's morals? At times he reads like a ruthless egoist, and at other times like an equally ruthless utilitarian; but he also embraced on the one hand what may be called common decency and on the other a sweeping pessimism about human nature which leds him to permit perfidy. I do not find him constant. Nor, incidentally, did his wife Marietta. I think it is safe to conclude, however, that those who see him as the Devil himself are mistaken. For in both his distaste for the likes of Agathocles, and his witting or unwitting acceptance of conflicting values and principles, Machiavelli shows himself capable of being quite human after all.

Further Reading

For Machiavelli's writings see, for example, Allan Gilbert's translation *Machiavelli: The Chief Works and Others*, 3 vols., (Durham, N.C., 1965,). A more accessible edition is the Everyman, *Machiavelli: The Prince and Other Political Writings*, selected and translated by Bruce Penman (London, 1981), from which my quotations are taken.

The literature is vast, but see perhaps Quentin Skinner's concise *Machiavelli*, (Oxford, 1981) and Sydney Anglo's critical *Machiavelli: A Dissection*, (London, 1969). Various interpretations are represented in De Lamar Jensen (ed.), *Machiavelli*, (Lexington, Mass., 1960) and illuminated in Sir Isaiah Berlin's essay 'The Originality of Machiavelli' in his *Against the Current*, (London, 1979).

Chapter Five

Luther and the Temporal Kingdom

Robert Young

Introductory Remarks

Martin Luther is best known as the most influential figure in the Protestant Reformation of the sixteenth century. As a political thinker he is known to historians of political ideas and in theological circles, but elsewhere, except on one main point, he is not taken to have been an influential political thinker.[1] That one main point concerns his commonly being taken to be the founder of the separation of Church from State. As we shall see, though, it is not accurate to attribute to Luther a doctrine like that of the modern one on the separation of the Church from a secular State. But neither is it accurate to maintain, as has so often been done, that he was just a reactionary political thinker of no particular interest.

The period from the late fifteenth century through to the first half of the sixteenth century was one of great political ferment in various parts of Europe. Peasants and labourers had become seriously disaffected because of their declining economic position. Many of them initiated struggles to better their condition and to achieve greater equality in society,[2] but were met with resistance by the ruling classes (nobility, clergy and merchants) who directed the forces of the State. The issue of the proper exercise of authority came to have renewed importance[3] and thus it was hardly surprising that

---

[1] *Pace* L.H. Waring in *The Political Theories of Martin Luther*, (Port Washington, New York, 1968).

[2] Cf. E.L.R. Ladurie, *Carnival in Romans*, (Harmondsworth, 1981) for an illustration of the point in a provincial city in France in the latter part of the sixteenth century.

[3] Cf. J.W. Allen, *A History of Political Thought in the Sixteenth Century*, (London and New York, 1957), chs. 1, 2.

in Germany various of the peasants would look to Luther as their champion given certain of his declared political ideas (e.g. those about the liberty and conscience of the individual Christian and those concerning the obligations and responsibilities of the State). Luther sought to outline a philosophy of government that would make clear the proper limits of worldly rule but he did so as a theologian not as a practical politician. At the level of practical politics he gave strong support to the princes[4] and though he also endeavoured to temper their harshness, his support tended to reinforce rather than check their power. One consequence of this was the loss of some of his popular appeal, because his position came to be understood as neither radical nor apocalyptic but moderate. He was, of course, developing a theological position rather than a *realpolitik*[5] but it is unlikely that the loss of his popular appeal can be explained by this fact. Once his main political ideas are before us the nature of the enterprise in which Luther was engaged will, I think, become clearer. I shall, therefore, turn now to the task of elaborating those ideas.

The Doctrine of the Two Kingdoms

Probably the key notion for an understanding of Luther's political thought is his doctrine of the two kingdoms. In the kingdom of God, God (as redeemer) rules all regenerate believers. In the kingdom of men, God (as creator) rules all sinful but rational creatures through Caesar and the law. God is at once the lord of both kingdoms, the Christian is at once a subject of both kingdoms. For Luther the distinctiveness of these two kingdoms was evident (as evident as the related distinction between the heavenly city and the earthly city had seemed to Augustine a thousand or so years before[6]). But while he took the two kingdoms to be distinguishable Luther certainly did not think of them as separate and self-contained – society contained few Christians and so could not be thought of as Christian but equally it was unthinkable that it should be allowed to be secularized.

The concerns of the kingdom of men are with the physical body

---

[4] Cf. especially 'Against the Robbing and Murdering Hordes of Peasants' in *Luther's Works*, H.T. Lehman, (ed.) (Philadelphia, 1967) vol. 46.

[5] For interesting discussion of the activities of others more concerned with such *realpolitik* see R. Bainton, *Here I Stand: A Life of Martin Luther*, (New York and London, 1971), pp. 195ff, and R. Friedenthal, *Luther: His Life and Times*, (New York, 1967), esp. ch. 31.

[6] Augustine's distinction (like Luther's) does not always work as clearly as it might. See e.g. F.E. Cranz, '*De Civitate Dei*, XV, 2, and Augustine's Idea of the Christian Society' in R.A. Markus (ed.), *Augustine*, (Garden City, New York, 1972).

and with property. Accordingly the temporal authorities are to
restrain those who would wickedly threaten life, limb and property.
Law was instituted for the sake of the lawless and the upholding of
the law serves to restrain the wicked and maintain the sort of peace
needed for tolerable social existence. The concern of the kingdom of
God is the soul. The Church is charged with the responsibility of
teaching, preaching and administering the sacraments so that people
might be brought to faith in God and thence to live righteously.[7]
Thus far it may well seem that Luther was right to affirm the evident
distinctiveness of the two kingdoms. But, as I previously indicated,
he does not take the kingdoms to be separate and self-contained and
matters therefore sometimes become more complicated than he
implies. For instance, Luther held, as we shall see, that the State is
not authorized to compel anyone to do wrong against God *or* man.
This conviction does pose difficulties for some of his contentions
about the distinctive authority of the temporal kingdom though it
might be thought to sit more easily with his notion that the
kingdoms are not separate. Again, Luther's strong support for the
princes would seem to have been thoroughly in line with his view of
their distinctive role but, as Allen and others have pointed out, he
came in the 1530s, when religious toleration declined markedly, to
urge the princes to maintain pure religion by force and this would
not appear to line up well with the continued insistence in his
writings on the distinctiveness of the temporal and spiritual kingdoms.

Still, if it be allowed that Luther's distinction is not altogether
bereft of value, it becomes clear why and how Luther was enabled to
give positive acceptance to the temporal order. At the same time
it also becomes clear why his stated position did not encourage
Christians to see themselves as having an urgent social responsibility to work for the transformation of existing social structures. If
God is believed to be lord of the fallen world and to make use of
its institutions, laws and offices graciously to preserve it from even
greater chaos, injustice and suffering, the believer will have a
powerful motive to respect the integrity of those institutions, laws
and offices.

Nonetheless Luther's position is not that of the political quietist.
He insists that rulers exercise their role under God's judgment just
as the Church does. Each is of divine origin and has its sphere of
authority but the individual is not bound to obey in everything.
While Luther did for the most part strongly support the princes (and

---

7   On the distinction between the two kingdoms see especially, 'To the Christian
     Nobility of the German Nation Concerning the Reform of the Christian Estate' in
     Luther's Works, vol. 44, pp. 91ff, 130; 'Temporal Authority: To What Extent It
     Should Be Obeyed' in *Luther's Works*, vol. 45, pp. 85–105; 'An Open Letter on
     the Harsh Book Against the Peasants' in *Luther's Works*, vol. 46, pp. 70ff.

this despite his generally low view of them as individuals[8]), it is well to remember that he himself refused to comply with the order of the highest temporal authority, the emperor, when at Worms in 1521 he would not recant his various writings. It is true that this related to a matter of faith and thus Luther saw the order of the emperor as encroaching on God's kingdom and government.[9] But Luther also rebuked rulers who disregarded their responsibility to God for their subjects' economic and social welfare (and called upon others to do so as well).[10] And he made it clear that where the prince is in the wrong (e.g. in waging a particular war) the people are not bound to follow him for 'it is no one's duty to do wrong'.[11] This accords well with the fact that Luther himself practised a form of civil disobedience when he thought his faith and conscience were imperilled by an order of the State which would have required him to give up the truth. (Interestingly he urged that where the citizen was unable to tell whether the prince was in the right, and could not with all possible diligence find out, he could obey with a clear conscience.) Luther did not see his claim as any justification, however, for revolutionary activity. What he says about rebellion in the various places where he addresses the question makes it clear that his concern is with the circumstances of his own time and place.[12] But he is quite constant in his opposition to violent resistance to the civil authorities – to violently resist is to rebel against the order instituted by God.

In summary, then, Luther's position is not (as has so often been said) that there can be no justification for any kind of resistance to civil authority. Those German Lutheran theologians (like Paul Althaus, Friedrich Gogarten and Emmanuel Hirsch) who sought to show there was a foundation in Luther's political ideas for Nazi totalitarianism certainly misread him.[13] So, too, did those who tried to trace what they saw as the easy acquiescence of the German clergy

---

[8]   Cf. 'Temporal Authority', op. cit, p. 113.

[9]   Cf. 'Temporal Authority', op. cit., especially part II, and his commentary on Psalm 82 in *Luther's Works*, vol. 13 pp. 42–72.

[10] *Luther's Works*, vol. 13, p. 50f. But see too, J.M. Tonkin, *The Church and the Secular Order in Reformation Thought*, (New York, 1971), p. 56f.

[11] 'Temporal Authority', op. cit., especially p. 125f.

[12] Cf. 'A Sincere Admonition by Martin Luther to All Christians to Guard Against Insurrection and Rebellion' in *Luther's Works*, vol. 45 and 'To the Christian Nobility' op. cit.,

[13] Luther was also cited as a forerunner of Hitlerian anti-semitism. While Hitler's policies toward the Jews were not justified by him by reference to Luther's writings it is necessary to say something about the relationship between their views. In one of Luther's most disreputable pieces 'On the Jews and their Lies' (*Luther's Works*, op. cit., vol. 47), Luther made various recommendations to the authorities to act against Jews (see especially pp. 267–92). These included confiscation of property obtained from usurious practices (which particularly angered Luther). Luther does not, however, seem to have passionately hated Jews

to Hitler's régime to Luther's having urged subservience by the people to the State as a political absolute. (This latter claim suffered as well from ignoring the evidence that the positive attitude of many clergy toward Hitler was mainly confined to the early part of his régime when he gave relief from the miseries of the Weimar republic, and that later it was frequently members of the clergy like Niemoller and Bonhoeffer who most strongly opposed Hitler.) While Caesar must be rendered his due, so, too, must God (cf. *Luke* 20:25). There can, therefore, be no thought for Luther of the State as a political absolute. Worldly government is autonomous relative to this worldly consideration but it is not absolutely autonomous. All rulers are subject to God (irrespective of whether they have theistic convictions), even though they are not subject to ecclesiastical rule (as was claimed by many of the medieval popes). Governments have their function under God, the Church has its function. While governments are, therefore, to exercise their function free of religious direction, there is in Luther's thought no licence for a State like the secular one of modern political thought. So even though Luther believed that violent resistance to the civil authority was not permissible in any circumstances, he carefully avoided any suggestion of the absoluteness of such authority. Where the civil authority issues orders that violate the law of God (which includes the natural law expressed in conscience) passive resistance is certainly justified. The law of God and of conscience is the final judge of the validity of *all* human law, it is not concerned merely with religious belief and worship.[14]

On Luther's account governments are chiefly charged with restraining evil – he specifically mentions such things as public immorality, usury, extortion and poverty – and thereby with preserving the decaying world in as good order as possible until the final denouement for this present age.[15] (Since civil government is to be in the interests of all and not just for the benefit of any particular group or class, governments are also charged, as we shall see, with positive responsibilities like upholding civil and religious liberties and educating the young in matters of the world, of morals and of religion.)

---

for all that he was ready to accept much of the popular prejudice about them. His frustration with them for what he deemed their obstinacy in refusing to turn to Christ put them in much the same stead as the papists and Turks. Though his recommendations to the authorities were unfeeling they were in no way to be compared with the policies of the Nazis. This is clearest in relation to his suggestion that if Jews would not become Christians and thus become an integral part of (German) society they should be repatriated to Palestine (p. 276). For further discussion of these matters see E.G. Rupp, *Martin Luther: Hitler's Cause – or Cure?*, (London, 1945).

[14] Cf. 'Temporal Authority', p. 83f, 112; Allen, op. cit., p. 20f.
[15] See Luther's exposition of Psalm 101 in *Luther's Works*, vol. 13, p. 164.

Importantly for Luther the central mandate to curb evil extended to evil or injury done by ecclesiastics (including the Pope)[16] and that of the maintenance of good order extended to crushing the rebellious Anabaptists. Luther could justify the actions of the State in such cases by reference to his doctrine of the two kingdoms: they were 'civic acts in the worldly realm for the sake of public order'.[17] But it is unlikely that the princes put such a fine theoretical point on, for example, quelling the Anabaptist disturbance – they did not see themselves as having the limited role Luther had marked out for them. To that extent Luther's attempt to maintain the independence and integrity of both Church and State did not always win out in practice. Indeed, as I have already mentioned, his very strong support for the princes on various occasions helped reinforce their own more absolutist views of their role. But it remains true that Luther's stated position represented a break with ecclesiastical claims to control of the State and with claims to absolute authority on the part of temporal rulers and of ecclesiastical leaders (like the Pope). Both the Church and the State must acknowledge their subjection to God and that each has a (distinctive) God-given role. I propose now to spell out more fully the scope of the State's role as Luther saw it.

The Functions of the State

I previously pointed out that Luther saw the main purpose of government to be the restraint of evil. Men are wicked and through their sin they have brought disorder and suffering into the world. God has thus ensured the establishment of instruments to preserve the decaying world. Luther's solemn outlook on the world and its need for law and order is, however, not the whole of the story. He had at the same time a positive and indeed joyful attitude to the created world because it was God's world. God has not been dethroned – he continues to rule despite the evil in the world and will ultimately restore the created world. Moreover the world is a good world for all that there is evil in it. There is no need, therefore, to retreat from the world. Hence as well as restraining evil[18] the temporal authorities are also to seek the good of their subjects.[19] Luther's writings contain a great deal of material which is directed

---

[16] 'To the Christian Nobility ...', op. cit., pp. 126ff.

[17] Tonkin, op. cit., p. 82.

[18] Luther had in mind immorality as well as crime. Thus he saw a need for the State to move against gambling, prostitution, extravagantly costly dress and conspicuous consumption. Cf. especially 'To the Christian Nobility', op. cit., especially p. 212ff.

[19] 'To the Christian Nobility ...', op. cit., p. 130.

at the authorities in an endeavour to get them to fulfil their responsibilities in this regard. Thus, against irresponsible merchants he
attacked economic injustice and proposed government controls to
halt unfair commercial and labour practices.[20] Against selfish parents
and lax public officials he fought for educational opportunities
to be more widespread and for reforms in the educational practices
of the day.[21] He argued for the establishment of community chests as
a way of eradicating the need for begging.[22] Perhaps most fundamentally of all he urged (Christian) rulers to 'give consideration
and attention to [their] subjects, and really devote [themselves] to
... being useful and beneficial to them'.[23] The good ruler, says
Luther, does not think that the land and the people belong to him
and hence that he may do what pleases him, but rather seeks to serve
the people by working for their advantage and not his own.[24]
Despite the hard line he took on the peasant uprisings,[25] Luther
urged the princes to deal more justly with the peasants by ceasing to
rob and cheat them in the pursuit of a life of luxury and extravagance. Indeed he lays the blame for the rebellion squarely at the feet
of the princes and lords.[26] In all of these writings and more, Luther
makes it clear that the authorities are to foster the good (as well as to
restrain the evil), and thus to enhance life in the kingdom of men
while ever that kingdom remains.

It will help in achieving a fuller appreciation of Luther's political
ideas if I outline a little more fully his views on some of these aspects
of the role of government. First, then, his concern for justice and
equity in the economic sphere. Luther took no special interest in the
changes that were taking place in the economy of his day. Chiefly
these changes were the move away from a peasant agricultural
society to one oriented toward trade, in particular foreign trade. This
required large accumulations of capital. Since the laws against usury
hampered the accumulation of capital (by deterring investment) they
were either evaded or ignored. Luther saw some of the manifestations of these changes, such as high prices and growing disparities
in wealth, as the result of the greed and avarice of sinful men.
Accordingly, his views about economic matters are mainly about
regulating economic agents and their practices so as to curb greed
and avarice, not to restructure the economy to achieve a more just
distribution of resources. Various practices which were accepted by

---

[20] See especially 'Trade and Usury' in *Luther's Works*, vol. 45.
[21] 'A Sermon on Keeping Children in School' in *Luther's Works*, vol. 46; 'To the
Christian Nobility', op. cit.
[22] 'Ordinance of a Common Chest' in *Luther's Works*, vol. 45.
[23] 'Temporal Authority', p. 120.
[24] Ibid., p. 120.
[25] 'Against the Robbing and Murdering Hordes of Peasants', op. cit.
[26] 'Admonition to Peace' in *Luther's Works*, vol. 46, p. 19.

others (including the early scholastics and the canonists) he saw as being akin to usury and thus to be outlawed.

One such practice was the cornering of a market so as to give monopolistic control over price.[27] Another was the selling of goods 'on time and credit for a higher price than if they were sold for cash'. Luther was critical of the governments of his day for failing to deal with these and similar abuses. He also urged reform of *Zinskauf* contracts. These were becoming increasingly common. They developed out of the idea of rental paid to a feudal landlord who turned over a piece of land as a fief in perpetuity. The main change was that money became the chief and ultimately almost the sole factor both in the original exchange and in the method of payment. In one variation the borrower retained the title to his land but gave the produce to his creditor; in another the debtor paid his creditor a specific interest on the principal using the land as security; in a third the entire property of the debtor was pledged for the interest due. Luther was realist enough to recognize that such contracts need not be unreasonable but he argued that there should be a specific collateral so that the entire person and property of the debtor might not be subject completely to the creditor's demands. He argued, too, that the early repayment of the principal should be an option of the debtor alone. The 'interest' was thus to be seen as a guard against loss by the creditor – and therefore was not subject to the condemnation on usury.[28]

Luther's views on economic life were primarily developed to instruct the Christian conscience about God's demands for equity for all. In a truly Christian society there would be no need for law or regulation but in a non-Christian society there have to be codes of behaviour and laws which will restrain evil. This is as true in the economic affairs of the kingdom of men as in any other. Hence the role of government in economic affairs is the same as its general one: to be a bulwark against evil and thus to regulate economic and business life so as to contain greed and corruption. Doing this indirectly promotes the good of all.

In relation to education, and the role of the State in making provision for it, Luther's views were very progressive. During the early Middle Ages education was almost wholly carried on by members of the clergy through the monastic schools. In subsequent centuries cathedral schools with a somewhat broader curriculum developed. In the later Middle Ages the chantry school and the guild

---

[27] 'Trade and Usury', op. cit., p. 262.

[28] Since Luther rejected the monastic ideal of asceticism and positively affirmed the place of private property – chiefly, it is true, as a means to implementing Jesus' command in the Sermon on the Mount (*Matthew* 5) to aid the needy – he was at odds with the scholastics and canonists who had to resort to casuistry to justify such 'interest'.

school emerged. The clergy continued to service all these forms of schooling. Changes began when some of the guild schools (which were originally established for the children of guild members) developed into municipal schools largely supported and controlled by the secular authorities and having some lay teachers.[29] In the fifteenth century the influence of Renaissance humanism led to the introduction of humanist subjects into the curriculum of some existing schools and the founding of new schools in which humanist ideas prevailed. Luther himself attended one of these schools for a time. Such schools and the course of study they followed had little appeal, however, for the common people. The standing of education in general was low in the eyes of the common people anyway, since it was professionally oriented and thus not seen as helpful in the world of trade and industry. Boys were indentured to learn a trade at an early age because this, rather than education, was thought to ensure a good livelihood.

It was against this background that Luther offered not an outline of a complete system of education[30] but practical advice to the responsible authorities and gave an apologia for education against its critics. Luther maintained that education was necessary for the spiritual growth of boys and girls and for their development as useful citizens.[31] It is worth making special comment on Luther's attitude to education for girls. Such education was not unheard of but was quite unusual. Luther urged the establishment of girls' schools in all towns. (In fact he offered to provide board and lodging to one particular lady should she be willing to establish a school for girls in Wittenberg.)

In his treatise directed to councilmen Luther argued for an amalgam of the best features of humanist education (history, literature, languages), the other liberal arts and training in the Christian religion. Unlike the humanists Luther wished for public education to be available to all. Indeed against those parents who argued that they could not spare their children from domestic duties he argued that education should be compulsory at least for some small part of each day. (In arguing for compulsory education Luther did, it is true, have an eye to the way in which schooling would provide the young with the capacity to resist the wiles of the Papacy. But mostly he was more nobly motivated.)

Luther also advocated the founding by the authorities of public libraries. He believed that this should be a matter for the public

---

[29] Cf. F.P. Graves, *A History of Education During the Middle Ages and the Transition to Modern Times*, (New York, 1920).

[30] As his colleague Philip Melanchthon later did.

[31] In 'To the Councilmen of All Cities in Germany That They Establish and Maintain Christian Schools', *Luther's Works*, vol. 45 and 'A Sermon on Keeping Children in School', op. cit.

authorities for, as with the funding of schools, it is the State's duty to ensure the availability in the community of the skills and knowledge needed for the efficient running of the community.

Luther was at once a man of the kingdom of this world as well as of God's kingdom. Thus just as he was motivated to make suggestions for the reform of the schools with a view to improving life in the kingdom of men so, too, did he suggest that every city should take care of its own poor, and that an organized system of poor relief be set up.[32] In his 'Long Sermon on Usury' (later republished in 'Usury and Trade') Luther declared that Christians were not to allow anyone to remain in want or to beg (an extremely widespread practice in the Middle Ages). Where a town or city could not manage this on its own, neighbouring villages should be called upon to contribute – with the abolition of begging this would become financially more possible. At the time the bulk of the funds for poor relief came from income-producing foundations or properties and though the income from these was used by the Church to relieve poverty, control of the foundations or properties was frequently vested in the local administrators. What Luther and others advocated required a complete reorganization of the parish financial system since it involved taking over all church properties within the parish and establishing an organization to administer them. The revenue thus derived, along with income from a parish tax, was to be used so as to provide for worship, schools and the assistance (via a community chest) of the poor and needy.[33]

Concluding Remarks

Luther was first and foremost a theologian. When he addressed political issues he did so as a theologian. This single point explains a good deal of the tension in his writings between his hankering for a temporal state ruled by God's word, the natural law and reason and his conviction that the flawed character of the temporal states he knew was unalterable given man's sinfulness. The former, theocratic ideal could only be hankered for; what must be sought, therefore, was a State free of ecclesiastical control but one with as much integrity as could be managed. To rule the world by the gospel would not be feasible. The best guidance for earthly rulers is in fact to be found in the reason and commonsense (the wisdom) of the 'pagan' philosophers.[34] Reason cannot gain one access to the king-

---

[32] 'To the Christian Nobility', op. cit., p. 189f.

[33] Cf. 'Ordinance of a Common Chest', op. cit. Included among the 'poor and needy' were the aged and infirm, those needing home help, newcomers to the area, orphans etc.

[34] 'Exposition of Psalm 101' in *Luther's Works*, vol. 13, p. 199f.

dom of God. Such access is by grace alone. But since it is reason that separates man from the animals and since it is reason that dictates how to live well in the kingdom of men, it is reason that is the best guide for the conduct of the business of government.[35] Good and just decisions and laws are given 'by love and by natural law, with which all reason is filled'.

Life in the earthly kingdom in all its guises – ecclesiastical, domestic, political, economic – is lived under the sovereign law of God but is at the same time (relatively) autonomous. Because worldly life has this degree of autonomy it is to be regulated by reason and justice. That is not to say that faith (which is regulative for the kingdom of God) has no place in the temporal realm. For the Christian such faith can illumine reason. But, for Luther, there were few Christians and thus the government of God's earthly kingdom (in all matters bar those of faith and conscience) properly turned on the exercise of reason in the pursuit of justice.[36]

Further Reading

In addition to the secondary works mentioned in the footnotes to chapter five there are other valuable discussions of Luther's political ideas in Gerhard Ebeling, *Luther: An Introduction to His Thought*, (London, 1972) and in E.G. Rupp, *The Righteousness of God*, (London, 1953). But there is, of course, no substitute for reading the primary sources themselves. The American edition of *Luther's Works* cited throughout chapter five is an admirable one.

---

[35] Cf. 'Temporal Authority', op. cit., p. 129.
[36] I am grateful to Walter Phillips and John Kleinig for their comments on a draft of this paper.

Chapter Six

Hobbes: Reason, Morality and Politics

C.A.J. Coady

'Fear and I', said Thomas Hobbes, 'were born twins'. Hobbes was referring to the fact that his mother gave birth to him prematurely on hearing the frightful news of the coming of the Spanish Armada but the joke turns on the central role played by fear in Hobbes' political theory. Some commentators have speculated that his political philosophy needs to be seen in the light of his supposedly timorous nature. Not only is this suggestion probably based on a misunderstanding of the man, for Hobbes liked to give the impression that fear played a greater part in his life than it really seems to have done, but it is certainly based on a misunderstanding of the philosophical theory. The sort of fear that Hobbes placed at the centre of his political philosophy is no quaking nervousness but a rational aversion from real dangers. It is significant that when he defined fear, in Chapter 6 of his great book *Leviathan*, as '*Aversion*, with opinion of HURT from the object' he continued in the next sentence to define courage as involving just that aversion but 'with hope of avoiding that hurt by resistance'.[1]

Thomas Hobbes was born in 1588, the son of a clergyman in Malmesbury, and he died in 1679, having lived through the turbulence of the English Civil War – though he did so at a prudent distance, spending the years 1640–1651 in France. He said himself, in the final paragraph of *Leviathan*, that his writing on political

---

[1] Thomas Hobbes, *Leviathan*, (New York, 1962), p. 50. *Leviathan* has been produced in many editions in recent years and several may be out of print at any given time so it is difficult to give page references with any confidence that they will be easily accessible. My practice will be to give chapter references in the text and more specific page references in footnotes, these being to the Collier edition with an introduction by Richard Peters.

theory was 'occasioned by the disorders of the present time' and
certainly the dangers of civil war provide a persistent theme in his
political theory. Hobbes was not only a great political philosopher,
probably the most important ever produced in Britain but he was a
significant thinker in optics, ethics, metaphysics and the philosophy
of mind. He raised some of the most acute objections to Descartes'
Meditations (published nowadays with Descartes' replies as the third
set of Objections) and his materialism about man and nature helped
make his name notorious in his own day and subsequently. He was
often accused of atheism, though, as I shall argue, the accusation was
probably unjust. He was witty, occasionally caustically so, but was
capable of inspiring loyalty and affection. John Aubrey, whose
account of Hobbes in his *Brief Lives* is well worth reading, makes a
point of Hobbes' generosity to those in need. · · · · ·

Hobbes' first publication was a translation of Thucydides' history
of the Peloponnesian War which is a work that tries to show that
Sparta triumphed over Athens *because* Athens was a democracy and
suffered from the weaknesses inherent in a democracy. Even at that
time (1628) Hobbes, according to his own word, was worried that
divisions between Charles I and his parliament would lead to Civil
War. Educated at Oxford under the prevailing Aristotelian system of
thought, Hobbes had been trained in classics although he had
encountered the growing dissatisfaction with Aristotelianism on
a visit to the Continent in 1610. Later visits in 1628 and 1634–
1636 made him familiar with the work of Galileo and aroused
in him a passion for the study of motion and a respect for and
devotion to geometric method. When he returned to England in
1636 he found the country in a state of political disturbance and
began to apply his mind to political theory bringing to it what he had
learned of the new mechanics. His idea was to draw forth certain
inevitable scientific consequences or rules from the analysis of the
nature of political society and of man, these conclusions to constitute
a science of politics. Here Hobbes thought of himself as totally
original and totally successful. Political society or the Commonwealth he viewed as a wholly artificial body created by those natural
bodies, men, who were themselves to be understood wholly in terms
of certain organizations of matter in motion. An account of men and
their passions in mechanical terms was to lead on to an account of the
State they must inevitably found and the constitution or make-up it
ought to have.

In 1640 Hobbes wrote *The Elements of Law* and published an
expanded version of it in Latin in 1642 entitled *De Cive*. This was
later translated into English in 1651 under the title of *Philosophical
Rudiments Concerning Government and Society*. In 1650 *The Elements
of Law* was republished in two parts called *Human Nature* and *De
Corpore Politico*. (Not to be confused with *De Corpore* published

much later.) In 1651 the book which most regard as his masterpiece, *Leviathan*, was published – two years after the execution of Charles I. The book's title makes reference to the great sea monster of the book of Job and Hobbes quotes the Old Testament description of Leviathan to describe that 'mortal God', the State:

> Upon earth there is not his like, who is made without fear.

> He beholdeth all high things: he is a king over all the children of pride.
>
>   (*Job*, ch. 41, v.33–34)

Hobbes spent most of his life as a tutor and, partly because he had been a tutor to Charles II when he was Prince of Wales, was identified with the monarchist cause. He returned to England after his self-imposed exile in Paris in 1651, shortly after the publication of *Leviathan*, some of the doctrines in which may have appealed to Cromwell. Soon after the restoration of the monarchy in 1660 he was invited to the court of Charles II and given a pension of 100 pounds a year. In 1666 *Leviathan* and *De Cive* were censured by Parliament and a Bill to punish atheism, which seems to have had Hobbes as a prime target, was put forward in the House of Commons but abandoned, probably at the King's request.

He was at the centre of many controversies during his long life (including his ill-starred attempt to square the circle) and controversy continues today about how he is best to be interpreted. The issue of Hobbes' supposed atheism is only one such bone of contention. There are those who believe that he was attempting to produce a wholly naturalistic ethico-political system to replace the medieval God-centred outlook but equally there are highly intelligent critics who portray him as seeking to establish a 'Divine politics' based on an ethic of obedience to Divine law. Some treat his account of the State as showing him to be the first theorist and advocate of liberal democracy while others see him as a defender of absolutism and tyranny, even of 'totalitarianism'. His ethical theory has been described as subjectivist but it has also been characterized as a traditional natural law ethic. Others think that he subordinates morality to law, seeing it as constituted by the ruler's decree. Some regard his psychological theory as central to his moral philosophy, and others see it as irrelevant. It is hotly debated whether his psychological theory allows for only egoistic motives. There are those who see him as a defender of bourgeois values and others who treat him as hostile to them.

These are some of the broad interpretive disputes, but one thing that is agreed upon is that Hobbes wanted both to exhibit the rationale of political life and also thereby show the way to maintaining a stable political order. Let us see how he does it.

The State of Nature

Hobbes did not invent the idea of a pre-political state of nature. Something very like it may be found in his medieval precursors (for example, Molina and Suarez) and even in the ancient Greeks. What he did was to construe the notion in a certain way and then make this construal central to his accounts of political obligation and of the nature of the State. His picture of this condition is more awful and unpleasant than any earlier or later theorist had supposed possible. He presents it as a condition of war 'of every man against every man' (*Leviathan*, ch. 13),[2] which arises first from the natural equality of all human beings which, for Hobbes, means their equal vulnerability – and is fuelled by competition for scarce resources and possessions, mutual mistrust and the love of glory. The first of these 'causes of quarrel' in man's nature 'maketh men invade for gain; the second for safety and the third for reputation' (*Leviathan*, ch. 13).[3] This state of war consists either in actual fighting or the known disposition to it and it produces a deprived, uncivilized life style in which there is no industry, trade, agriculture and 'no knowledge of the face of the earth; no account of time; no arts; no letters; no society; and which is worst of all, continual fear, and danger of violent death; and the life of man, solitary, poor, nasty, brutish and short'. (*Leviathan*, ch. 13).[4]

Hobbes' use of the state of nature is also original. He makes it a basic premise in both his derivation of the legitimacy of traditional moral duties and of political obligation; he also uses it to determine the proper nature of a legitimate state and to rank the different types of political constitution. The basic idea is that the horrors of a state of nature are such that it is a fundamental dictate of reason to seek a situation in which peace is assured. The only such situation consistent with the facts of human nature is the establishment through a social contract of a commonwealth presided over by a sovereign to whom the basic natural right to govern oneself is surrendered. The sovereign (who may be an individual or an assembly) is not party to the contract, he is merely its instrument and beneficiary. The contract is between the citizens and obliges them to obey the sovereign who, as their authorized representative, determines what is just or unjust, right or wrong, for the citizens. As for the sovereign, nothing he does can be unjust no matter how severe and oppressive it may seem (and be) to the citizen.

Hobbes is sometimes criticized for believing in the historical reality of the state of nature; it is objected that mankind was never in the a-social or anti-social condition that Hobbes so vividly describes.

---

[2]   Op. cit., p. 100.
[3]   Op. cit., p. 99.
[4]   Ibid.

Perhaps not, but the objection is mostly beside the point. To begin with, Hobbes is not firmly committed to the historicity of the state of nature. He considers the objection in chapter 13 of *Leviathan* and agrees that the condition of war of every man against every man 'was never generally so, over all the world', though he claims that 'the savage people in many places of America, except the government of small families, the concord whereof dependeth on natural lust, have no government at all; and live at this day in that brutish manner'.[5] Hobbes is interested in the supposed habits of American Indians not because he thinks any given civil society must have emerged from a state of nature by the process he calls sovereignty by institution but because he thinks that their life-style may provide evidence that in the absence of a commonwealth what you get is a state of nature. The crucial role of the state of nature is not to give a genetic account of how states actually arise but to provide a model of what life without them would inevitably be like. Neither is it, for Hobbes, a purely abstract device as it seems to be for Kant and Rawls but an all too urgent present possibility. So Hobbes goes on to argue, immediately after the discussion of savage life in America, that in any case it is clear from the degeneracy of life in the circumstances of civil war just 'what manner of life there would be where there were no common power to fear'.[6] Moreover, as he then points out, even if a state of nature has never existed between individuals it has always existed between sovereigns who in their 'continual jealousies' are in 'a posture of war' towards one another. It is precisely the absence of a world state which leads to the brutishness of the international 'order'.

The relationship between a philosophically illuminating explanatory model and an historical or genetic reality that it seems naturally to imply is difficult to elucidate though it arises in many different fields. Perhaps such theories are, at least, committed to the idea that the implied genesis is not logically or conceptually impossible and it is interesting to see whether Hobbes' state of nature can survive this test.

There seem to be two distinct problems for Hobbes' model here. The first is that the climate of fear and apprehension supposed by Hobbes seems to undercut the requirements of rational calculation which should lead to the institution of a civil state. No doubt the best outcome for all concerned is the establishment of a commonwealth but achieving that outcome requires trusting others sufficiently to suggest an assembly for that purpose and turning up to implement the proposal. Such trust may be too risky in what is still a state of nature. There are overtones here of the game-theoretic puzzle

---

[5] Op. cit., p. 101.
[6] Ibid.

known as 'the prisoner's dilemma' but much depends upon the balance of benefits and the relative likelihoods of outcomes. Hobbes would reply to the objection, as he does to a slightly different form of it in a footnote to chapter 1 of *De Cive*, that fear is a powerful motive to rational action in search of security and can be mutually known to be such by those in a state of nature.[7] It is at least not impossible that men in a state of nature could come to see that there was a much greater chance of security in taking the risk of trusting one another briefly enough to convene to set up a sovereign than in refusing to take the risk in the first place. They could also have good reason to believe that others can reason in the same way thereby making the risk of non-compliance less alarming. I think that a reply along these lines is both persuasive and available to Hobbes.

$\Rightarrow$ The second problem for the model is that human beings cannot be as a-social as it supposes. After all they are born of other humans and if they survive at all owe their lives and well-being to those who care for them when they are helpless and immature. The allegation is that Hobbes supposes the existence of atomistic individuals in the state of nature and yet this is impossible even as an imagined contrast situation to life in civil society. People are by nature involved in smaller communities, at the very least, the family. Now it must be conceded that Hobbes often speaks in a way that encourages this objection but he also allows that families constitute in the state of nature a sort of natural unit of pre-political society or even small political units of their own.[8] Hobbes' theory of the family, though fascinating, is certainly incomplete. He could however argue that since the family is held together by 'natural lust' and superior force (children being unequal by virtue of their greater vulnerability) but is clearly too small an association to provide the security of a commonwealth then families can be considered as atoms in the state of nature along with other individuals, who are without family, and even other small associations, gangs or alliances. In this way he could avoid much of the force of this objection but at the cost of allowing that the brutishness of the state of nature might be less extreme than he often supposes since life therein would not be totally solitary and

---

[7]   Cf. Thomas Hobbes, *Man and Citizen* Bernard Gert, (ed.), (Harvester, 1978), p. 113. There is the further difficulty for Hobbes' account that such calculations and implementation of them hardly seem available without a common language and the achievement of a common language may already take us beyond his state of nature. I think this is the principal difficulty for the conceptual possibility discussed above.

[8]   On the family and its manner of rule, see *Leviathan*, chapter 20 and *De Cive*, chapter 9. Hobbes believed, incidentally, that in a state of nature the mother is rightly the ruler of the children and not the father. As he says in *De Cive*, 'original dominion over *children* belongs to the *mother*: and among men no less than other creatures, the birth follows the belly'. (*Man and Citizen*, p. 213.)

non-communal. Alternatively he could hold that families are small states and the original state of nature is like the present international order. His discussion of paternal dominion, especially in *De Cive*, certainly tends in this direction – in chapter 6 he says in a footnote that 'a family is a little city'[9] – but even this concedes a good deal to the idea that there is a certain 'political' sociability natural to man. Let us now turn to other aspects of his political theory in which the state of nature is put to work.

Obligation and Right

One basic question for political philosophy is: what reason do we have for obeying the laws or edicts of the state? An answer to this will tell us about the nature and extent of political obligation. Hobbes thought that he could show that there was a moral rationale for such obligation and that its demands were very wide ranging.

One simple answer to the basic question might just be that disobeying the state is simply too risky. A popular impression of Hobbes' philosophy would have it that this is his answer and there is, I think, a kernel of important truth in that impression. Nonetheless Hobbes does not simply claim that 'might is right'. He does not hold, as some might think, that our obligation is constituted by our apprehension that we will be caught and punished for Hobbes thinks that we are still obliged even if we are certain that we shall not be detected in our disobedience. If he grounds our obligation in self-interest, it is a rather deeper self-interest than this. Actually there have been roughly four different theories of obligation attributed to Hobbes by scholars. Since Hobbes usually treats the obligation to obey the state or the sovereign as equivalent to the duty to be just, I will follow him and talk of political obligation interchangeably with the obligations of justice. There are some problems in doing so but they do not affect our interpretive enterprise.

1   The obligation to be just is a matter of self-interest, or more specifically self-preservation, based on the undesirability of the state of nature which Hobbes sees as the only alternative to life in a commonwealth. One is obliged to be just because one is bound by the dictates of reason to seek peace and the self-preservation that goes with it. In a state of nature, one has what Hobbes calls a right of nature or *jus naturale* which is 'the liberty each man hath, to use his own power, as he will himself, for the preservation of his own nature' (*Leviathan*, ch. 14).[10] In a state of nature every person has a right to everything 'even to one another's body' but it is a

---

9   *Man and Citizen*, p. 184.
10   Op. cit., p. 103.

fundamental law of nature to seek peace (though its corollary is to defend ourselves by all available means if others will not co-operate) and it is another basic law of nature to lay down one's right to all things where others will do so as well and these two dictates of reason, labelled by Hobbes the first and second laws of nature, lead to setting up the civil State. This account of Hobbes' theory of obligation could fairly be called the traditional one.

2   The obligation of justice is essentially a matter of obedience to God's command and we are here bound by the sort of inevitability that goes with bowing to 'irresistible power' (*Leviathan*, ch. 21).[11] The obedience to God's commands is analogous to the 'natural obligation' whereby a weaker must yield to the stronger 'despairing of his own power to resist'.[12] This account has been most forcefully urged by Howard Warrender but F.C. Hood has argued a similar case though with more emphasis on Hobbes' views about revelation rather than his natural theology.[13]

3   The only kind of obligation is that created by the sovereign's commands. To be obliged is just to be under the constraint of the state's laws. This interpretation fastens upon the way Hobbes insists (for example at the beginning of chapter 15 of *Leviathan*) that 'justice and propriety begin with the constitution of commonwealth' and he seems at times to extend this idea to the whole of morality. So in *De Homine* ch. XIII sect. 9 he says, 'a common standard for virtues and vices does not appear except in civil life'.[14] Yet few scholars adopt this interpretation without qualifications; the one who comes nearest to it is J.W.N. Watkins.[15]

4   The obligation to be just, like all obligations, is a matter of being bound by one's word. This theory keeps close to the letter of Hobbes' statements about the nature of obligation in *Leviathan* and particularly in the discussion in chapter 14 of covenants, rights, liberty and transfer of right where Hobbes says:

> And when a man hath ... abandoned, or granted away his right; then he is said to be OBLIGED or BOUND, not to hinder those, to whom such right is granted or abandoned, from the benefit of it: and that he *ought*, and it is his DUTY, not to make void that voluntary act of his own: and that such hindrance is INJUSTICE, and INJURY, as being *sine jure*; the right being before renounced, or transferred.[16]

The basic idea here is that to be under an obligation is simply to

---

[11] Op. cit., p. 262.
[12] *De Cive*, chapter XV. In *Man and Citizen*, p. 294.
[13] H. Warrender, *The Political Philosophy of Hobbes*, (Oxford, 1957); F.C. Hood, *The Divine Politics of Thomas Hobbes*, (Oxford, 1964).
[14] *Man and Citizen*, p. 69.
[15] J.W.N. Watkins, *Hobbes' System of Ideas*, (London, 1965).
[16] *Leviathan*, pp. 104–5.

have given up a right or freedom to act. In the central case, it is a matter of being bound by one's word though there are other cases where the self-binding is implicit. Brian Barry has done most to give prominence to this strand in Hobbes' thought and he marshals an impressive body of evidence for his interpretation and for the associated view that, contrary to the received opinion, there *can* be moral obligations in a state of nature.[17] Barry admits that there is a 'secondary' sense of obligation to be found in Hobbes – the sense in which one is rationally obliged to self-preservation and what conduces to it. This sense, however, (which is required by interpretation 1 and perhaps derivatively by 2 and which I shall term 'rational obligation') is claimed by Barry to be a 'left-over' from the *De Cive* period.

The best way to proceed in assessing these diverse interpretations will be to confront Barry's subtle and powerful case for 4. It must be conceded that in *Leviathan*, ch. 14, Hobbes does tie obligation to the binding of oneself that goes with renouncing a right to act but far from this being the primary sense of the term for Hobbes, I think it is clear that, even in *Leviathan*, Hobbes relies more significantly upon the sense which Barry claims to be secondary. At the start of chapter 15, for instance, we find Hobbes talking of the laws of nature *obliging* in the very sentence which establishes the third law of nature which calls on men 'to perform their covenants made'.[18] Moreover, Hobbes needs such obligations in order to constrain the sovereign. Since the sovereign is not a party to the social contract he cannot be obliged to make good laws or behave well by covenant – he has not bound himself to do so. For this reason he cannot do anything unjust since (in *Leviathan* at least) Hobbes operates with a definition of justice and injustice which relates them directly to keeping covenants.[19] Yet it seems obvious that sovereigns can behave badly and indeed one of the major problems of political theory is what should be done about it. Hobbes likes to sneer at those who worry about tyranny – he says in chapter 19 that tyranny is merely a name for monarchy 'misliked'[20] – but he knows that there is a world of difference between good and bad rulers and he would like there to be some constraints on misrule. So in chapter 30 of *Leviathan* when he discusses 'the procuration of the good of the people' he says that to this end the sovereign 'is obliged by the law of nature, and to render

---

[17] Brian Barry, 'Warrender and His Critics', *Philosophy*, 1968, vol. XLII, no. 164. Reprinted in Maurice Cranston and Richard Peters, *Hobbes and Rousseau*, (New York, 1972). Page references will be to this reprinted version.

[18] Op. cit., p. 113.

[19] But in earlier works he is less careful. See particularly *The Elements of Law*, F. Tonnies, (ed.) (London, 1928), p. 120, part II, ch. II, p. 93, where he says, 'divers actions done by the people, may be unjust before God Almighty, as breaches of some of the laws of nature'.

[20] *Leviathan*, p. 142.

an account thereof to God, the author of that law, and to none but him'.[21] The sovereign's violations of natural law are not indeed injustices but they are what Hobbes calls 'iniquities'. In this same chapter Hobbes says that the laws of nature 'oblige all mankind'.[22]

These references are enough to refute interpretation 3 and they surely constitute a severe obstacle to the acceptance of 4. If, as I claim, Hobbes sees obligation principally in terms of the requirements of self-preservation via the laws of nature then the demands of justice will be a special case of this, namely, the case mediated by the entering into covenants as indeed the third law of nature specifically declares (cf. *Leviathan*, ch. 15).

In any case the problems confronting interpretation 4 are more than textual. If the primary importance of the analysis of obligation is the light it throws upon political obligation and our original question why obey the laws of the state?, then an answer in terms of the obligations imposed by (implicit or explicit) contract or promise seems insufficiently deep. As Hobbes recognizes nothing is easier to break than one's word and although this is no doubt a point about human weakness it also naturally leads to our asking for the rationale behind keeping promises. On Barry's interpretation no answer in terms of obligation can be forthcoming. To give one's word *is* to be obliged to keep it. Yet if someone admits that we have agreed, or have exhibited in our behaviour our agreement, to obey the sovereign he may go on to ask why we should continue to do so. It is surely small comfort to be referred to the meaning of the word 'promise', 'commitment' or 'covenant'.

Hobbes seems to recognize this problem in the very paragraph on which Barry rests his interpretation because he goes on to argue that there is a sort of irrationality in going back on one's word like the absurdity involved in contradicting oneself.

> So that *injury*, or *injustice*, in the controversies of the world, is somewhat like to that, which in the disputations of scholars is called *absurdity*. For as it is there called an absurdity, to contradict what one maintained in the beginning: so in the world, it is called injustice and injury, voluntarily to undo that, which from the beginning he had voluntarily done.[23]

But Hobbes' argument here is surely unconvincing. One is involved in absurdity by maintaining two contradictory propositions but one can resolve the absurdity by abandoning one of them. Similarly one cannot rationally will both to obey this law now and not to obey this law now or to obey all laws and not to obey this law but one can

---

[21] Op. cit., p. 247.
[22] Op. cit., p. 260.
[23] *Leviathan*, p. 105.

resolve the absurdity by abandoning one of the conflicting resolutions. If there is good reason not to obey this law now, why not give up one's earlier resolution? There is nothing intrinsically irrational or absurd in changing one's mind or one's intentions.

I conclude then that Hobbes' theory of moral and political obligation is best viewed as one of long-term, enlightened self-interest in which peace and self-preservation are the fundamental values and their securing is promoted by the detailed prescriptions of his laws of nature. A full account of interpretation 1 would show how Hobbes' innovative genius was to reconstruct a traditional list of virtues and vices and to underpin a natural law account of them on the basis of the fundamental rationality of a concern for self-preservation.

Hobbes and God

Warrender and Hood argue that God has a central role in Hobbes' moral and political theory but until recently the received picture was that Hobbes was an atheist who merely pretended to believe in God to avoid trouble. The view of Hobbes as an atheist, though it also had considerable currency among his contemporaries, has always seemed to me incredible but God's role is not quite as central as Warrender and Hood make out.

Hobbes is certainly anti-clerical and his religious beliefs are somewhat heterodox but there is no real reason for treating his consistent affirmations of faith as insincere. To convict him of atheism on the basis of many of his contemporaries calling him an atheist would be rather like taking seriously Mr Bjelke-Petersen's characterization of Bob Hawke as a communist. In the seventeenth century the charge of atheism had a similar looseness and political value to the charge of socialism or communism today or in Senator McCarthy's America. In *Leviathan*, Hobbes not only declares the laws of nature to be commands of God in his natural kingdom and offers a proof for the existence of God but more than half the book is taken up with scriptural exegesis. The idea that all of this is a pretence is even more curious than Bertrand Russell's claim that Leibniz's theology was insincere. Leibniz's theology was at least pretty orthodox so might have made a 'front' but many of Hobbes' expressed beliefs were so far from conventional doctrine that it is bizarre to see his affirmations as a way of keeping out of trouble. A charge of heresy was just as dangerous as a charge of atheism in seventeenth century England so that Hobbes' evasion of the orthodox doctrine of the Trinity, for example, can hardly be viewed as a piece of timid time-serving.[24]

---

[24] For good discussions of Hobbes' religious views see Paul Johnson, 'Hobbes'

Nonetheless the Warrender thesis, and the even stronger Hood thesis, exaggerate the theoretical role played by God in Hobbes' political philosophy. Hobbes does say, as Warrender stresses, that the laws of nature are 'improperly' called laws unless considered 'as delivered in the word of God that by right commandeth all things'[25] (*Leviathan*, ch. 15) and Hobbes thinks of this as something that can be discovered by natural reason as well as by revelation. Yet natural laws as 'dictates of reason' or theorems relating to self-preservation would be, and are thought by Hobbes to be, compelling as rules for conduct independently of any belief in God. Whether, so understood, they are strictly to be called 'laws' or 'obligatory' is less significant than whether they provide rationally compelling considerations for conduct. Moreover, it seems that, prior to treating them as commanded by God, Hobbes thinks of them as giving the essentials of morality. The passage about their being laws, 'properly' speaking, only under the aspect of Divine Commands comes in a short paragraph at the end of chapter 15 which has something of the appearance of an afterthought. In any case, in the previous paragraph, prior to any references to God, Hobbes draws together the threads of his discussion of the 19 laws of nature by concluding that the science of these laws:

> is the true and only moral philosophy. For moral philosophy is nothing else but the science of what is *good*, and *evil*, in the conversation, and society of mankind... Now the science of virtue and vice, is moral philosophy; and therefore the true doctrine of the laws of nature is the true moral philosophy.[26]

Warrender attempts to meet the objection that Hobbes' system of morality seems to rest on a basis of enlightened self-interest independently of a primary role for God by treating that dimension of Hobbes' thought as concerned with psychology rather than ethics proper. He argues that Hobbes is really sketching the motivation behind morality rather than its rationale. We have insufficient space to deal with this claim fully here but, as the quotation from Hobbes about true moral philosophy indicates, this manoeuvre has slim prospects of success. It can, however, be remarked that there is a version of interpretation 2 which is not at odds with interpretation 1 and the compatibility of the two interpretations raises a further problem for Warrender's view. Suppose that someone who discovers that obedience to the laws of nature is commanded by God then asks

---

Anglican Doctrine of Salvation' in *Thomas Hobbes in His Time*, Ralph Ross. Herbert W. Schneider and Theodore Waldman, (eds), (Minneapolis, 1974) and P.T. Geach, 'The Religion of Thomas Hobbes', *Religious Studies*, vol. 17, December 1981.

[25] *Leviathan*, p. 124.
[26] Op. cit., pp. 123–4.

himself why he should obey God's commands. One might hold that for the case of Divine command this question is unaskable since it is palpably rational to obey God but surely the more plausible Hobbesian answer is the one he does seem to give in his talk of God's 'irresistible power', namely, that one's self-preservation dictates obedience to the Almighty. If so, interpretation 2 merely reinforces interpretation 1 and is not a rival to it.

Hobbes and Absolutism

Hobbes has been hailed as a forerunner of modern liberal democracy and denounced as the first theorist of totalitarianism. Neither view is anywhere near the truth. Hobbes' theory of sovereignty is absolutist in that he allows for no constitutional checks on the exercise of legitimate sovereign power and for no division of powers within the state. Nonetheless the requirement of obedience to the sovereign is not unconditional. The social contract requires one to surrender one's natural right to self-government and the associated right to deal with others as one thinks fit but the right to self-protection *in extremis* is inalienable and one may exercise it even against the sovereign power if the occasion arise. This leads to the curious consequence that a self-confessed murderer is morally entitled to resist with violence the sovereign's attempts to put him to death or even to imprison him although, of course, the sovereign and his agents are equally morally entitled or even obliged, to proceed against him. Hobbes' general theory of rights as freedoms is so constructed as to allow that A may have a right to do something and B may equally have a right to prevent him, but we cannot now embark upon a discussion of the moral and conceptual difficulties it creates. In the face of severe enough punishment the relations between a criminal and the sovereign relapse into those of a state of nature. This chink in Hobbes' absolutism has led some to see him as a supporter of citizens' rights against the Government. Roger Masters has claimed him as an advocate of the 'rights to life, liberty and the pursuit of happiness' boldly announced by the American revolutionaries.[27] Hobbes would, however, have regarded Jefferson and the rest as seditious rebels. Mere matters of burdensome taxation and unresponsiveness constituted nothing like sufficient grounds for resisting the sovereign in Hobbes' eyes. Yet the fact that he allows the one inalienable right to life and that he grounds political legitimacy on the rights and consent of the governed makes the treatment of him as a kind of liberal thinker not altogether

---

[27] Roger Masters, 'Hobbes and Locke' in *Comparing Political Thinkers*, Ross Fitzgerald, (ed.), (Sydney, 1980), pp. 131–2.

fanciful. He also had a theory of representation whereby the sovereign represented the people but, characteristically, it binds the citizen and not the sovereign. (See *Leviathan*, ch. 16.) This theory deserves more discussion than I can give it, but its point is to insist that the sovereign's acts are really the citizen's acts by virtue of the social contract, and so cannot be complained of even where the citizen suffers from them. It is only fair to add that Hobbes envisaged, in practice, plenty of scope for the liberty of citizens but, in principle, the sovereign's writ was unrestricted except by his own prudential reasoning, concern for the moral law and fear of God.

Why did Hobbes allow the sovereign such dominion? The basic answer is that he thought it the only way to hold the state of nature at bay. Once you allow for divided authority, citizens' rights to reject unjust laws or to dispute sovereign decisions, or a right to replace the ruler then you allow for dissension, strife, disorder and ultimately civil war. I have heard it argued that Hobbes was guilty of the logical fallacy, somewhat akin to that supposedly committed by Aristotle's argument that there is one ultimate good for man, of thinking that it followed by logical necessity from the concept of arbitration or decision-making that a society must have a single ultimate arbitrator. Perhaps there is a trace of this sort of thinking in Hobbes but I doubt it. What he really insists upon are the awful longer-term consequences of divided power and he draws his argument from two sources – history and his analysis of human nature. Opinion is likely to be divided about his historical examples of national collapse consequent upon less than absolute sovereignty. It is certainly common to say that whatever may have been the case in the ancient world, modern political society refutes Hobbes' claims since division of power and constitutional checks have proved compatible with stable government. Of course Hobbes did not mean to say that a society with divided sovereignty would collapse immediately but only that it contained the seeds of its own destruction. Even so, the historical record does not appear to support him.

His argument from human nature is also suspect. Hobbes does not paint human nature in wholly dark colours for he recognizes altruistic motives and admires large spirited men such as his friend, Sidney Godolphin, to whose brother Frances *Leviathan* is dedicated but he had a realistic appreciation of man's capacity for evil and his overall picture of our proclivities is certainly gloomy. This is reflected in the fact that Hobbes defines the expressions 'good' and 'evil' in terms of individual desire and argues that in a state of nature there can be no 'common rule of good and evil, to be taken from the nature of the objects themselves'. (*Leviathan* ch. 6.[28]) He then gives such an account of human passion and the lack of harmony between

---

[28] *Leviathan*, pp. 47–8.

the desires and projects of different individuals that it seems unbelievable that reason and common judgement could prevail to maintain the peace and promote common objectives in the absence of an absolute decision-maker.[29] There is only one object of desire fundamentally common to men, dictated by the necessities of their nature and that is the preservation of life and the peace that is a precondition of it. Earlier and later natural law thinkers were more generous in their attribution of basic common desires, needs or goals to human nature and hence could be more concessive about the interplay between subject and ruler and about the positive potentialities of public disagreement, argument, dissension and about limitations upon the sovereign power thus arising. For Hobbes such recourse is simply an invitation to 'diverse measures' of good and evil with all the dangers attendant upon the inevitably divergent verdicts. Hobbes' pessimism provides a permanently useful check upon the various rosy optimisms with which political thinking is plagued but, in the end, it suffers the fate of so many 'realisms' in becoming itself unrealistic. Human inclinations are not as diverse or incommensurable as Hobbes likes to make out and it does not seem that the divergence that does exist is sufficient to ensure a state of war in the absence of an absolute arbitrator, nor even, possibly, in the absence of a civil state.

Hobbes' fear of civil war and his sense of the fragility of human sociability caused him to minimize the horrors of tyrannical rule. Locke was later to comment on Hobbes' belief that absolute rule was needed to protect us from the state of nature: 'This is to think that men are so foolish that they take care to avoid what mischiefs may be done them by pole cats or foxes, but are content, nay think it safety, to be devoured by lions.'[30] This comment surely has particular point in the century of Hitler and Stalin. Hobbes is at his least convincing when, as at the end of chapter 18 of *Leviathan*, he tries to make light of this sort of difficulty. What he does rightly remind us of, however, is that even a bad and despotic government *may* be preferable to the feasible alternatives, especially where these include civil war or violent revolution.

---

[29] Hobbes' subjectivism about good and evil comes out very strongly in *De Cive*, chapter 3: 'good and evil are names given to things to signify the inclination or aversion of them, by whom they were given. But the inclinations of men are diverse, according to their diverse constitutions, customs, opinions... They are, therefore so long in the state of war, as by reason of the diversity of the present appetites, they mete good and evil by diverse measures'. (*Man and Citizen*, p. 150.)

[30] John Locke, *Two Treatises of Government*, ed. with introduction by Thomas I. Cook, (New York, 1947). This quotation is from section 93 of *The Second Treatise of Civil Government*.

Hobbes Today

In recent years there has been a great upsurge in Hobbes studies and an increased awareness of his importance as a social and political thinker. Hobbes appeals to modern political analysts just because he takes the anti-social tendencies of human nature so seriously and because his concern with the role of power and rational self-interest in political life strikes a sympathetic chord in the hearts of modern devotees of political 'realism'. Modern political 'realists', however, are uncomfortable with morality where they are not positively contemptuous of it and some of the contemporary relevance of Hobbes arises from the fact that he does not share this attitude. For all his tough-mindedness, Hobbes' outlook on politics is very much that of a moralist; for him, morality is not irrelevant to political security and social peace nor is such security indifferent to moral constraint. Political power is a precondition for morality to function fully but there can be no secure political order which is not shaped by the moral dictates of the natural law revealed by reason. Hobbes may base morality upon self-interest but he does so in a fundamental and complex way in the confidence that communal and individual interests can with effort be brought into beneficial co-incidence. He is no advocate of the hidden wonders of 'laissez-faire' or of Randian 'selfishness'. One may well doubt that his project can succeed but it is an impressive attempt and where it fails its failure instructs as only major philosophical work can.

Bibliography

Thomas Hobbes, *English Works*, W. Molesworth (ed.), 11 volumes, (London, 1839–45).

Thomas Hobbes, *Leviathan*, M. Oakeshott (ed.), with an introduction by R.S. Peters, (Collier, London, 1962). (There are many other good modern editions including the Everyman.)

Thomas Hobbes *The Elements of Law*, M.M. Goldsmith (ed.), (London, 1969). (There is also an earlier edition by E. Tonnies.)

Thomas Hobbes *Man and Citizen*, with introduction by B. Gert. (ed.), (New York, 1972). (This contains a translation of parts of *De Homine* and Hobbes' own complete translation of *De Cive*.)

Thomas Hobbes *Body, Man and Citizen*, R.S. Peters (ed.), (New York, 1962). Extracts from a number of Hobbes' less accessible works.

Further Reading

Books on Hobbes:

Leo Strauss, *The Political Philosophy of Hobbes – its Basis and its Genesis*, (Chicago, 1963). First published in 1936 Strauss' book marked – or at least coincided with – the modern revival of interest in Hobbes' political thought. It has the virtue of paying attention to the texts and of making the business of understanding Hobbes seem exciting and worthwhile. There are some interesting, if somewhat intangible, speculations about the development of Hobbes' thought. Strauss also argues that Hobbes' political philosophy is independent of his general metaphysics.

R.S. Peters, *Hobbes*, (Harmondsworth, 1956). A useful, general account of Hobbes' views.

Howard Warrender, *The Political Philosophy of Hobbes: His Theory of Obligation*, (Oxford, 1957). Places Hobbes in the tradition of natural law theory and gives God a primary role in Hobbes' theory of obligation. Impressively argued and set a new standard for close attention to the text.

C.B. McPherson, *The Political Theory of Possessive Individualism: Hobbes to Locke*, (Oxford, 1962). A stimulating Marxist analysis, which casts Hobbes (as does Strauss) as an advocate of bourgeois morality. McPherson's basic thesis, particularly with regard to the characteristics of man in a state of nature, is highly debatable and many aspects of Hobbes' thought are hostile to a middle-class ethic but the book is well worth reading.

F.C. Hood, *The Divine Politics of Thomas Hobbes*, (Oxford, 1964). Argues that Hobbes' political theory depends not only on God but specifically on Christianity.

J.W.N. Watkins, *Hobbes' System of Ideas*, (London, 1965). Tries to show, against Strauss and others, that Hobbes' ideas in general philosophy logically dictated his political theory.

M.M. Goldsmith, *Hobbes' Science of Politics*, (London, 1966). Clear and readable. Emphasizes the role of Hobbes' theory of scientific method.

F.S. McNeilly, *The Anatomy of Leviathan*, (London, 1968). Excellent philosophical discussion of Hobbes. Particularly interesting on the role of psychological egoism in Hobbes' account of human nature.

David Gauthier, *The Logic of Leviathan*, (Oxford, 1969). A good philosophical book on Hobbes. Especially interesting on his theory of authorization. Also has interesting though controversial views on the interpretation of Hobbes' key terminology.

D.D. Raphael, *Hobbes, Morals and Politics*, (London, 1977). An admirable little book. Probably the best introduction to Hobbes' thought.

Collections and articles:

K.C. Brown (ed.), *Hobbes Studies*, (Oxford, 1965). A good collection containing important articles by A.E. Taylor, Willis Glover and Brown.

Maurice Cranston and Richard Peters (eds), *Hobbes and Rousseau*, (New York, 1972). Contains Barry's excellent article and Quentin Skinner's provocative essay.

R. Ross, H. Schneider and T. Waldmann (eds), *Thomas Hobbes in His Time*, (Minneapolis, 1974). Contains a neglected essay by John Dewey and Paul Johnson's interesting article.

Brian Barry, 'Warrender and His Critics', *Philosophy*, 1968, (reprinted in Cranston and Peters above).

M.T. Dalgarno, 'Analysing Hobbes's Contract', *Proceedings of the Aristotelian Society*, 1975–6.

P.T. Geach, 'The Religion of Thomas Hobbes', *Religious Studies*, 1981.

Greg Kavka, 'Hobbes's War of All Against All', *Ethics*, 1983.

F.S. McNeilly, 'Egoism in Hobbes', *Philosophical Quarterly*, 1966.

A.E. Taylor, 'The Ethical Doctrine of Hobbes', *Philosophy*, 1938, (reprinted in Brown above).

Chapter Seven

Locke on Political Authority, Property, and Toleration

C.L.Ten

Introduction

The political theory of John Locke (1632–1704) dealt with three major issues: the limits of political authority, property rights, and the basis of religious toleration. His plea for toleration, though well-known, has not received the same degree of critical discussion as his views on the first two issues. There are many different and incompatible interpretations of his theories of political obligation and property, and his views have also inspired important developments in contemporary political philosophy.

Locke's book *Two Treatises of Government* was published anonymously in 1689 shortly after the Revolution of 1688 which resulted in William III becoming the king of England. Locke's work has often been regarded as an attempt to justify the Revolution that had just taken place. But there is strong evidence to show that it was mostly written several years earlier with the aim of justifying the opposition of Locke's patron, the Earl of Shaftesbury, to the rule of King Charles II.[1]

Natural Rights and the Limits of Political Authority and Political Obligation

Locke's starting point is a pre-political state of nature in which people had natural rights conferred on them by the law of nature. His account of the law of nature, on which the *Two Treatises* relies, is

---

[1] See Peter Laslett's 'Introduction' to his edition of Locke's *Two Treatises of Government*, (Cambridge, 1960), Section III. Laslett assigns 'the important part of the work of composition to the years 1679–80', p. 35.

set out in greater detail in the *Essays on the Law of Nature*.[2] The law of nature is the expression of God's will which humans can discover by reflecting on their function in a teleological world in which everything is designed to perform a special function. Humans, being the creation of God, are subject to His will just as clay is subject to the potter's will.[3] But humans differ from animals in the possession of reason and are therefore required to act in accordance with the dictates of reason. The law of nature has a rational foundation which all humans, except 'lunatics and idiots', can discover and use as the basis for guiding their conduct. The fundamental law of nature is that mankind ought to be preserved.[4] This is evident from the fact that people are in no position to carry out God's purposes unless they continue to survive. A similar consideration shows that the law of nature requires people to enter into society and to maintain it, for they are dependent on a society for their existence and for the satisfaction of their needs.

In the state of nature everyone has the right to execute the law of nature since there is no superior authority who can perform this function. So everyone has the right of punishing those who violate the law of nature, whereas only the injured party has the right to receive reparation from offenders. But attempts by each person to execute the law of nature lead to uncertainties and insecurities. In order to escape from these uncertainties and insecurities, people in the state of nature agree to move into a political society. This is done by transferring to the political authority the right to be one's own judge and executor of the law of nature. In the light of the reason for moving out of the state of nature, it is obvious that an arbitrary and absolute government will be unacceptable. Such a government will subject people to the same sorts of uncertainties and insecurities from which they have tried to escape. Indeed a government with absolute power will have greater power than anyone in the state of nature, and it is inconceivable that people are 'so foolish that they care to avoid what mischiefs may be done them by polecats or foxes, but are content, nay, think it safety, to be devoured by lions.'[5]

Locke thus imposed limits on political authority. These limits require that the laws enacted by the government should take the form of known and established rules applied by impartial judges. They also require that the laws enacted should be confined to certain

---

[2] John Locke, *Essays on the Law of Nature*, W. von Leyden, (ed.) (Oxford, 1954).
[3] ibid., p. 157.
[4] ibid., pp. 157–8. See also the illuminating discussion in James Tully, *A Discourse on Property*, (Cambridge, 1982), ch. 2.
[5] *Two Treatises*, II, 93. References to the *Two Treatises* will be to the relevant sections. Thus 'II, 93' means the Second Treatise, section 93. I have taken quotations from the Everyman edition. There are slight differences in punctuation etc. in the edition by Peter Laslett.

functions, those of securing 'the peace, safety, and public good of the people'. The government has only whatever rights have been transferred to it by the people moving from the state of nature into political society. In the state of nature people have obligations under the law of nature not to harm the lives, liberty, and possessions of others. These same constraints therefore apply to the government.

In Locke's view a right conferred by the law of nature can be forfeited when a person violates the law of nature. The only other type of situation in which a person can lose a right is when he or she consents to its being taken away. It is in this way that some rights are handed over to the government thereby establishing political authority. Rights are transferred by the giving of explicit, or what Locke called 'express', consent. But Locke did not believe that all rights can be transferred in this way. The right to self-preservation can only be forfeited through gross violations of the law of nature. On the other hand, the express consent given in order to establish political society and to acquire full membership of that society cannot be revoked once it is given. A person will only cease to be a member of a political society, and thereby be discharged of his or her political obligation to obey the government of that society, if he or she is expelled from the society for violations of its rules, or is granted permission to leave, or if the society is dissolved. But a unilateral renunciation of membership on the part of the person who is a full member will not be effective.

The limitations on political authority mean that members of political societies have a right to resist a government that violates the terms of the social contract by usurping powers that have not been handed over to it. So Locke's doctrine of express consent embodies a doctrine about the functions and limits of governmental activity, and ultimately a doctrine of resistance to government if it exceeds these limits. This is the basis of Locke's strong opposition to an absolute and arbitrary monarchy. He attacked the analogy drawn between governmental power and parental power. Children lack the capacity to discover and understand the law of nature and hence to be guided by it. So they are to be looked after by their parents until such time as they acquire the relevant capacity. But once children grow up and are capable of exercising their reason, the authority of parents ceases. The relationship between adult parents and their children is therefore different to that between different adults who are each capable of understanding the law of nature and of directing their conduct in accordance with it.

Once political society is established by the unanimous express consent of those who thereby become members of that society, a problem arises with respect to the form that the government of that society should take. Here Locke's argument is that a society 'being one body, must move one way', and this should be the way 'whither the greater force carries it, which is the consent of the majority, ... "[6] Locke's acceptance of majority consent in this context does not imply support for democracy as a system of government based on majority rule. It has been illuminatingly suggested by John Kilcullen that Locke's argument committed him at most to the view that 'the form of government must be chosen by the majority, not that it must be a democracy ... Majority rule applies in the constitutional convention but it need not apply in the constitution the convention chooses.'[7]

Foreigners who live in a political society also have obligations to obey the government, but these obligations are based on tacit rather than express consent. Tacit consent is given when one enjoys the use of one's property in the society, or when one resides in that society, or even when one is merely travelling on one of its highways. Tacit consent does not however make one a full, or as Locke put it, a 'perfect' member of the society. One is not therefore permanently obligated to the government of that society. Those resident non-members who own property in a society are free to leave that society once they have, through gift or sale, transferred their property to others. But it is unclear whether in some other respects the obligations of non-members are more stringent than those of members. Do they have to accept the form of government in the society as given, and do their obligations to the government hold good even when the government is one which violates the terms of the contract made between it and its full members?

In his account of express consent and the obligations of membership of a political society to which it gives rise, Locke seems to equate express consent with a kind of promise. This explains why for Locke the obligations of membership, once accepted, cannot be renounced, for a promise has a binding character from which normally one cannot simply release oneself, and can only be released by the promisee. If political obligation is to be a species of the obligation of promise-keeping, then it is important that there should be deliberate and explicit acts of promising to enter into political society. But it is difficult to discover acts which all members of an existing society would have engaged in that could plausibly count as acts of making the relevant promise. Some commentators have suggested that the relevant consent is hypothetical, although different versions of hypothetical consent have been given.[8] One version

---

[6]   *Two Treatises*, II, 96.

[7]   John Kilcullen, 'Locke on Political Obligation', *The Review of Politics*, 45, 1983, p. 333.

[8]   See the interesting discussion in John Dunn, 'Consent in the Political Theory of John Locke', *The Historical Journal*, (X, 1967), pp. 153–82, and in Hanna Pitkin, 'Obligation and Consent' in *Philosophy, Politics and Society*, Fourth Series, Peter Laslett, W.G. Runciman and Quentin Skinner (eds) (Oxford, 1972).

is that if members of an existing political society were asked whether they would wish to be incorporated into that society, they would give an affirmative answer. Another version locates the hypothetical consent in the consent which any rational person in the state of nature, with full knowledge of the relevant facts, would have given. These interpretations will not however be ultimately helpful because if they succeed in explaining political obligation then they will do so only on a basis different to that of the obligation of promise keeping. A hypothetical consent, in any version, is not an actual consent, and nothing less than actual consent can count as an obligation generating promise. The fact that, if asked, I would have made a certain promise, or the different fact that if I were fully rational and in possession of all relevant information, I would have made the promise, does not in either case show that I have in fact made such a promise.

An account of express consent in terms of hypothetical consent may however show that political obligation is a species of the different duty of fairness or fair play. John Rawls expounds the duty of fair play as a duty that arises from one's acceptance of the benefits of a just scheme of social co-operation. Citizens of a political society accept, and intend to continue accepting, the benefits of the system of social cooperation constituted by the laws of that society. If the scheme of social co-operation is a just one, then citizens have a duty of fair play to obey the laws.[9] For Rawls the principles which define a just scheme of social co-operation are those which would be chosen by rational and mutually disinterested people acting behind a 'veil of ignorance' which deprives them of knowledge about their personalities and their specific interests. Rawls calls this hypothetical situation in which principles of justice are selected the original position.[10]

David Richards has brilliantly reinterpreted Locke's accounts of express and tacit consent to make them yield a Rawlsian basis of political obligation as the obligation of fairness.[11] In Richards' view the passages describing express consent imply that a necessary condition of political obligation is that the institutions of society are just, and the test of justice is the hypothetical consent of rational people in a state of nature where there is equal liberty. But a further condition has to be satisfied for there to be sufficient grounds for political obligation. This is that a person takes advantage of the benefits of the legal system of the society. This condition is satisfied whenever tacit consent, in Locke's sense, is given to the government. On Richards' interpretation of Locke, the two requirements

---

[9]   John Rawls, 'Legal Obligation and the Duty of Fair Play' in *Law and Philosophy*, Sidney Hook (ed.) (New York, 1964), pp. 9–10.

[10]   Rawls' much discussed theory of justice is developed at great length in his *A Theory of Justice*, (Oxford, 1972).

[11]   David A.J. Richards, *A Theory of Reasons for Action*, (Oxford, 1971), pp. 152–7.

that the institutions of society are just by the test of hypothetical consent, and that tacit consent has been given, are both necessary, and together sufficient, for there to be political obligation. But Richards criticizes the incompleteness of Locke's test of justice in that the baseline of equal liberty from which hypothetical consent is given is too low. Since the conditions prevailing in the state of nature are undesirable, everyone will benefit from contracting out of that state even if the resulting political society is unjust in the distribution of economic, social, and political goods. Richards suggests the strengthening of the test of justice by incorporating the features of Rawls' original position into the situation from which hypothetical consent is given. Richards also wants to strengthen Locke's concept of tacit consent by requiring that the benefits of the legal system should be voluntarily accepted in the sense that they are accepted 'with the intention and expectation of encouraging others to rely on you to do your part in bearing the burdens, so that they will be encouraged to do their part.'[12]

Although Richards' account is an excellent reconstruction of a Lockean theory of political obligation, it suffers from some weaknesses as an account of Locke's intentions in so far as these can be gleaned from the text. Locke's concept of express consent is modelled too closely on promising for it to be reducible to a version of hypothetical consent. But more importantly, Locke's account of the law of nature is a theological account which presupposes the existence of a Christian God who is the creator of mankind. Injustice for Locke involves the violation of God's will as embodied in the law of nature. This heavily theological conception of justice is not reflected in Richards' notion of hypothetical consent. But those who find Locke's theological presuppositions unattractive or unacceptable as the basis of political obligation in pluralistic societies, may prefer Richards' secular reconstruction.

Property

Apart from his discussion of political authority and political obligation, Locke's *Two Treatises* is well known for his views on property. Very often the term 'property' is used by Locke to refer broadly to the totality of a person's rights to life, liberty, and property in the narrow sense which Locke also called 'possessions'. The famous chapter on property is largely an account of the right to property in the narrow sense which covers the possession of land and various goods. Here, as elsewhere, Locke's starting point is theological: God has given the world to mankind in common to use for its preserva-

---

[12] ibid., p. 155.

tion. Locke's argument for property rights seeks to explain how each person is entitled to take from the common property something for his or her own exclusive use. Locke points out that the consent of others is not necessary, for otherwise people will starve while waiting for the express consent of others.

Locke maintains that 'every Man has a Property in his own Person', and this entitles him to the 'labour of his Body, and the work of his Hands.' Thus when he 'mixed his labour with' something in the common estate, he is entitled to the products of his labour.[13] Many commentators have asked why 'mixing my labour' with an object should give me an exclusive right to that object. It is not intuitively obvious why this should be a way of gaining possession of the object rather than a way of losing my labour. Thus in *Anarchy, State, and Utopia*, Nozick points out that if I mixed my tomato juice with the sea by pouring a can of juice into the sea, I would have lost the tomato juice and not gained property rights over the sea.[14] Locke's use of the notion of 'mixing labour' has also been criticized by Jeremy Waldron. Waldron argues that we mix objects with other objects, and not with labour which consists of actions. In an ordinary case of mixing, the cook mixes the egg with the batter. The action of mixing is distinct from the cook, the egg, and the batter. But suppose now we consider an apparently similar case of a labourer 'mixing his labour' with an object. The labourer is the analogue of the cook, his labour is analogous with the egg (the ingredient) which is mixed with the batter (the object). But there is no distinct action of mixing. But if we treat the labouring as the analogue of the action of mixing, then the missing item is the ingredient which is mixed with the object.[15]

In a book of outstanding scholarship, James Tully maintains that Locke meant by 'labour' any intentional action, and that a person owns his labour in the sense that he is conscious of being the author of his action.[16] As author of his actions he has rights over the things he makes, just as God has the maker's right in His workmanship. This explains God's rights in man, and why man's body is God's property. Similarly man, as creator or maker, acquires property rights to the things that he has transformed by his labour or actions. However Tully's account raises as many problems as it solves. It establishes an analogy, based on the workmanship model, between a person's actions and God's creation. But it does not really answer the question as to why the creator of something should have exclusive rights to it. If our bodies are God's property simply because He is

---

13 *Two Treatises*, II, 27.
14 Robert Nozick, *Anarchy, State, and Utopia*, (New York, 1974), pp. 174–5.
15 Jeremy Waldron, 'Two Worries about Mixing One's Labour', *The Philosophical Quarterly*, 33, 1983, pp. 40–1.
16 James Tully, *A Discourse on Property*, (Cambridge, 1982), pp. 104–21.

their creator or maker, and if, as Tully suggests, Locke regarded intentional actions as a species of making, then parents who deliberately procreate have the same property rights over their children that God has over us. But this conclusion is unacceptable to Locke. It seems necessary to modify the workmanship model to the extent that God's rights to His creations arise not simply from His role as creator, but also perhaps from His omnipotence and omnibenevolence. But any modification of the workmanship model along these lines will make it inapplicable as an account of how a person, without God's unique properties, can acquire any property rights at all.

Locke's argument can perhaps be rescued from these and other objections by making it much more modest. Thus the argument may lead only to the conclusion that others have no cause for complaint if I appropriated something from the common estate by labouring on it. If God intended all of us to use the common estate, and if the only way in which I can use something is by transforming it into something valuable by my labour, then they have no cause for complaint. They can perform similar acts for their own benefit. Moreover, my appropriation of land for cultivation involves the more efficient use of land, and will thereby release more land for others to use.[17] If I had not appropriated land but merely appropriated the animals that I hunt and the food that I gather from the land, then I need to use more land to satisfy my needs. But interpreted in this way, Locke's argument does not give me exclusive property rights to use whatever I have appropriated, nor does it explain how I can acquire, or retain, property rights in situations of scarcity of resources. So long as others do not interfere with me while I am actually using the land, and so long as their use of my land does not defeat my longer term plans, there would seem to be no need for them to ask my permission to use the same land for their own purposes.

Locke maintains that a person may appropriate only as much as he can use without the goods spoiling, for 'Nothing was made by God for Man to spoil or destroy.'[18] This restriction on appropriation was removed by the invention of money which does not spoil. A person can thus exchange vast amounts of perishable goods for money without violating the spoilage proviso. Locke's remark that a person's appropriation of goods left 'enough and as good' for others has often been taken as laying down a further constraint on

---

[17] See David Lyons, 'The New Indian Land Claims and Original Rights to Land', in *Reading Nozick: Essays on Anarchy, State and Utopia* Jeffrey Paul, (ed.) (Oxford, 1981), p. 362, and Alan Ryan, 'Locke and the Dictatorship of the Bourgeoisie', in *Locke and Berkeley: A Collection of Critical Essays*, C.B. Martin and D.M. Armstrong, (eds) (New York, 1968), pp. 250–1.
[18] *Two Treatises*, II, 31.

legitimate acquisition. But it has been acutely argued by Jeremy Waldron that the remark merely states a fact about the effects of acquisition in the early stages, and is not intended as a restriction on acquisition.[19] However Waldron rightly points out that a stronger constraint is in fact embodied in Locke's view that when a person's own survival, or the survival of his family, is not at stake, he is required to assist in the survival of others.

The most well-known recent attempt to apply a Lockean theory of original acquisition of unowned goods and resources is to be found in Nozick's provocative historical entitlement theory of justice.[20] Such a theory requires a theory of original acquisition to supplement its accounts of justice in transfer and in rectification: if the justice of a distribution of goods depends not on its structure but on how it came about, then injustice in the acquisition of goods in the distant past will be transmitted to the current distribution. As we have seen, Nozick rejects Locke's 'mixing labour' criterion of property rights, but he accepts a version of what he calls 'the Lockean proviso' that the original acquisition of goods and resources should leave 'enough and as good' for others. Nozick's version states that a person can acquire as much as does not worsen the condition of others. In deciding whether others are made worse off, Nozick does not use the test of whether their needs and welfare are sufficiently catered for. Instead Nozick's test involves a comparison of their position before the relevant acquisition with their position after it. Thus Nozick points out that if by chance I come across a new substance in a distant place and I appropriate the total supply because the substance is effective in treating a certain disease, I do not worsen the condition of others.[21] It is unlikely, at least in the short run, that anyone else would have discovered the substance. Presumably within the period that others are unlikely to make the discovery, I can charge whatever I wish for the substance even if patients who cannot afford to pay the exorbitant price will die. Death does not make the patients worse off in the required sense for they would have died in any case had I not made the discovery. Nozick confirms the existence of this harsh edge to his theory of justice when he points out that property rights circumscribe the content of the right to life. If, in acquiring what I need to survive, I violate the property rights of others, then my right to life does not give me the right to such acquisition.[22] Nozick's Locke-inspired theory of justice does not however seem wholly compatible with Locke's account of the fundamental law of nature which enjoins the preservation of man-

---

[19] Jeremy Waldron, 'Enough and as Good Left for Others', *The Philosophical Quarterly*, 29, 1979, p. 326.
[20] Robert Nozick, op. cit.
[21] ibid., p. 181.
[22] ibid., p. 179 footnote.

kind. It would seem to be an implication of Locke's view that, except when the owner's life or those of his family are at stake, there can be no property rights, which if exercised, will deprive others of what they need in order to survive. The right to life circumscribes property rights, and Locke's account of the right to life does not merely impose negative duties on others not to interfere with my survival, but it also requires that they accept positive duties to help me to survive.[23]

Toleration

Locke's *A Letter Concerning Toleration* was originally written in Latin, and published in 1689. The English translation was also published in the same year. His defence of religious toleration remains one of the classics.

Locke argues that neither the government nor the dominant religious group in society is in a better position to know the religious truth than the ordinary citizen because every one is fallible. So it is best to leave people to judge for themselves where the truth lies. Locke believes that the truth will ultimately prevail in the free competition of ideas:

> For the truth certainly would do well enough if she were once left to shift for herself. She seldom has received, and I fear never will receive, much assistance from the power of great men, to whom she is but rarely known and more rarely welcome. She is not taught by laws, nor has she any need of force to procure her entrance into the minds of men. Errors indeed prevail by the assistance of foreign and borrowed succors. But if truth makes not her way into the understanding by her own light, she will be but the weaker for any borrowed force violence can add to her.[24]

Part of this passage is quoted and criticized by the recent Williams Report on Obscenity and Film Censorship. The Report argues that the truth may need help to emerge from the free market of ideas. It cites against Locke's argument the opposite view embodied in a cultural version of Gresham's Law: just as bad money drives out good, so too, the Report suggests, perhaps the most interesting ideas or the most valuable works of art may not survive commercial competition.[25] Locke's remark is taken by the Report as laying down

---

23 This account of Locke's view is, I think, in line with the arguments of Jeremy Waldron in 'Enough and as Good Left for Others', op. cit., pp. 326–7.

24 John Locke, *A Letter Concerning Toleration*, The Library of Liberal Arts, (New York, 1955), pp. 45–6.

25 Bernard Williams (ed.), *Obscenity and Film Censorship: An Abridgement of the Williams Report*, (Cambridge, 1981), p. 55.

a sufficient condition for the emergence of truth, and, if this interpretation is correct, then it certainly shows Locke to be unduly optimistic about the power of truth and goodness. But today most of those who support the free market of ideas regard it at most as a necessary condition for the emergence of truth or of valuable ideas. In any case they would doubt whether the 'commercial competition', to which the Report refers, is wholly compatible with the operation of the free market of ideas, for such competition often leads to a concentration in too few hands of ownership and control of the media of communications.

But the eloquent statement from Locke does not contain his main argument for religious toleration, which is that even if the religious truth were known, it should not be imposed on those who did not accept it.

He maintains that the use of force can only change the conduct of a person, but it cannot change his beliefs. True belief can only be produced by 'light and evidence', and without true belief there will be no salvation.

> I may grow rich by an art that I take not delight in, I may be cured of some disease by remedies that I have not faith in; but I cannot be saved by a religion that I distrust and by a worship that I abhor. It is in vain for an unbeliever to take up the outward show of another man's profession. Faith only and inward acceptance are the things that procure acceptance with God.[26]

Locke's argument is, as often, couched in colourful language which seems on this occasion to hide its weakness from him. For the argument relies on a crude psychological account of the way in which true beliefs are produced, and it is open to the objection that acting as if you believe in God can sometimes lead to genuine belief. Pascal, in presenting his famous Wager, was much closer to the truth when he maintained that religious disbelief, which was for him a kind of sickness, could be cured by acting as if one believed in God. But Locke's argument can be restated as a normative account of the requirements for salvation. Perhaps God is not impressed by the mere fact that a person happens to hold the true religious belief: what matters is how he or she arrived at it. It is doubtful, for example, that a just God would care much for Pascal's rather obnoxious character who succeeded in acting his way into true belief. On moral grounds such a believer is not to be preferred to the conscientious atheist who allowed his fallible conscience to guide his conduct. This is an argument that Locke could very nearly accept if it were not for the fact that he foolishly believed that toleration should not be extended to atheists because they could not be relied

---

[26] ibid., p. 34.

upon to keep their promises, which were for him the cement of political society. The other group to whom Locke did not extend religious toleration was that of Roman Catholics. Locke argued that their allegiance to a foreign Pope made them a threat to national security.

Locke's other major argument for religious toleration relies on his doctrine about the limits of political authority. The State's function is to protect the life, liberty, and property of its citizens, and so 'the care of men's souls' falls outside the scope of its proper functions. Not all sins should be punished by the state, but only those which threaten the peace of society and the rights of its members. This line of argument is developed with admirable lucidity into a case for limiting the type of reasons which may justifiably be used to interfere with the conduct of individuals. Thus Locke points out that the sacrifice of a calf in a religious ceremony should not be prohibited if it does not harm the members of a society. (Locke of course lived before the campaign for animal liberation.) However if it can be shown to be in the interest of society to build up the severely depleted stock of cattle, then the legal prohibition on the killing of calves is justified. 'Only it is to be observed that, in this case, the law is not made about a religious but a political matter; nor is the sacrifice, but the slaughter of calves, thereby prohibited.'[27] Contemporary liberalism has relied on the distinction between crime and sin, but this distinction has often been misstated as a distinction between different areas of conduct, with certain types of sinful conduct absolutely immune from legal prohibitions. Liberalism needs to be restated in terms of different types of reason for interfering with conduct in any area.[28] Only some reasons for intervention are relevant. A careful reading of Locke shows that his case for religious toleration espouses the more defensible form of liberalism.

Locke's deep commitment to religious toleration went hand in hand with an equally passionate belief in the truth of Christianity. Here his position is again instructive, and should help to dispel the common view that religious toleration is the product of religious scepticism.

Conclusion

The framework of Locke's political thinking is Christian. But some who have been influenced by him have either not noticed the

---

[27] ibid., p. 40.
[28] In *Mill on Liberty*, (Oxford, 1980), I have given an interpretation of J.S. Mill's liberalism along these lines.

theological underpinnings of his political theory, or they have somehow extracted from his writings views which do not require support from his Christianity. Perhaps he has inspired most where he has been most misunderstood. This is paradoxical, but it is a measure of the depth and complexity of his contribution as a major political thinker.[29]

Bibliography

John Locke, *Two Treatises of Government*. The definitive edition is that by Peter Laslett, (Cambridge, 1960). The Everyman edition, called *Two Treatises of Civil Government*, is also useful.
John Locke, *a Letter Concerning Toleration*, (New York, 1955).
John Locke, *Essays on the Law of Nature*, W. von Leyden (ed.), (Oxford, 1954).

Further Reading

Lawrence C. Becker, *Property Rights: Philosophic Foundations*, (London, 1977).
Maurice Cranston, *John Locke: A Biography*, (London, 1966).
John Dunn, 'Consent in the Political Theory of John Locke', *The Historical Journal*, X, 1967, pp. 153–82.
John Dunn, *The Political Thought of John Locke*, (Cambridge, 1969).
John Kilcullen, 'Locke on Political Obligation', *The Review of Politics*, 45, 1983, pp. 323–44.
David Lyons, 'The New Indian Claims and Original Rights to Land', in *Reading Nozick: Essays on Anarchy, State, and Utopia*, Jeffrey Paul (ed.), (Oxford, 1981).
C.B. MacPherson, *The Political Theory of Possessive Individualism*, (Oxford, 1962). This provocative book includes an interpretation of Locke's political theory from a Marxist point of view. It is criticized by Dunn in *The Political Thought of John Locke* and also by Ryan and Tully.
C.L. Ten, *Mill on Liberty*, (Oxford, 1980).
Robert Nozick, *Anarchy, State, and Utopia*, (New York, 1974).
Hanna Pitkin, 'Obligation and Consent' in *Philosophy, Politics and Society*, Fourth Series, Peter Laslett, W.G. Runciman and Quentin Skinner (eds), (Oxford, 1972).
John Plamenatz, *Man and Society*, vol. 1, ch. 6, (London, 1963).
John Rawls, 'Legal Obligation and the Duty of Fair Play', in *Law and Philosophy*, Sidney Hook (ed.), (New York, 1964).
John Rawls, *A Theory of Justice*, (Oxford, 1972).
David A.J. Richards, *A Theory of Reasons for Action*, (Oxford, 1971).

---

[29] I am indebted to Barbara Younger and the members of the Monash University Philosophy Seminar for their comments.

Alan Ryan, 'Locke and the Dictatorship of the Bourgeoisie' in *Locke and Berkeley: A Collection of Critical Essays*, C.B. Martin and D.M. Armstrong (eds), (New York, 1968).

James Tully, *A Discourse on Property*, (Cambridge, 1982).

Jeremy Waldron, 'Enough and as Good Left for Others', *The Philosophical Quarterly*, 29, 1979, pp. 319–28.

Jeremy Waldron, 'Two Worries about Mixing One's Labour', *The Philosophical Quarterly*, 33, 1983, pp. 37–44.

Bernard Williams (ed.), *Obscenity and Film Censorship: An Abridgement of the Williams Report*, (Cambridge, 1981).

Chapter Eight
Hume on Justice
G.D.Marshall

I

On the death of David Hume in 1776 at the age of sixty-five, Adam Smith wrote:

> Thus died our most excellent and never to be forgotten friend; concerning whose philosophical opinions men will, no doubt, judge variously, every one approving or condemning them according as they happen to coincide or disagree with his own; but concerning whose character and conduct there can scarce be a difference of opinion. His temper, indeed, seemed to be more happily balanced, if I may be allowed such an expression, than that perhaps of any other man I have ever known... Upon the whole I have always considered him, both in his lifetime and since his death, as approaching as nearly to the idea of a perfectly wise and virtuous man, as perhaps the nature of human fraility will permit.[1]

'Le bon David', as he was known to many on both sides of the English Channel, was a man of letters who first became widely known through the publication in 1741 and 1742 of his *Essays Moral and Political*. In the preface to them he expresses what is in fact his greatest contribution to the politics of his day:

> Public Spirit, methinks, should engage us to love the public and to bear an equal affection to all our countrymen; not to hate one half of them under the pretext of loving the whole. This party-rage I have endeavoured to repress as far as possible and I hope this design will be

---

[1] Letter from Adam Smith, LL.D., to William Strahan, Esq., in Hume's *Essays, Moral, Political and Literary*, T.H. Green and T.H. Grose (eds), (London, 1875), vol. I, pp. 13–14.

acceptable to the moderate of both parties; at the same time that, perhaps, it may displease the bigots of both.[2]

Hume was the impartial observer of the politics of his time and its past – a position he had already decided was necessary to any properly moral judgement on anything. But amidst all his philosophy and history he was still a man, as he enjoined us all to be. In his middle years and public life as secretary to General St Clair's expedition to Canada and later military embassy to the courts of Vienna and Turin, and then as secretary to the English Embassy in Paris, where he was for a time chargé d'affaires, he could not stay removed from the political matters of his day. Witness, for example, his portrait of Sir Robert Walpole which he concludes by saying:

> He would have been esteemed more worthy of his high station had he never possessed it; and is better qualified for the second than for the first place in any government. His ministry has been more advantageous to his family than to the public, better for this age than for posterity, and more pernicious by bad precedents than by real grievances. During his time trade has flourished, liberty declined, and learning gone to ruin. As I am a man, I love him; as I am a scholar, I hate him; as I am a Briton, I calmly wish his fall. And were I a member of either house, I would give my vote for removing him from St James's; but should be glad to see him retire to Houghton-Hall, to pass the remainder of his days in ease and pleasure.[3]

Hume was philosophical about politics. The *Essays Moral and Political* have a style of thought that penetrates the fogs of ideology. Of course, an impartial observer neither ever was nor is entirely impartial; but Hume reminds us more than anyone of the possibility of being so. One may explain away the arguments and critical analyses of Hume and those like him, but one does not thereby dispose of the strict necessity of meeting them. In the ordinary course of life and letters they are not answered by causal explanations for them. Ideology is exactly the place to hide when one has dodged an issue, and Hume is exactly the person to expose the transparency of such a manoeuvre.

Hume is arguably the greatest of the British philosophers and for that reason alone what he has to say about politics is worth attending to. His thought is very much all of a piece though it does not present as an overpowering system as does that of Plato, Hegel or Marx. His political philosophy is part of his moral philosophy and rests on his metaphysics and epistemology. What most characterizes him is an original kind of scepticism. He said that he would be entirely

---

[2] ibid., vol. I, p. 41.
[3] ibid., vol. II, p. 396.

sceptical if nature were not too strong for him. These two points are the poles on which all his thought turns. He was sceptical particularly about *a priori* philosophizing and about how much in general reason alone can disclose. His scepticism is the realization of the limitations of reason to secure its own hegemony. His naturalism, on the other hand, provides what he calls a sceptical solution to sceptical doubts and rests on the clear apprehension that the deepest problems vanish into the ordinary course of life. We cannot get behind how things naturally are. 'Nature breaks the force of all sceptical arguments in time.'[4]

Hume is an empiricist: all our knowledge is generated by and confined to what we can experience. The furthest we can go towards general truths is ideal laws based on induction from facts, itself based on nothing but our own experience of causal relations determined by custom and habit. And Hume is a positivist; at least he was claimed as an ally by the Logical Positivists in the 1930s, with some justification, given the conclusion to his *Enquiries Concerning Human Understanding*:

> When we run over libraries persuaded of these principles, what havoc must we make? If we take in our hands any volume, of divinity or school metaphysics, for instance; let us ask, Does it contain any abstract reasoning concerning quantity and number? No. Does it contain any experimental reasoning concerning matter of fact and existence? No. Commit it then to the flames, for it can contain nothing but sophistry and illusion.[5]

Yet he was a very complex and sophisticated positivist, if he was really one at all. His intention was not to limit egregiously the objects of genuine thought and reflection but to point out, first, that there is no ground on which to suppose the existence of certain things, and second, that there is no necessity to do so. And while he had no time for what he called the pernicious nonsense of religion and superstition, and inveighed against grand statements defended on the supposed ground of absolute obviousness, his rich moral psychology and the importance he accords to the manifold interrelated sentiments in human knowledge and action, fits ill with the crudities of recent positivism. He did not, for example, confine truth-confirming experience to the perception merely of mind-independent facts. He stresses, on the contrary, both the contribution that habits of mind make to the understanding of the world, and the enormous impor-

---

4   David Hume, *A Treatise of Human Nature*, L.A. Selby-Bigge (ed.), (Oxford, 1888), 1st edn, I, IV, II, p. 187.

5   David Hume, *Enquiries Concerning the Human Understanding and Concerning the Principles of Morals*, L.A. Selby-Bigge (ed.), (Oxford, 1902), section XII, part III, p. 165.

tance of moral experience, of sympathy and fellow-feeling. He rejects rationalistic and idealistic metaphysics not fundamentally because it requires its professors to cross the bounds of sense but because there is nothing natural connected with it to solve sceptical doubts that arise within it. Reasons come to a stop somewhere, he believes, but not in first principles or self-evident axioms; only in experience, where rational connections and relations give place to causal ones, the operation of which, though not beyond critical reflection, is independent of any reasoning. His positivism, like his empiricism, derives from his scepticism.

These are the attitudes and principles Hume takes into his political philosophy.

II

Hume is credited, first, with the final destruction of Natural Law Theory through a mortal attack on the doctrine of Natural Rights. Second, he produces a compelling argument against contractual theories of allegiance or political obligation by way of an attack on the primacy of obligation in general and promise keeping in particular. But third, his central concern is with justice, the province of which he restricts to property and the substance of which is given in the extablished rules and practices governing it. He saw that there is no natural reason or motive in humankind to act justly and from this his arguments under the first and second heads are generated. They are not entirely conclusive, as we shall see in the end.

Hume's views on justice are consequential on his views about morality and moral obligation. Hume firmly believed that morality, whatever precisely it encompasses, serves human nature; it regulates human behaviour in order to enhance human life as we know it through our capacities. There must, therefore, be a sense in which morality is perfectly natural to humankind, in sympathy with human nature and not set over against it, judging, condemning, forbidding it, in the assurance of some transcendent ideal or law. But though morality is in this sense natural to humankind in general, moral acts, whatever they may be precisely, may not be natural to any particular human being. Hence, certain acts may appear as obligatory and not in sympathy with the nature of any particular person, as those exemplified in the desires, interests, feelings and beliefs he or she actually has, for all that such acts are consonant with human nature generally considered. It is, for example, clearly not inhuman to be generous though someone may go through life only grudgingly so. It follows that no act could be morally obligatory unless there is, for acts of that sort, a reason or motive which is natural for humankind: one to be commonly found amongst people or clearly associated with what is so found, and readily comprehended as a recognizably human reason or motive. So it would be quite unintelligible to suppose that we should ever be morally obliged to have regard to those less fortunate than ourselves, for example, if we did not, at least sometimes, have a perfectly natural concern for them.

If there is no natural reason amongst humankind to act justly, it would appear to follow that there is no moral obligation upon one to be just and no moral virtue to be found in it. Hume's way out is to make justice a social or political virtue. In so doing, he laid the foundation for a social-theoretic account of its origin and just-ification.

Hume contends that there is no natural motive for acting justly. He considers several possibilities and dismisses them. What could such a natural motive be? Not simple self-love or the desire for one's own advancement or advantage, since that, Hume rightly says, is the source of all injustice and violence. Not solely the benevolent regard we may have for the advantage of another, or humankind in general, for questions of justice may arise when we do not feel benevolently disposed: when the other is an enemy, for example, or when we are suddenly ashamed of our species. Neither is it the inclination to religion or the motive of piety, as Francis Hutcheson and the Natural Law writers thought, for that inclination and motive is itself not natural.[6] Hume makes this contention in the introduction to his *The Natural History of Religion* and the reason he gives is that piety is not like love of progeny, gratitude and resentment.

> Every instinct of this kind has been found absolutely universal in all nations and ages and has always a precise determinate object which it inflexibly pursues. The first religious principles must be secondary, such as may easily be perverted by various accidents and causes, and whose operation too, in some cases, may, by an extraordinary concurrence of circumstances, be altogether prevented.[7]

Whether piety, justice, or indeed anything else is natural depends, of course, on how that term is understood, as Hume is very much aware. As this last quotation reveals, Hume believed the natural motives and feelings to be those that are both universal and have a determinate object. Whatever may be thought about Hume's list and the evidence upon which it or any revision of it is drawn up, it is quite plain that the inclinations to religion and justice are not in this sense natural. One may wonder, indeed, whether anything is. But the point is that the existence of such inclinations and the uniqueness of their objects, cannot be *relied upon* without the assistance of education, sanction, or enlightenment. So, as Hume construes the natural, it is entirely reasonable to say that there is no natural motive

---

6   C.F. Duncan Forbes, *Hume's Philosophical Politics*, (Cambridge, 1975).
7   David Hume, *The Natural History of Religion*, H.E. Root (ed.), (London, 1956), p. 21.

to justice. What is natural, however, even in this regimented sense, is that rules of justice should come to be made by humankind in the ordinary development of society.

Justice, Hume agrees, has long been defined as giving each man his due. But what is his due? Hume says that each of us values three different species of goods: 'the internal satisfaction of our minds, the external advantages of our body, and the enjoyment of such possessions as we have acquired by our industry and good fortune.'[8] He sees no threat to the first by anyone or anything. The second, he says, 'may be ravished from us but can be of no advantage to him who deprives us of them'. Only our possessions, he concludes, can be taken from us for another's advantage. This is to be remedied by 'putting these goods as far as possible on the same footing with the fixed and constant advantages of the mind and body.'[9]

This is a curious argument, to which we shall return. But, setting aside the momentous question of our minds and bodies, which Locke made central in the matter of our natural rights, are our possessions our due? We have them and will fight to enjoy them if not to increase them at the expense of others unless we are constrained. There is no natural motive towards justice; our own 'partiality for ourselves' sees to that. Why should we be so concerned about the matter ? We would not be if everything we wanted were available in great abundance like the air we breathe (it is only really fresh air we get concerned about). The obvious answer is that our possessions we have in proportion to our wants; and 'tis to restrain relative to our wants. 'The selfishness of men is animated by the few possessions we have in proportion to our wants; and 'tis to restrain this selfishness that men have been obliged to separate themselves from the community and to distinguish betwixt their own goods and those of others.'[10] This clearly explains our *interest* in our possessions but it goes no way at all to explain our *right*. Indeed, says Hume, there is no right prior to our developing a sense of justice. His major contention is that what is a person's due, what are his or her rights, is entirely dependent upon and derived from the prior establishment of rules and practices of justice.

The rules arise slowly through the experience of living in societies gradually enlarging with and from the development of families. In the satisfaction of sexual needs is the beginning of society and in the perception of the advantages of co-operation in society the beginnings of justice. Conventions are needed to control 'the inconveniences of our selfishness and limited generosity and the use of scarce goods'. These conventions are such as can be accepted by all

---

[8] *A Treatise of Human Nature*, op. cit., III, II, I, p. 487.
[9] ibid., p. 489.
[10] ibid., p. 495.

members of a small enough society and constitute the rules of justice for that society. The recognition by members of that society of the need for such conventions and the advantages to be enjoyed by observing them, is the emergence of the sense of justice and the source of its value. The rules of justice must bind everyone in the society and do not exist as such until they are accepted as doing so. The moral value of justice lies in the sympathetic recognition by each member of the society that justice is in the interests of all and therefore of each. Hume's view is that justice, so conceived, is the unintended consequence of individual human actions. As Haakonssen says, this must be one of the boldest and most ingenious moves in the history of the philosophy of law.[11] Justice is an empirical consequence of human interactions and as such it arises without the need of Hobbes' sovereign or any other intervention.

This is not yet civil society or the state; but it is co-operative society. If anything is a state of nature beyond the fictions of Hobbes and Locke this is more properly to be called so. Justice is perfectly natural in this state of nature, though that is not to say that everyone now has his or her natural due. There are still no natural rights, even though in the natural course there will emerge societies in which rights are created by the formation of conventions concerning property, though achieving that happy result is not the intention with which the conventions are accepted.

Hume can now give, after all, a natural motive for justice and therefore a ground for the obligation towards it. It is nothing other than one's own enlightened and redirected self-interest. Herbert Simon could have been expounding Hume's view (with a touch of Adam Smith) when he was expressing his own:

> In our formation of public policy and in our own private decision making it is probably reasonable to assume, as a first approximation, that people will act out of self-interest. Hence a major task for any society is to create a social environment in which self-interest has reason to be enlightened. If we want an invisible hand to bring everything into some kind of social consonance, we should be sure first that our social institutions are framed to bring out our better selves, and second, that they do not require major sacrifices of self-interest by many people much of the time... [12]

It might be thought that enlightened self-interest is not natural in the sense used earlier for the self-love that Hume said was the source of all injustice. Indeed, there is a difficulty here. Either enlightened self-interest is not natural, in which case we need a natural motive to become enlightened, or basic self-love itself is sufficient for justice

---

[11] Knud Haakonssen, *The Science of a Legislator*, (Cambridge, 1981), p. 20.

[12] Herbert A. Simon, *Reason in Human Affairs*, (Oxford, 1983), pp. 105–6.

when it is also said to be the cause of injustice. But enlightened self-interest must be natural because unless it is as universal and precisely directed as Hume thought natural motives and feelings are, it could hardly be the foundation of co-operative societies, and Hume's account of their development would therefore be at fault. But if it is natural, what is its distinction from basic self-love which is destructive of society? This cluster of problems we shall return to later in dealing with the prisoner's dilemma.

III

Promise keeping has been thought to show much about foundations of morality and society. Hume does not deny that we have an obligation to keep promises, indeed, on the contrary makes much use of it; but he does deny characteristically that we have any natural motive to make promises, or once made, to keep them. Both are unintelligible without co-operative society. Again, it is the development of conventions which establishes the institution of promise keeping. 'The self-interested commerce of men' becomes so many conventions that create new motives. In a small enough society with common offices and the possibility of exacting the consequences of broken promises, the new motives of enlightened self-interest should be plain enough. The conventions here, Hume sees cleverly, include those governing the use of certain forms of words. The acceptance of a convention is the declaration of an intention to act in a certain way, and if that declaration is public and the right conditions are fulfilled, that constitutes the making of a promise obligatory upon one. There is no prior, original, moral obligation beyond this. Therefore, the promise-based contractual theories of civil allegiance must be inadequate.

Once, however, co-operative society flourishes and conventions equally of justice and promise keeping are established in the natural course of the development of such societies, then we have a real basis for civil society. Allegiance to government is, Hume says, 'grafted on' to the obligation of promises but then becomes distinct. Government, in the growth of society, is a new invention by men to secure what, in a smaller co-operative society, they could secure for themselves, namely the stability of possessions, the control of the transfer of them, and 'the advantages of peace, commerce and mutual succour'.

Hume has a dozen arguments to prove that our duty of allegiance to government is not derived from our duty to keep promises, despite being 'grafted on' to them, and that it is not the case that our political obligation derives from a contract we have tacitly made. His main line of thought is that self-interest supports both duties in different ways. Government was invented from the need to preserve order in 'large and polished' societies whereas promises were invented from the need for 'mutual trust and confidence in the common offices of life': the ends and the means are distinct, and so are the advantages. However, the duties are also too alike for the one to be derived from the other. 'As these two rules are founded on like obligations of interest, each of them must have a peculiar authority independent of the other.'[13] Moreover, even if there had been

> no such thing as a promise in the world, government would still be necessary in all large and civilized societies; and if promises had only their own proper obligation without the separate sanction of government, they would have but little efficacy in such societies. This separates the boundaries of our public and private duties and shows that the latter are more dependent on the former than the former on the latter.[14]

Hume adds some empirical considerations. 'The greatest part of the nation' believe they were born to obedience to their rulers even if those rulers were such that 'no man, however foolish, would voluntarily choose them'. Furthermore,

> a man living under an absolute government would owe it no allegiance since by its very nature it depends on no contract. But as that is as natural and common a government as any, it must certainly occasion some obligation; and 'tis plain from experience that men who are subjected to it, do always think so.[15]

He concludes with the reflection that 'where no promise is given, a man looks not on his faith as broken in private matters upon account of rebellion, but keeps those two duties of honour and allegiance perfectly distinct and separate.'[16]

In commenting on this, Jonathan Harrison says:

> I find all the arguments which Hume uses to show that our duty to obey the government is not a special case of an antecedently existing duty to keep our promises, and that, in consequence, we have a duty to obey the government whether we consent to do this or not, absolutely conclusive, and can only wonder that the contrary view has survived until the present day, in spite of his arguments.[17]

Perhaps the contrary view has survived because Hume's conclusions are more compelling than his arguments, which are quite inconclusive. The needs secured by government and promises may be

---

[13] *A Treatise of Human Nature*, op. cit., III, II, VII, pp. 545–5.
[14] ibid., p. 546.
[15] ibid., p. 549.
[16] ibid., p. 549.
[17] Jonathan Harrison, *Hume's Theory of Justice*, (Oxford, 1981), p. 191.

different, but a cause must also be different from its effects, as Hume himself has taught us. Political obligation and promise keeping may be ever so alike but so may be the successive years of a course of study. And the most shown by the need for government in the absence of an institution of promise keeping is that the latter is not necessary for the former, but not that it is not sufficient nor that it might not have always been empirically so. Nevertheless, Hume is quite right to rubbish the contractual theory, and in the end his empirical observations carry the most weight. But as J.L. Mackie observes, there is an irony about those observations: 'At least a vague form of the view that government derives its legitimacy from the consent of the governed is now widely held, and even tyrannical rulers try to maintain the fiction that they are supported by some kind of popular will.'[18]

IV

There are some difficulties in Hume's position. Two of the problems Mackie isolates are crucial.

> First, does Hume show that self-interest together with understanding is sufficient to make each man accept the system of justice without Hobbes's device of sovereignty? Secondly, has he a plausible account of how a convention can grow up and gradually establish itself; or is what he says appropriate only to the solving of co-ordination problems, not to the solving of a problem of prisoners' dilemma type, such as we repeatedly encounter in the relations between men in social groups?[19]

The second is of prime importance and an answer to it solves the first as well.

Co-ordination problems presuppose that there is no conflict of real interest between the people concerned. It is plain that Hume's emerging conventions plausibly enough solve problems of this sort. But, as he points out so often himself, the partiality of each to himself or herself makes it highly likely that the interests of each will at least sometimes conflict so that in order to achieve co-operative society we shall have to be able to solve partial conflict problems as well. The so-called prisoners' dilemma is a paradigm of such problems, especially in its many-person form. The dilemma can be generally put as the question: what is it rational for each person to do if it is in the interests of all to do one thing but in the interests of each to please themselves? In a small fishing community, for example, where there is a danger that the waters will become over-fished, it

---

[18] J.L. Mackie, *Hume's Moral Theory*, (London, 1980), p. 110.
[19] ibid., p. 86.

would seem to be in the interests of all that each fisherman should be limited to a restricted catch, yet in the interests of each to exceed the limit. Or, as is the case in so many of our towns with easily congested roads, it would seem to be in the interests of all to have efficient public transport for all to use; but it would seem to be in the interests of each not to use it if everyone else does.[20] Of course, we have to add considerations dependent upon being found out. The social sanctions in small fishing communities might well make it in the interests of each to keep within the limits after all, but in many such cases it would appear conventions are not going to prevent 'free riding' completely. It is quite natural to try to make an exception of oneself and to advantage oneself at the expense of others if one can get away with it. That might well be harder to do in small societies but, as Hume notes, it is highly likely to occur to some extent in all large ones. Appeal to enlightened self-interest may not always be successful. Indeed, if public benefits are going to be provided by a large enough number of people, enlightened self-interest would appear to dictate that one make no contribution oneself: why should one, at some cost to oneself, if there is little risk of being found out and the public benefits are going to be provided anyway? Enlightened self-interest does not yield morally good or socially useful actions in all cases unless one defines enlightenment tendentiously in such a way that it must.

It might not matter in large generally law-abiding societies that some quiet law-breaking occurs. But the question for Hume is how such societies could ever have developed if enlightened self-interest alone is insufficient to solve the partial conflict problems that might occur on the way. An answer could be developed along two lines. One is, that prisoners' dilemmas only arise for those who think of people as self-interested atoms governed entirely by their desires to maximize their pleasure as determined by purely calculative reasoning. But for Hume, to see people that way is false, pernicious and absurd. As well as being self-interested, people abound in natural virtues that spring from their sympathy and fellow-feeling with other people. In the *Enquiries* he says: 'It is needless to push our researches so far as to ask why we have humanity or a fellow-feeling with others. It is sufficient that this is experienced to be a principle in human nature.'[21] That is, empirically, human nature is co-operative, caring and concerned enough to be able to trust and be generous. It is also of course, mean enough to be grossly selfish and vicious. If it were only the latter, life in a state of nature would indeed be nasty, brutish and short, and we should need Hobbes'

---

[20] Derek Parfit's examples. Cf. his 'Prudence, Morality, and the Prisoner's Dilemma', *Proceedings of the British Academy*, 1978.

[21] *Enquiries*, op. cit., V, II, p. 219 fn.

sovereign to get us out of it. But though Hobbes must not be forgotten, he may also be corrected. Enough prisoners' dilemmas are naturally solved through trust to make sure that we do not remain imprisoned by the narrow artificiality of too economical a definition of self-interest. That is, *normally*, basic self-love is enlightened and sympathetic enough to make the kind of trust possible without which our lives would hardly be viable.

A second line of thought begins with the fair assumption that in small co-operative societies the benefits one receives from others in one's own enterprises will depend upon the contributions one is seen to make to their enterprises. Thus Mackie suggests that actions become 'tied together'. In his discussion of Hume's own example of two men rowing a boat he says:

Each man can say to himself, '*Perhaps* the other chap will row if and only if I do; it can do no harm to find out'. So one of them begins to row, just a little bit, without straining himself and watches to see what the other will do. The other, in a similar experimental spirit, wondering whether his rowing too will encourage the other, tries rowing gently; if the first then rewards him by rowing a bit harder, they will soon both be fully at work. But perhaps one starts to slack, when the other has got going; the other notices this, and eases off at once as a warning. The slacker will then, for purely selfish reasons, put more effort into it; they can thus keep each other up to the mark. In circumstances like those outlined here, co-operation can be maintained by each party's readiness to use the sanction of non-co-operation... In this way, even partial conflict problems can be solved by 'convention', without explicit contract, without an external sanctioning authority, and even without any specifically moral feelings.[22]

A third central question for Hume's position concerns his restriction of the province of justice to property, and even so, his failure to consider the justice of different systems of property distribution. On owning the fruits of one's own industry, he does not go as far as Locke who defines private property as that which one has mixed one's labour with, but more soundly suggests that one 'who has hunted a hare to the last degree of weariness' has a greater right to his quarry than one who is idly about to pick an apple.[23] However, he has not considered the main rules which in fact determine property: 'the working principles of the economic system which allocate to some rather than others what are in reality, the products of the industry of many people in complex and indirect forms of co-operation.'[24] Hume gives what he calls general rules for determin-

---

[22] J.L. Mackie, op. cit., pp. 89–90.
[23] *A Treatise of Human Nature*, op. cit., III, II, III, pp. 506–7 fn.
[24] J.L. Mackie, op. cit., p. 96.

ing property but they do not touch the matter of the just distribution of goods. He says that we may legitimately take something not yet owned by anyone, and properly own something one has merely possessed for a long time as well as a natural increase of something else one owns, and one may properly own what one inherits. But the inclusion of this last, for example, shows what he ignores, for there needs to be an argument why any one person's good fortune should not be more widely shared.

Hume's reply to this objection of omission would be that 'it is the proper business of municipal laws to fix what the principles of human nature have left undetermined'.[25] And since principles of justice are not natural, there is no point outside the emerging conventions themselves from which to judge of their justice or injustice. But the further objection must be that there surely is. It is not obvious that one cannot raise and discuss the question of whether, for example, capitalistic conventions are less just than socialistic ones, nor that one cannot write a utopia of a perfectly just society.

Hume's rejoinder would be fourfold. First, there is no reason why he should not allow comparisons between different co-operative conventions nor a ranking of them. The common coin is their utility, their usefulness to humankind in the circumstances in which they are, on the one hand; and the approbation or pleasure called forth by the even working of the conventions, on the other. It is with regard to these that we may prefer socialistic conventions to capitalistic ones, if that is how the utility considerations detail out. What is rejected is that the comparisons are made in terms of a concept of justice itself which we have prior to the acceptance of any set of principles. And we might go some way towards agreeing with Hume here. Justice does not intelligibly admit of degrees: an act is either just or it is not, and one set of principles is more or less acceptable than another insofar as fewer or more acts of injustice are prevented by them. Hume might have some difficulty in giving a clear sense to this last, but the imagination is not confined to what actually obtains within a particular society at any one time.

Secondly, justice is not the sole or principal moral concept we have to employ. This is shown well in a case Hume considers in the *Enquiries*.

> Were there a species of creatures intermingled with men, which, though rational, were possessed of such inferior strength, both of body and mind, that they were incapable of all resistance, and could never, upon the highest provocation, make us feel the effects of their resentment; the necessary consequence, I think, is that we should be bound by the laws of humanity of give gentle usage to these creatures,

---

[25] *A Treatise of Human Nature*, op. cit., III, II, III, p. 513 fn.

but should not, properly speaking, lie under any restraint of justice with regard to them...[26]

That is, if a rule of justice comes with sanctions and if there are some who cannot exact the penalties by virtue of their inferior powers, then we cannot act either justly or unjustly towards them, because some of the necessary conditions for the establishment and maintenance of co-operation with them are not satisfied. Conventions constitutive of justice could not have arisen in the first place. But Hume says emphatically that we should still be under an obligation to treat such beings gently. In such a way, too, may Hume deal with one person's physical attack on another. There may be no issue of injustice here but that is not to say that such an act is not grossly immoral. Similarly with the injustice of punishing an innocent. Restricting justice to matters concerning property does not confine morality to those limits as well. There are more grounds for moral repugnance than the breaking of co-operative conventions.

But the doubts persist. Why is punishing an innocent so repugnant? These doubts are increased by reflecting on Hume's 'curious argument' that our possessions must be put on the same footing as the mental and bodily goods we value. Hume cannot mean that we must own our possessions as we own our minds and bodies; that would be absurd, since our possessions could not then constitute property, as Hume is concerned with it, at all: it could not be transferred, for example. And he cannot mean that we should be able to *enjoy* our possessions as we enjoy the 'internal satisfaction of our minds' and 'the external advantages of our bodies', presumably in complete security and peace; for he admits that those external advantages can be 'ravished from us', and, though he denies it, he should have said the same about the internal satisfaction of our minds. He must mean, therefore, that the *agreeableness and usefulness* of our possessions, like those of our minds and bodies, must be conserved. This can be achieved by having rules governing the ownership and transfer of property. But the obvious lacuna in the argument is that we must have as well rules ensuring the agreeableness and usefulness of one's mind and body; that is, rules protecting one's life and liberty. It is hard to avoid the conclusion that Hume has not shown that we have no natural rights to life and liberty; he has rather failed to carry his argument to the point where he must concede them. That is, his arguments for the artificiality of justice do not, after all, show that we have no natural rights, though they do emphasize that the only natural laws we are governed by are the empirical laws of our own human nature.

However, thirdly, if justice is morally valuable because it is in the

---

[26] *Enquiries*, op. cit., p. 190.

public interest and therefore in the real interests of each, it is open to Hume to argue that it is not in the public interest for each to feel insecure in mind and body; it is certainly not in their real interest. So questions of the right to life and liberty can be settled within society; they are as socially secured as the rights to property. And what need we of *rights* to life and liberty without society?

Fourthly and finally, if the point is pressed that we do have a sense of justice that is altogether larger than a concern with property, Hume may say, as he often does, that the dispute becomes merely verbal. He does not wish to deny, for example, that there are acts and responses which are appropriate to humankind in various circumstances, and others which are not; he only denies that such relations as appropriateness can be determined by reason alone or seen to be intuitively obvious. On the contrary, he asserts that such judgements and perceptions are made out of our natural sympathy with our fellows and feeling for ourselves. Love of others and pride in ourselves are the stuff of morality and both are generated by our natural sentiments. If one wants to call love of others and pride in oneself a sense of justice, then there may be loss of felicity but none of substance. If it be insisted that we do have an innate sense of the rightness of things, then Hume would rest content to let his opponent make the argument. For himself, being sceptical of what is not given in experience, he lets the question vanish back into our common political and moral life, which is rich and diverse enough in convention and practice and natural concern to show that the question need never arise.

Bibliography

David Hume, *Enquiries Concerning the Human Understanding and Concerning the Principles of Morals*, L.A. Selby-Bigge (ed.), (Oxford, 1902).

David Hume, *Essays, Moral, Political, and Literary*, 2 vols, T.H. Green and T.H. Grose (eds), (London, 1875).

David Hume, *The Natural History of Religion*, H.E. Root (ed.), (London, 1956).

David Hume, *A Treatise of Human Nature*, L.A. Selby-Bigge (ed.), (Oxford, 1888).

Further Reading

Duncan Forbes, *Hume's Philosophical Politics*, (Cambridge, 1975).

Knud Haakonssen, *The Science of a Legislator*, (Cambridge, 1981).

Jonathan Harrison, *Hume's Theory of Justice*, (Oxford, 1981).

John Laird, *Hume's Philosophy of Human Nature*, (London, 1932).

J.L. Mackie, *Hume's Moral Theory*, (London, 1980).

Herbert A. Simon, *Reason in Human Affairs*, (Oxford, 1983).

Chapter Nine

Rousseau and the General Will

David Muschamp

The Man, The Writer and His Task

Jean-Jacques Rousseau supposed that he was a very remarkable man, and he was right. We can gain something of an insight into his character, as he wanted us to, by reading his autobiography *The Confessions* which he wrote between 1765 and 1770 and which was published four years after his death on 2 July 1778.

> I know my own heart and understand my fellow man. But I am unlike any one I have ever met: I will even venture to say that I am like no one in the whole world. I may be no better, but, at least I am different. Whether nature did well or ill in breaking the mould in which she formed me, is a question which can only be resolved after the reading of my book[1] (C, p. 18).

His mother died a few days after his birth in Geneva in 1712, and because of it, 'so my birth was the first of my misfortunes'. A sister of his father Isaac an indulgent, erratic and irascible man, assisted in his early upbringing, his parents having left him only one endowment 'a sensitive heart. It had been the making of their happiness, but for me it has been the cause of all the misfortunes in my life' (C, p. 19).

---

[1] Unless otherwise stated references will be from the three Rousseau volumes cited in the Bibliography at the end of this chapter: *The Confessions* (C), *Emile* (E), *A Discourse on the Moral Effects of the Arts and Sciences* (DAS) *A Discourse on the Origin of Inequality* (DOI), *A Discourse on Political Economy* (DPE) and *The Social Contract* (SC). All but the first two are collected in the revised 1973 version of *The Social Contract and Discourses*.

On the same page of his autobiography he tells us that his suffering, like most of his experiences, was unique: 'I suffered before I began to think: which is the common fate of man, though crueller in my case than in another's'. Why this should be so he does not tell us. He does, however, tell us about many of his other characteristics: 'My melancholy imagination took alarm, for it always paints things at their blackest' (C, p. 325).

> My warm-heartedness, my acute sensibility, the ease with which I formed friendships, the hold they experienced over me, and the cruel wrench when they had to be broken; my innate goodwill towards my fellow men; my burning desire for the great, the true, the beautiful, and the just, my horror of evil in every form...
>
> (C, p. 333.)

> I have told the truth. If anyone knows anything contrary to what I have here recorded, though he prove it a thousand times, his knowledge is a lie and an imposture; and if he refuses to investigate and inquire into it during my lifetime he is no lover of justice or truth. For my part, I publicly and fearlessly declare that anyone, even if he has not read my writings, who will examine my nature, my character, my morals, my likings, my pleasures, and my habits with his own eyes and can still believe me a dishonourable man, is a man who deserves to be stifled.
>
> (C, p. 606.)

While one may not agree with Rousseau that he was 'like no one else in the whole world', one can see even from these snippets that he was probably exceptional as a man (introspective, egocentric, passionate, uncomfortable and prickly) and that he was certainly exciting as an essayist (sensitive, extravagant, elegant, energetic and pugnacious). He is also an infuriating writer, not least because one can often have very good reasons for saying of any account of his views the opposite of what one did say. He seems to be, as Dylan Thomas said of himself, a boily boy in love with the shape and sound of words and also, one might add, of boily and boiling ideas. Moreover, while he is keen to make many points, Rousseau seems at least as keen not to be required by the arguments of anyone else to modify let alone retract any of them. All of this makes it easier to be excited than to be rationally persuaded by him.

A prolific littérateur, Rousseau also wrote musical opera, one of which, *The Village Soothsayer*, was performed in 1752 at court before Louis XV, his Queen, family and Mme de Pompadour, with Rousseau himself present 'dressed in my usual careless style, with a rough beard and an ill-combed wig'. His knowledge of musical composition and theory may have assisted the production of his political theory. In 1749 Diderot and d'Alembert had undertaken to produce *The Encyclopaedic Dictionary* and asked Rousseau to write the articles on music. The project was, however, soon interrupted by the imprisonment of Diderot at Vincennes, near Paris, for some personal allusions he had made in his *Letter to the Blind*. Rousseau often walked to the prison.

> One day I took the *Mercure de France* and, glancing through it as I walked, I came upon this question propounded by the Dijon Academy for the next year's prize: Has the progress of the sciences and arts done more to corrupt morals or to improve them? The moment I read this I beheld another universe and became another man... What I remember distinctly about this occasion is that when I reached Vincennes I was in a state of agitation bordering on delirium. Diderot noticed it: I told him the cause... He encouraged me to give my ideas wings and compete for the prize. I did so, and from that moment I was lost. All the rest of my life and of my misfortunes followed inevitably as a result of that moment's madness.
>
> (C, pp. 327–8.)

Rousseau's essay won the prize. Its theme was that, so far from ennobling man, the sciences and the arts have corrupted him by replacing the innocence, simplicity, self-reliance and honesty of the ancients with the artificial and mannered dissembling of modern times.

> In our day, now that more subtle study and a more refined taste have reduced the art of pleasing to a system, there prevails in modern manners a servile and deceptive conformity,... sincere friendship, real esteem, and perfect confidence are banished from among men. Jealousy, suspicion, fear, coldness, reserve, hate and fraud lie constantly concealed under that uniform and deceitful veil of politeness...
>
> (DAS, p.6.)

> Harsh Sparta 'as famous for the happy ignorance of its inhabitants as for the wisdom of its laws,' ... 'eternal proof of the vanity of sciences' should be preferred over elegant Athens 'the seat of politeness and taste, the country of orators and philosophers'.
>
> (DAS, p.10.)

Human nature is not worse now than it used to be, but it has been diseased by false culture to such a degree that the people, as if addicted to their baubles, have become enslaved by them and have lost their sense of their own natural and authentic worth.

The accusation that modern society distorts what it does not suppress of the real (or at least the best) part of man had been made many times before and has been made many times since Rousseau's *Discourse on the Arts and Sciences* (1750) and if he had written nothing more we would be not much interested in either him or the essay. The charge, however, became a theme to which he returned in all his later political works: man has been forced by social institutions to become less virtuous than he had been and less virtuous than he can be. In most of his subsequent writings, Rousseau seeks to give the true account of man's virtue, how it was lost and how it can be regained.

Natural Man and Social Man

Following Aristotle, Rousseau supposes that man's virtue will be found not by looking at distorted men but by examining men who are rightly ordered according to nature. Again the Academy of Dijon provided the occasion for a thesis, its question being: 'What is the Origin of Inequality among Men, and is it Authorized by Natural Law?' In reply, Rousseau, who this time did not win the prize, distinguishes between natural or physical differences and moral or political inequalities and proceeds to discuss how the second type of inequalities came about and what if anything could justify which of them. He begins the account by writing of man's evolution from savagery to society.

Like Descartes and Hobbes before him, Rousseau regards an animal as merely an ingenious machine 'to which nature hath given senses to wind itself up, and to guard itself against anything that might tend to disorder or destroy it' (DOI, p. 53). Humans were always distinguishable by their capacity to make free choices. 'Nature lays her command on every animal, and the brute obeys her voice. Man receives the same impulsion, but at the same time knows himself at liberty to acquiesce or resist: and it is particularly in his consciousness of this liberty that the spirituality of his soul is displayed' (DOI, p. 54).

It is in this, then, that man's natural liberty consists, that he is neither a mere object in the hands of nature nor the subject of the will of any other person. In these respects he is his own master. Nature who gives the savage his appetites secures his autonomy by providing him with the objects of their satisfaction. Since all men possess natural liberty equally and since nature herself takes care of all alike, the savage 'breathes only peace and liberty', respecting his own self and feeling at home in his world, innocent of pride and greed, having compassion for all. Rousseau argued that Hobbes was wrong in supposing that savage man was rapacious and cruel, at war with all his fellows: 'nothing is more gentle than man in his primitive state, as he is placed by nature at an equal distance from the stupidity of brutes, and the fatal ingenuity of civilised man' (DOI, p. 82). In this state, 'the happiest and most stable of epochs', man is moved by two innate and complementary springs of action, healthy self love (*amour de soi*) which motivates every person to seek his own good, and compassion (*pitie*) which produces generosity and friendship and the general sentiment which we call love of humanity and which was also called fraternity. 'Savage man, when he has dined, is at peace with all nature, and is the friend of all his fellow creatures.' (DOI, p. 107.)

Rousseau is unclear, though very eloquent, about some aspects of the nature and the life of savage man, as he also is about the evolution from savagery to society. Three slightly different but quite compatible accounts are given of the emergence of society and oppression. One account proposes that men compared their skills with the animals and with those of other men and began feeling pride and began behaving proudly, desiring and striving for what they had previously not wanted, reputation and glory, as the basis of their own self respect. This foundation for self-worth was utterly treacherous because it required that every man depended upon the assessment of others for his valuation of his own worth. Vanity, the desire to be admired, was paid for by dissemblance, by appearing to be what one is not, and thus lying and deceit were fostered and grew with contempt and conspiracy and vengeance. This vanity, which Rousseau calls *amour propre*, a term likely to mislead English and even French language readers (it is improper self-love, and unnatural since it did not exist in the true and happy state of nature), is the source of man's corruption and the cause of the state of society in which alone it occurs (DOI, footnote to p. 66). It is this vanity which is the cause of the ridiculous sense of honour, that potent and corrosive destroyer of fraternity and equality in society.

A second account is of contented hunters living independent lives in rustic huts who, having been beguiled by the apparent benefits of metallurgy and agriculture and needing the assistance of other people in developing these arts began to dominate and be dominated by their fellows. Where some gained by co-operative work, some lost and natural equality disappeared. The more aggressive men prospered, appropriating not only the fruits of the earth but the earth itself (DOI, p. 85). The enriched grew richer and squeezed out their partners who became their impoverished servants and at length their slaves.

The third account is that the believed claim to the ownership of land was the cause of mankind's misery.

The first man who, having enclosed a piece of ground, bethought himself of saying 'This is mine,' and found people simple enough to believe him, was the real founder of civil society. From how many crimes, wars, and murders, from how many horrors and misfortunes might not any one have saved mankind, by pulling up the stakes, or filling up the ditch, and crying to his fellows: 'Beware of listening to this impostor; you are undone if you once forget that the fruits of the earth belong to us all, and the earth itself to nobody'.

(DOI, p. 76.)

The greed and the power of landowners increased, as did the misery of those who were dispossessed both of the land and its wealth. This, not the earlier state, was the violent epoch which Hobbes had so vividly described, the war of every man against every man. 'Usurpations by the rich, robbery by the poor, and the unbridled passions of both, suppressed the cries of natural compassion and the still feeble voice of justice, and filled men with avarice, ambition, and vice.' (DOI, p. 87.)

The chaos and the terror united with self-interest so that the rich and corrupt proposed what the poor and wretched accepted, the establishment of political society. 'Instead of turning our forces against ourselves, let us collect them in a supreme power which may govern us by wise laws, protect and defend all the members of the association, repulse their common enemies, and maintain eternal harmony among us.' (DOI, p. 89.) The trick worked. 'All ran headlong to their chains in hopes of securing their liberty' (ibid).

Rousseau does not mind whether the account he has given is true or not. What matters to him is that he has given a plausible explanation for the origin of political societies and that in showing that savage man contentedly rabbiting about in the bush possessed natural liberty equally, he has also shown that this liberty has been stolen from him by greedy society which has been founded upon the vanity (*amour propre*) of the rich instead of the healthy compassion and self-love (*amour de soi*) of everyone.

Rousseau's account of the natural goodness of man and of his almost accidental yet almost historically inevitable departure from original innocence is confirmed in many of his other writings and, in the manner of many rationalists of the time, it challenged the orthodox Christian account that man's fall from grace and expulsion from Eden was the consequence of God's anger at the disobedience of man. It was not disobedience, rebellion and ungodliness which caused the misery of mankind, as the theologians proposed,[2] but

---

[2]   Article IX of the 39 Articles of Religion in the *Book of Common Prayer* of the Church of England expresses orthodox Christian doctrine in appropriately severe and Calvinistic in fashion: '. . . it is the fault and corruption of the Nature of every man . . . and therefore in every person born into this world, it deserveth God's wrath and damnation. . .' The need for a supernatural redeemer, a need denied by Rousseau, is thus evident.

unnatural and vicious social arrangements which produced the inequality, the injustice, the loss of freedom and the consequent degradation of civilized mankind.

Julie or The New Heloise (1761), a novel immensely influential in shaping and invigorating the romantic movement, restates the view that freedom is impossible if one is dependent upon other persons' wills when they are tainted with vanity, as does *Émile* (1762), a romantic philosophy for the education of a child-boy-man-citizen. Always a stylish opener, Rousseau begins *Émile* in characteristic declamatory fashion: 'God makes all things good; man meddles with them and they become evil'. Again the theme is that society has perverted humanity. Like the other great book of the same year, *Émile* offers hope of redemption by proferring a recipe for reconciliation. A child is a child, not a homuncule; his perfectable nature can develop and flower only if its stages of growth are appropriately tended by his tutor-gardener. Nothing may be rushed; for every season there is a thing to do and an activity to engage upon.

In *Émile* Rousseau brings the good news of redemption for the child who will be a man. Is there any corresponding hope for mankind; can we all be set free from our social bondage, liberated to be as at our most perfect we would be? Rousseau's good news is that we can become perfect and that this will happen and that it will only happen in society, when we have transformed the chains of the present corrupt and corrupting society making from them fraternal bonds of liberty. The volume which bears the good news of the liberation of all is *The Social Contract* (1762), and its vehicle is the majestic carriage the General Will.

The General Will and True Liberty

> I mean to enquire if, in the civil order, there can be any sure and legitimate rule of administration, men being taken as they are and laws as they might be. In this inquiry I shall endeavour always to unite what right sanctions with what is prescribed by interest, in order that justice and utility may in no case be divided.
>
> (SC, p. 165.)

Rousseau begins his major political writing, *The Social Contract or Principles of Political Right* (1762), with these clear words and with this clear intention.

How men are, that is to what condition they have been taken, he has already set out in the two *Discourses* and other works mentioned in this chapter. Rousseau encapsulates his view of the condition of civilized mankind in his celebrated and ringing denunciation:

'Man is born free; and everywhere he is in chains. One thinks himself the master of others, and still remains a greater slave than they' (SC, p. 165).

It is important to Rousseau, as later to Marx, that all civilized people are in chains, not merely, as more obviously, the wretched of the earth, the exploited peasants and labourers and lackeys, but also the ruling aristocracy in Paris or London or Moscow, Beijing or Brasilia or Brazzaville. One might see what Rousseau and other radical reformers saw if one thinks of society as some type of large ship, as Plato and many others had sometimes done. The rowers, manacled to their oars and in constant peril of being starved or flogged are clearly unfree. But so too are the flagellators, so too the sailors, the navigators, the helmsmen: even the captain is required to obey the orders of others. While it may appear that the wealthy passengers, and certainly the owners of the ship who spend their days lying around and their evenings gorgeously dressed dining and dancing to the music of the hired orchestra enjoy complete freedom, even these people are really unfree, for if they were to behave otherwise than conventions require, rebellion and mayhem would follow. Nor does it matter which person is the captain and which the rower; all arrangements will be tainted by the greed and the desire to dominate – the *amour propre* – of all the people. What is required is a just and stable social system in which everyone is both free and secure. 'The problem is to find a form of association which will defend and protect with the whole common force the person and goods of each associate, and in which each, while uniting himself with all, may still obey himself alone, and remain as free as before' (SC, p. 174). The form of association must be voluntary, based upon the will of every individual who is a part of it, and yet it must have the power to ensure that the individual does not sell himself into servitude, thereby improperly disposing of his fundamental natural liberty.

The problem is solved by the social contract in which every individual person hands over to the community, the public person, all his power and all his rights. The conditions of the contract 'may be reduced to one – the total alienation of each associate, together with all his rights, to the whole community...' (ibid).

It may seem at first sight that Rousseau's institutional remedy is worse than the social disease which it is supposed to cure, for it might seem that a Leviathan of unlimited power and authority, more absolute than Hobbes' sovereign, has been created. Rousseau, of course, supposes that, so far from producing a tyrannical monster, his social contract has opened up a pathway to a new and splendid liberty and that this will have happened because of the unique nature of the public person formed by the free willing of the individual persons.

In his *Discourse on Political Economy*, written for Volume V of the *Encyclopédie* and published in 1755, Rousseau argues that the corporate being created by the private individuals itself possesses a will; 'and this general will, which tends always to the preservation and welfare of the whole and of every part' (DPE, p. 120) is the sole source of all just laws. Wherever there are constraints upon a person's will, the person is not free; for example one is not master of one's own property if another person can remove it without penalty, one is not master or mistress of oneself if one can be compelled to do what one abominates.[3]

The transformingly splendid quality of the general will is that it always requires and decrees the true liberty of all. How can this be so? How can service be perfect freedom? The answer is that the social contract, where 'each of us puts his person and all his power in common under the supreme direction of the general will' (SC, p. 175) creates an inalienable, indivisible and infallible sovereign whose commands are really liberating laws. 'It is to law alone that men owe justice and liberty. It is this salutary organ of the will of all which establishes, in civil rights, the natural equality between men' (DPE, p. 124).

'What man loses by the social contract is his natural liberty ... what he gains is civil liberty ... the obedience to a law which we prescribe to ourselves' (SC, p. 178). In obeying the dictates of the general will a person is obeying himself, and because obedience to one's own true will, rather than obedience to one's own mere instincts or desires, is what moral liberty, the distinctive mark of humanness, consists in, one is thus free in obeying the sovereign general will and unfree when disobeying it. Consequently, said Rousseau in a celebrated passage:

> Whoever refuses to obey the general will shall be compelled to do so by the whole body. This means nothing less than that he will be forced to be free; for this is the condition which, by giving each citizen to his country, secures him against all personal dependence. In this lies the key to the working of the political machine; this alone legitimates civil undertakings, which, without it, would be absurd, tyrannical and liable to the most frightful abuses.
>
> (SC, p. 177.)

---

[3]   Rousseau's 'That man is truly free who desires what he is able to perform, and does what he desires' (E, p. 48) seems compatible with being resigned to one's manacles and oar. It is inconsistent with such servile acquiescence to a demeaning condition only if the 'truly free' truly desires what he is truly able to perform. Existential authenticity is one of two necessary conditions for emancipation, the other is that there be no malefactors at large. Nothing more is needed; the kingdom of heaven is truly within us all.

Thus, the general will is, like the true vanguard of the people, the infallible and emancipating will of the corporate being, the body politic, the public person which was created by all the individual people when they willed to the sovereign all their powers and rights. 'No one', says Rousseau in a phrase whose idea was much used by Kant and Hegel, 'will disagree with the view that the general will is, in each individual, a pure act of the understanding which reasons, when the passions are silent, about what a man can ask of his fellows and what his fellows have the right to ask of him' (*The Geneva Manuscript*, p. 160). But it does not follow that the general will is always the same as the will of each individual; how could it be when individual wills so often clash? An individual's will is the same as the general will only when he wills correctly, that is, when he wills not from his particular interest (*amour propre*) but in accordance with the common interest (from *amour de soi* and compassion plus a concern for justice). Then and only then is his will identical not to anyone else's particular and self-interested will but to the general will, the one true sovereign, incorruptible, infallible, inalienable and indivisible, at once the necessary and the sufficient condition for the perfecting of mankind.

Fundamental as it thus is to his political thinking, it seems incumbent upon Rousseau that he gives us an account not only of the nature of the general will but also of how it declares itself and how it may thus be discovered.

Though from some partial readings, (especially PE, p. 145 and SC, Book IV, Chapter 11, p. 250), one might conclude that the general will is the same as the majority will, the better reading is that the general will, not being an immediate empirical item discoverable by a simple majority vote (or even a complex empirical item discoverable by a Hare-Clark or an electoral college system) cannot be discerned by any electoral measures. Rousseau's general will has, in common with Plato's Forms and Hegel's rational organic state, the characteristic that it exists and has definite qualities even though people ignorantly or maliciously (the latter because of the former) deny its pervading presence.

It is important to Rousseau that the distinctions can be made between what is the majority will, what is the unanimous will and what is the general will. The difference, he tells us, is that whereas the general will considers only the common interest the will of the majority and even the will of all 'takes private interest into account and is no more than a sum of particular wills: but take away from these same wills the pluses and minuses that cancel one another, and the general will remains as the sum of the differences' (SC, p. 185).

It may at first sight seem that Rousseau has here distinguished majority will and unanimous will and general will and has proposed some arithmetical way of determining what the general will is.[4]

While there may be much to be said for finding out about people's real wishes by letting them try to tell us what these are (it respects their autonomy), and while there may be much to be said for letting everyone try to express their wills (it seems to involve us in treating people as equals), all we get from this procedure is a number of expressions of wills.

To say that your will to increase the level of taxation is 'cancelled out' by my will to reduce it, and that both our wills are 'cancelled out' by Fred's will that the status quo be preserved, is to engage in prosaic empirical discourse unfitted to the nobility of mankind and much removed from the poetical metaphysics of Rousseau whose general will shines with its own light, unconnected to the generators of the generations of man.

In the paragraph succeeding the last passage quoted, Rousseau flirts a little longer with quasi-empirical conditions for establishing the pronouncements of the general will.

> If, when the people, being furnished with adequate information, held its deliberations, the citizens had no communication one with another, the grand total of the small differences would always give the general will, and the decision would always be good.

> (SC, p. 185.)

Here again the suggested method of determining the existence and the decrees of the general will is quintessentially vague. Who are 'the people'? – only the educated? only property owners? only the sans culottes? only adults? only male adults? only (but all) those affected by the outcome of the decision? Then present and future French and Polish and Russian peoples must be allowed to express their wills on the matter of German re-unification as must all the people of Hong Kong about unification with China. Of what are the people citizens – villages like Woodstock or Wychwood or towns like Arras or Amritsar, cities like Geneva or Djakarta or nations like Portugal or Peru? Or are people citizens of the world? How would one know and why should that answer be preferred to another? If Rousseau is only a village man, or even only a town or a city man, he can be of no great use to us as a political theorist since mankind would not and could not go back to pre-city days. If he is a nation

---

[4] Something similar (and additional) is proposed in *Émile*: 'The citizen is but the numerator of a fraction, whose value depends on its denominator; his value depends upon the whole, that is, on the community' (p. 7).

If we suppose (what I do not think is true) that Rousseau has some mathematical procedure in mind we will find that it is a singularly silly system, since all we can get from the sums is an account or set of accounts of how many want this, how many want that and how many want neither.

man, as is the more likely, or an internationalist, as there are some
reasons for saying that he is, how can the people's deliberations be
held and how can who know that they have been held? Who draws
up the agenda? What sorts of items may, and what may not, appear
on the agenda? May we decide about freeways and brothels and
parking meters and public rubbish tips? Why so, or not? How could
one know when the people had been furnished with adequate information? Who furnishes the information? May there never be
'communication one with another'? If so, what civil liberties and
what rational procedures prices will have been paid, and by whom?
Since 'partial associations' are forbidden, must trade unions and employers' groups and leagues of lettuce lovers be banned? What can
'the grand total of the small differences' mean? How does one total
differences? Are all differences small? (You want peace, I want a
limited war, he wants a total war; is there only a small difference
between us all?) How could we know that all differences are small
ones or, if they are not, that they are not and by how much they are
not?

It seems evident either that Rousseau was unable to give a
satisfactory account of the empirical methods of discovering the
general will and its decrees or that he didn't want to do so. A
footnote on the same page (p. 185) as well as many similar
intimations in many other places confirms the view that the general
will is the proper province not of the social statistician but of the
political poet. 'If there were no different interests, the common
interest would be barely felt, as it would encounter no obstacle; all
would go of its own accord, and politics would cease to be an art.'

Politics is an art, not a science; the common interest is felt, not
calculated. The same view is expressed in *Emile*, perhaps especially
in the large passage 'The Creed of a Savoyard Priest' which forms the
centre of Book IV, and of all this, perhaps especially p. 254 which is
principally a panegyric to Conscience, Divine instinct and 'infallible
judge of good and evil which makes man like to God!... Thank
heaven ... [that] we may be men without being scholars.' Timid
conscience 'speaks to us in the language of nature, and everything'
(in corrupting social life) 'leads us to forget that tongue.' This is
mainstream Rousseau, as is 'the heart has its reasons, which are
unknown to the head' (though it was Pascal, Rousseau's predecessor
by a century, who wrote that). The same romantic appeal can be
found at the beginning of Book IV of *The Social Contract*, and it is a
picture of what we might suppose is Rousseau's Utopia. Here
upright, simple and happy 'bands of peasants are seen regulating
affairs of State under an oak, and always acting wisely... A State so
governed needs very few laws; and, as it becomes necessary to issue
new ones, the necessity is universally seen. The first man to propose
them merely says what all have already felt...' (SC, p. 247.)

Rectitude is recognized by feeling, not by cogitation, and only after the decadent vanities of diseased and corrupting society have been pruned by a master gardener, burned out by a gifted metallurgist, excised by the scalpel of a skilful surgeon. The political chains which everywhere bind and enslave can be removed only after men have destroyed the social tyrannies which inhabit their minds and distort their lives.

A host of questions raise themselves. Who will be the (sea-green?) incorruptible gardener – metallurgist – surgeon? How will he be recognized, and by whom? Rousseau misnames this august and sinister being 'the legislator' and describes him in Book II, chapter VII as having a superior intelligence 'wholly unrelated to our nature' and 'capable of changing human nature, of transforming each individual . . . into part of a greater whole . . . of altering man's constitution for the purpose of strengthening it' (SC, p. 194). People who see Rousseau as a progenitor of totalitarianism and as a source of inspiration for ghastly totalitarian monsters don't need to look much beyond this section, though they can with profit do so. They can look to the compulsory civil religion proposed in Book IV, chapter VIII and to the death penalty to be imposed upon anyone who, having publicly recognized the simple dogmas of the religion (as one must if one is to be a good citizen) 'behaves as if he does not believe them' (SC, p. 276). They can look to the second footnote on p. 250:

> At Genoa, the word 'Liberty' may be read over the front of the prisons and on the chains of the galley-slaves. This application of the device is good and just. It is indeed only malefactors of all estates who prevent the citizen from being free. In the country in which all such men were in the galleys, the most perfect liberty would be enjoyed.

Eternal vigilance is indeed the price of liberty, itself the eternal spirit of the chainless mind and brightest in dungeons; error, having no rights, must not be tolerated.

We might usefully remind ourselves of Rousseau's intention 'to inquire if, in the civil order, there can be any sure and legitimate rule of administration, men being taken as they are and laws as they might be' (SC, p. 165). We have seen that he proposes that the general will can uniquely unite justice and utility by creating the framework of liberty upon the foundations of fraternity and equality. Perhaps his proposal is successful, though, as may be evident from the preceding discussion, I think that it has failed. Another reason for this opinion may be found in comparing the intention to take men 'as they are' with a principal thrust of the educational, social and political programme which, as we have seen, does not deal with people 'as they are' (generous and greedy, kind and cruel, wise and foolish, courageous and cowardly) but which requires that they be transformed into at least principally agapeistic beings. Many of us may wonder whether people who have been purged of *amour propre* would be recognizably people, and whether such beings would have the morally and socially interesting characteristics that people do, for better and for worse, possess.

Concluding Remarks

Few writers have attracted more devotees and few have enraged more detractors than has Rousseau: few writers are richer than he; even those who find him appalling find him fecund and fascinating, even those who regard him as right find the need to restate what others find wrong.

Rousseau's vices and virtues lie in his diversity. He is both Dionysius and Apollo. He can with good grounding be seen as a seminal source for romanticism and for rationalism, for anarchism and for statism, for individualism and totalitarianism, for liberalism and despotism, democracy and monarchism, consensualism and élitism. Rousseau is a man for all theories and a theorist for all men. This is not because there are two almost clear and almost distinct Rousseaux (Saul Paul; wicked Augustine saintly Augustine, young Marx old Marx) but because there are many and simultaneous and quite inconsistent Rousseaux. It is a commonplace to say that there are two incompatibles: Jean-Jacques the romantic revolutionary and J.J. Rousseau Esq., the champion of property-owning, middle-class decency; and that both were dedicated, the one through the dictates of the heart the other through the commands of the head, to Fraternity and Equality and Liberty, but Rousseau is more than such a Janus for he looks and applauds and denounces and attacks everywhere.

Bibliography

Jean Jacques Rousseau: *The Confessions*, translated with notes by J.M. Cohen, (Harmondsworth, 1953).

Jean Jacques Rousseau: *Émile*, translated by Barbara Foxley, (London, 1972).

Jean Jacques Rousseau: *The Social Contract and Discourses*, translated with introduction by G.D.H. Cole, revised and augmented by J.H. Brumfitt and John C. Hall, (London, 1973).

Further Reading

Books on Rousseau (all of which contain extensive bibliographies).

David Cameron, *The Social Thought of Rousseau and Burke*, (Birkenhead, 1973). Argues that there is more in common between Rousseau and Burke than generally supposed.

Lester G. Crocker, *Rousseau's Social Contract*, (Cleveland, 1969). Highly critical of the arguments, the models and the influences of Rousseau.

Stephen Ellenburg, *Rousseau's Political Philosophy*, (London, 1976). A disciple's defence of Rousseau against charges that he is inconsistent in his arguments and an enemy of individual liberty.

Joan McDonald, *Rousseau and the French Revolution*, (London, 1965). A lively and detailed discussion of the effects of Rousseau's writings upon the course of the French Revolution.

Judith N. Shklar, *Men and Citizens, A Study of Rousseau's Social Theory*, (Cambridge 1964). A sympathetic account and defence of Rousseau which argues that the general will is the will against inequality and one that each citizen ought to possess.

Jacob Leib Talmon, *The Origins of Totalitarian Democracy*, (London, 1952). Argues that Rousseau is a principal intellectual forebear of twentieth century totalitarianism.

Chapters and articles

Brian Barry, 'The Public Interest' in Anthony Quinton (ed.), *Political Philosophy*, (Oxford 1973). An explication of 'the public interest' sympathetic to and approving of 'the general will' as a coherent and ingenious unity.

Jacques Maritain (ed.), *The Social and Political Philosophy of Jacques Maritain*, Selected Readings, (London, 1956). Chapter X, 'Solitude and the Community', is a savage and often intemperate attack on Rousseau from a Natural Law position.

Bernard Mayo, 'Is there a Case for the General Will?' in Peter Haslett (ed.), *Philosophy; Politics and Society*, (Oxford, 1956). Argues that some alleged ambiguities in 'the general will' are really sources of strength to the theory.

J.P. Plamenatz, 'The General Will', chapter III of his *Consent, Freedom and Political Obligation*, (Oxford, 1968).

Leonard Schapiro, *Totalitarianism*, (London, 1972). In chapter 4 argues that 'The Social Contract' is a fount of totalitarianism.

Chapter Ten

Burke and Conservatism

Brian Costar

Edmund Burke was born in Dublin, Ireland in 1729 to a Roman Catholic mother and a Protestant father. By all accounts the family was not wealthy but was comfortable enough to allow Burke to attend Trinity College, Dublin where he took a first class honours degree in classics. He then displayed an inclination to follow his father's profession and commenced legal studies in London in 1750. These studies, however, were never completed and by the middle of the 1750s Burke had seemingly settled upon a literary career. In 1757 he manifested the religious tolerance of his upbringing and married the daughter of an Irish, Roman Catholic physician. Burke's literary endeavours were soon coupled with an increasing interest and involvement in political affairs which were to persist until his death in 1797. His formal political career commenced in 1765 when he was appointed secretary to the Marquess of Rockingham. Britain in the eighteenth century possessed only an embryonic political party system. Lords and Commons were titularly divided into Whigs and Tories.[1] Party lines were never clearly drawn but the prominent, contentious issue was the relationship between king and parliament. Here the Whigs were the radicals wishing to curb the prerogative powers of the monarch and establish the constitutional dominance of parliament. Factions within the two 'parties' were usually centred around a prominent member of a traditional noble family. Lord Rockingham headed a liberal group within the Whigs to which Burke attached himself.

---

[1] After 1832 it became commonplace to use the terms Tory and Conservative Party synonymously, but it is misleading to link the Tories of Burke's age with the later Conservatives.

In 1774, at the age of forty-five, Burke entered the House of Commons as the member for Bristol, but he forfeited the seat at the elections of 1780. Through the grace and favour of Rockingham he then transferred to the constituency of Malton which, unlike Bristol, was a 'rotten' or 'pocket' borough requiring little but noble patronage to win and retain.[2] He sat for Malton continuously until his retirement in 1794. Burke's twenty years of parliamentary experience placed him amongst that very small group of political thinkers who were also practising politicians. While he held governmental office for only two brief periods, Burke was an active and influential parliamentarian who was to be found at the centre of all the major political controversies of the later eighteenth century. Surprising as it may appear at first, Burke's political ideas and activities marked him as a progressive and, to some, even a radical.

Space does not permit a full account of Burke's political activities, but a brief summary of some of them is necessary better to understand his political beliefs. Burke was an admirer of the so-called Glorious Revolution of 1688–89[3] and sought regularly to defend and advance its achievements. These he believed involved the establishment in England of a balanced constitutional monarchy and the defeat of the tyrannical pretentions of despots such as James II. Burke has rightly been criticized for an excessive servility, and even sycophancy, towards those he perceived as his superiors;[4] yet, at the same time, he could be courageous in his championship of unpopular and even dangerous causes. He never forsook his heritage and was a regular critic of British policy in Ireland; even to the extent of questioning the wisdom of establishing the English church there. Another of his famous parliamentary crusades concerned the impeachment moves against Warren Hastings, who had been Governor General of Bengal (1772–1785), on the grounds that his application of British colonial policy usurped the traditional rights of the Indian inhabitants. His pursuit of Hastings, who was acquitted on all charges, was not totally altruistic since personal animosity and

---

[2] Because eighteenth century Britain lacked a broad franchise (as late as 1831 only 5 per cent of the population aged over twenty held the franchise) abuses abounded. 'Rotten' boroughs were ones which contained a paltry number of voters. 'Pocket' boroughs were those which were in the pockets of landed noblemen.

[3] In 1688 the English parliament acted against James II's absolutist pretentions (and his Roman Catholicism) and invited William of Orange to lead an army to Britain and re-establish a free parliament. James was eventually enabled to flee to France. The major impact of the glorious revolution was to establish the parliament above the monarch. The settlement was embodied in an Act of Parliament known as the Bill of Rights.

[4] Karl Marx called him 'a sycophant ... in the pay of the English oligarchy'. Quoted in Conor Cruise O'Brien (ed.), Edmund Burke, *Reflections on the Revolution in France*, (1790), (Harmondsworth, 1968), p. 9.

the desire to assist the dubious financial schemes of two relatives seem also to have been motivating factors.

Burke's opposition to the slave trade was, however, genuine and probably contributed to his electoral defeat in the slave port of Bristol in 1780. Similarly, he was a consistent and articulate advocate for the north American colonists in their disputes with the administration of George III. Burke believed them to be suffering genuine and serious grievances at the hands of an autocracy which was contemptuous of their rights. His preferred solution was to extend to the colonists the privileges and responsibilities of the British constitution. When the government displayed little inclination to do so, Burke supported the revolution of 1776.

Burke's political career until the year 1790 well justifies his own remark that 'almost the whole of [my] public exertion has been a struggle for the liberty of others;'[5] an opinion that would have been shared by most of his political colleagues. Imagine then, their surprise (and for some such as Charles James Fox,[6] horror) when in November 1790 he published his major political work *Reflections on the Revolution in France* which contained a thoroughgoing repudiation and condemnation of the revolution which had broken out in the previous year. Enlightened opinion in Britain was generally approving of the revolution, seeing it as liberating France from the stifling political environment of the *ancien régime*. Most expected Burke to be of similar opinion, especially given his views on the earlier revolutions in England and America. The fact that he took the diametrically opposite position inevitably gave rise to accusations of inconsistency which have persisted to the present. Burke anticipated such charges and sought to refute them in the *Reflections*. He distinguished the two earlier revolutions from that in progress in France by arguing that the former were embarked upon in order to protect 'antient indisputable laws and liberties' against usurpacious tyrants whereas the latter was a 'revolution in sentiments, manners and moral opinions'[7] certain to destroy all that was good in the old order.

At first glance, the distinction may appear thinly drawn but for Burke it was crucial. He opposed the French revolution because he believed that it was caused principally by the teachings of abstract metaphysicians such as Rousseau who lacked empirical experience of political reality and who held false and dangerous ideas about rights, the State and democratic government. On a more parochial level he

---

[5]   ibid, p. 376.
[6]   Charles James Fox (1749–1806) was one of Britain's most brilliant and influential eighteenth century politicians. His close friendship with Burke was shattered in a vitriolic exchange on the floor of the House of Commons in May 1791.
[7]   Burke/O'Brien, op. cit., p. 117 and 175.

feared that the French revolutionary idea, if it were not refuted, might spread like a contagion to England and destroy his much-cherished British constitution.[8] In fact, the *Reflections* is as much a celebration and commendation of the British constitution (as interpreted by Burke) as it is an attack on the French revolutionaries. He dismissed French attempts to 'make' a constitution since he believed such a task to be impossible; constitutions require time to evolve and grow, they cannot be cobbled together overnight. The concepts of State and constitution are central to Burke's political thinking. He favoured a strong centralized government and castigated the proposed federalist administrative arrangements of the French National Assembly[9] because they would dismember the nation and render it impossible to govern 'as one body'.[10] The organic analogy employed by Burke to refer to the State has remained popular with conservative writers and Roger Scruton has been prepared to assert that 'the State is not a machine, but an organism – more, a person'.[11]

Burke was grudgingly prepared to concede that the revolutionaries might succeed in creating a government and even that they must grant some degree of freedom to the people, but he insisted that their methods rendered them incapable of securing the elusive necessity of a civil society – a free government:

> To make a government requires no great prudence. Settle the seat of power; teach obedience: and the work is done. To give freedom is still more easy. It is not necessary to guide; it only requires to let go the rein. But to form a *free government*; that is, to temper together these opposite elements of liberty and restraint in one consistent work, requires much thought, deep reflection, a sagacious, powerful, and combining mind. This I do not find in those who take the lead in the national assembly.[12]

On the general issue of rights Burke appears most vulnerable to the charge of inconsistency; how could the defender of the rights of the Irish, Indians and Americans deny them to the French? Because, for Burke, the French revolutionary theory of abstract rights was a chimera and quite foreign to those traditional liberties of which he prided himself as an advocate.

Burke argued that while rights are 'indefinable, they are discernible' and he insisted that he loved 'a manly, moral, regulated

---

8   Eighteenth century Britain was plagued by a series of riots and disorders, the worst of which were the Gordon Riots of 1780.
9   The National Assembly was a deliberative body established by the Third Estate in June 1789. It changed its name to the Constituent Assembly in July.
10 ibid., p. 142 and again p. 297.
11 Roger Scruton, *The Meaning of Conservatism*, (Harmondsworth, 1980), p. 50.
12 Burke/O'Brien, op. cit. pp. 373–74.

liberty'[13] as much as any supporter of the French revolution. Where he parted company with the revolutionaries was with his rejection of their theory that rights can and should be derived from metaphysical abstraction. He was thus at odds with the Enlightenment dictum that man can be liberated by reason alone. Rather, Burke on rights was a circumstantialist in that he held that enduring rights can emerge only within the protective environment of a well-ordered civil society. Government is as important as liberty for without stable government there can be no true liberty:

> But I cannot stand forward, and give praise or blame to anything which relates to human actions, and human concerns, on a simple view of the object, as it stands stripped of every relation, in all the nakedness and solitude of metaphysical abstraction. Circumstances (which with some gentlemen pass for nothing) give in reality to every political principle its distinguishing colour, and discriminating effect. The circumstances are what render every civil and political scheme beneficial or noxious to mankind...
> ... I should therefore suspend my congratulations on the new liberty of France, until I was informed how it had been combined with government; with public force; with the discipline and obedience of armies; with the collection of an effective and well-distributed revenue; with morality and religion; with the solidity of property; with peace and order: with civil and social manners. All these (in their way) are good things too; and, without them, liberty is not a benefit whilst it lasts, and is not likely to continue long.[14]

Because the concept of government was so important for Burke, he was naturally concerned with discovering which was the best form of government. Again he was deeply suspicious of the French experiment. At the time the *Reflections* was being written the revolutionaries were in the process of dismantling the absolutist monarchy of the *ancien régime* and instituting a system of government which they supposed democratic. While Burke was highly critical of this process his position regarding the ideal form of government was more complex and sophisticated than might be imagined. In short, he preferred a constitutional monarchy of the British type in which sovereign, lords, church and commons occupied defined and balancing places under the law. While he was certainly capable of cloying sycophancy towards monarchs and held as subversive the view that all power should proceed from the people, he rejected the theories of those 'old fanatics of single arbitrary power'[15] who insisted that a divinely-ordained, absolutist

---

[13] ibid., p. 89.
[14] ibid., pp. 89–90.
[15] ibid., p. 111.

monarchy was the only legitimate form of authority. Again Burke
was a circumstantialist; constitutional monarchy is the desired form
of government, but it is possible for monarchs to usurp the
constitution and if they attempt to do so it is both necessary and
desirable to replace them – as the English revolutionaries did in
1688.

The French revolutionaries of 1789 were not, however, similarly
justified in rebelling against such a 'mild and lawful' monarch as
Louis XVI. Burke was adamant that Louis and his queen, Marie
Antoinette, were not 'inexorable and cruel tyrants'; had they been he
would have agreed with their punishment for 'the punishment of real
tyrants is a noble and awful act of justice'.[16] Burke conceded that the
French monarchy was not without fault but he denied that it was so
corrupt as to justify its destruction – it could and should have been
reformed. He accused the revolutionaries of maliciously exaggerating the failings of the monarchy as a contrivance to justify a
revolution that was based on nothing more than the speculative
theories of evil-intentioned metaphysicians.

Burke was equally trenchant in his criticisms of the French
revolutionaries' advocacy of what he regarded as an extreme form of
democracy. While perhaps not fully agreeing with his contemporary
John Wesley's opinion that 'the greater the share the people have in
government, the less liberty, civil or religious, does a nation enjoy',[17]
Burke warned against allowing 'the humbler part of the community'
becoming the 'depositaries of all power' and he was a life-long
opponent of attempts to extend the right to vote to the lower classes.
Instead he preferred a moderate democracy, in which the power of
the 'people' was tempered by other constitutionally entrenched
institutions of monarch, lords and church. For Burke the French
revolutionaries embraced false panaceas such as extreme democracy
because they were incapable of discerning the true nature and
sources of tyranny:

> Have these gentlemen never heard..., of anything between the
> despotism of the monarch and the despotism of the multitude...
>   Have they never heard of a monarchy directed by laws, controlled
> and balanced by the great hereditary wealth and hereditary dignity of
> a nation; and both again controlled by a judicious check from the
> reason and feeling of the people at large acting by a suitable and
> permanent organ? Is it then impossible that a man maybe found who,
> without criminal ill intention, or pitiable absurdity, shall prefer such a
> mixed and tempered government to either of the extremes; and who
> may repute that nation to be destitute of all wisdom and of all virtue,

---

[16] ibid., p. 178.
[17] Quoted in J.H. Plumb, *England in the Eighteenth Century*, (Harmondsworth,
1950), p. 94.

which, having in its choice to obtain such a government with ease, or rather to confirm it when actually possessed, thought proper to commit a thousand crimes, and to subject their country to a thousand evils, in order to avoid it? Is it then a truth so universally acknowledged, that a pure democracy is the only tolerable form into which human society can be thrown, that a man is not permitted to hesitate about its merits, without the suspicion of being a friend to tyranny, that is, of being a foe to mankind?[18]

'Pure' democracy, in Burke's view, meant unfettered democracy and was 'the most shameless thing in the world.' His case against democracy of this type was essentially a case against majoritarianism or tyranny by the majority.

Of this I am certain, that in a democracy, the majority of the citizens is capable of exercising the most cruel oppressions upon the minority, whenever strong divisions prevail in that kind of polity, as they often must; and that oppression of the minority will extend to far greater numbers, and will be carried on with much greater fury, than can almost ever be apprehended from the dominion of a single sceptre. In such a popular persecution, individual sufferers are in a much more deplorable condition than in any other. Under a cruel prince they have the balmy compassion of mankind to assuage the smart of their wounds; they have the plaudits of the people to animate their generous constancy under their sufferings: but those who are subjected to wrong under multitudes, are deprived of all external consolation. They seem deserted by mankind; overpowered by a conspiracy of their whole species...[19]

Given these strongly held beliefs it is perhaps surprising to learn that Burke was nevertheless prepared to concede that occasions could arise when a purely democratic form of government may be both necessary and desirable. He explained this apparent contradiction by asserting that 'I reprobate no form of government merely upon abstract principles'.[20] Pure democracy is clearly inferior to a mixed and balanced system of government, but what was required above all else was a legitimate government capable of creating and maintaining civil order; if in certain circumstances democracy was the only system capable of so doing then Burke was prepared to support it.

Legitimacy of government was a central concern of Burke's and he castigated the French revolutionaries for their foolish actions in 'having industriously destroyed all the opinions and prejudices which support government'.[21] He proceeded to the prophetic

---

[18] Burke/O'Brien, op. cit., pp. 227–8.
[19] ibid., p. 229.
[20] ibid., p. 229.
[21] ibid., p. 344.

observation that, in destroying the sources of governmental authority, the new rulers of France would soon be required to resort
regularly to naked violence to enforce their decisions on the people.
This, Burke predicted, would result in the army becoming a
deliberative institution, thus promoting the degeneration of the state
into the worst form of tyranny imaginable – a military democracy.

Edmund Burke has been described by Ian Gilmour as 'the most
intensely religious of all British political writers'.[22] This is not to
imply that Burke derived his political principles solely and always
from theological precepts. He did believe in the concept of original
sin and thus held that the Enlightenment notion of man's perfect-
ability on earth was dangerous cant. Burke was, however, no bigot –
he practised religious toleration in an age when to do so was
unpopular in many quarters. His was a rational faith and he was
coldly dismissive of superstition as 'the religion of feeble minds'.[23]
He held that man was a 'religious animal' and that 'religion is the
basis of civil society'.[24] Not surprisingly, Burke was highly critical of
the French National Assembly's treatment of the Catholic clergy,
in particular of its confiscation of church property. He was convinced that the revolutionaries, motivated by a naive faith in Reason
alone, were planning the eradication of the Christian religion. The
folly of such a course of action lay in the failure of the revolutionaries
to comprehend that organized religion was an all-important force
which sustained the civil order by conferring legitimacy upon
government. Burke leaves the reader in no doubt that he commends
the English system of church establishment because:

> The consecration of the state, by a state religious establishment, is
> necessary also to operate with an wholesome awe upon free citizens:
> because, in order to secure their freedom, they must enjoy some
> determinate portion of power. To them therefore a religion connected
> with the state, and with their duty towards it, becomes even more
> necessary than in such societies, where the people by the terms of
> their subjection are confined to private sentiments, and the manage-
> ment of their own family concerns. All persons possessing any portion
> of power ought to be strongly and awefully impressed with an idea
> that they act in trust; and that they are to account for their conduct in
> that trust to the one great master, author and founder of society.[25]

It has been the purpose of this chapter thus far to suggest that
Burke's political thinking was more subtle and complex than has
often been imagined. Popular misconception of Burke's beliefs is

22 Ian Gilmour, *Inside Right: A Study of Conservatism*, (London, 1978), p. 61.
23 Burke/O'Brien, op. cit., p. 269.
24 ibid., pp. 186–7.
25 ibid., p. 190.

nowhere more apparent than in regard to his theory of political change. Burke was an implacable opponent of the French revolution of 1789, but he was not an opponent of all revolutions and he most certainly did not deprecate necessary processes of political transformation. This much is clear from his statement that 'a state without the means of some change is without the means of its conservation'.[26] Burke's first priority was the preservation of the state and he opposed the French revolution because it was on a path which would lead to the destruction of the civil order. Out of such chaos would emerge a despotism immeasurably more terrible than that of the *ancien régime*. He chided the revolutionaries for wishing to destroy the old order simply because it was old. On the contrary, Burke contended that the age of an institution constituted a *prima facie* case for its retention, since by its persistence it had demonstrated its utility. He cites as an example the English ecclesiastical forms and institutions which, he proudly proclaims, have not altered greatly since the fourteenth or fifteenth centuries.

This reluctance to embrace every current and passing political fashion Burke saw as the essential strength of Britain's constitution. He praised 'our old settled maxim, never entirely nor at once to depart from antiquity'.[27]

Nonetheless, Burke was not so naive as to be ignorant of abuses and injustices within the civil order. But again the French revolutionaries were deserving of censure because they wrongly believed they could root out evil by destroying its ephemeral manifestations:

> You would not cure the evil by resolving, that there should be no more monarchs, nor ministers of state, nor of the gospel; no interpreters of law; no general officers; no public councils. You might change the names. The things in some shape must remain. A certain quantum of power must always exist in the community, in some hands, and under some appellation. Wise men will apply their remedies to vices, not to names; to the causes of evil which are permanent, not to the occasional organs by which they act, and the transitory modes in which they appear. Otherwise you will be wise historically, a fool in practice. Seldom have two ages the same fashion in their pretexts and the same modes of mischief. Wickedness is a little more inventive. Whilst you are discussing fashion, the fashion is gone by. The very same vice assumes a new body. The spirit transmigrates; and, far from losing its principle of life by the change of its appearance, it is renovated in its new organs with the fresh vigour of a juvenile activity. It walks abroad; it continues its ravages; whilst you are gibbeting the carcass, or demolishing the tomb. You are terrifying yourself with ghosts and apparitions, whilst your house

---

[26] ibid., p. 106.
[27] ibid., p. 198.

is the haunt of robbers. It is thus with all those, who attending only to the shell and husk of history, think they are waging war with intolerance, pride, and cruelty, whilst, under colour of abhorring the ill principles of antiquated parties, they are authorizing and feeding the same odious vices in different factions and perhaps in worse.[28]

Granted that political remedies are sometimes required, how, in Burke's opinion, should they properly be applied? Slowly and deliberately, because to act in haste will surely fail to achieve that 'union of minds which alone can produce all the good we aim at'. Since man is by nature imperfect so are his social and political organizations. The faults of the established political institutions are obvious and the irresponsible criticisms of speculative metaphysicians will easily destabilize them to the ultimate disadvantage of all:

> To avoid therefore the evils of inconstancy and versatility, ten thousand times worse than those of obstinancy and the blindest prejudice, we have consecrated the state, that no man should approach to look into its defects or corruptions but with due caution; that he should never dream of beginning its reformation by its subversion; that he should approach to the faults of the state as to the wounds of a father, with pious awe and trembling solicitude. By this wise prejudice we are taught to look with horror on those children of their country who are prompt rashly to hack that aged parent in pieces, and put him into the kettle of magicians, in hopes that by their poisonous weeds, and wild incantations they may regenerate the paternal constitution, and renovate their father's life.[29]

Because 'rage and phrenzy will pull down more in half an hour, than prudence, deliberation and foresight can build up in a hundred years', the more difficult but essential task is 'at once to preserve and reform'.[30] Change should occur when and because circumstances require, not in response to the speculations of political 'magicians' untutored in the practice of politics.

Given what has been revealed of Burke's political ideas is it profitable to label him a 'conservative'? In a literal sense it is because he was forever at pains to defend what was valuable against those who, in their eagerness to reform the imperfect, were happy to destroy equally the good with the bad. In a contextual sense, however, the description fails to do him justice. During the nineteenth and twentieth centuries the term 'conservative' became debased and distorted by the actions and writings of a diverse assortment of absolute monarchists, reactionaries and racial supremacists many of whom were pleased to invoke Burke's name but

---

[28] ibid., pp. 248–9.
[29] ibid., p. 194.
[30] ibid., pp. 279–80.

whose ideas and methods would have appalled him. Burke has suffered by being associated with these later ideologues and it is for this reason that Charles Parkin has argued that it would be preferable if we 'could break the association of his name with the conservative tradition'[31] so that we can assess him free from the distorting preconceptions engendered by his later so-called disciples.

Nevertheless the central difficulty for Burke and Burkeans alike remains the question of political change. Burke's position of supporting change when and to the extent dictated by circumstance begs the question, how can we discern which circumstances require how much, if any, change? Burke is unhelpful here because he made no attempt to provide anything approaching a set of criteria which might give guidance to the conservative reformer. Of course, it was completely in keeping with Burke's practical approach to politics that he would not regard it necessary to lay down such a scheme. His concern in the *Reflections* was to oppose the French revolutionary idea, not to develop an abstract theory of revolutions or political change.

Bibliography

Edmund Burke, *Reflections on the Revolution in France*, (1790), Conor Cruise O'Brien (ed.), (Harmondsworth, 1968).

Further Reading

Ian Gilmour, *Inside Right: A Study of Conservatism*, (London, 1978).
Noel O'Sullivan, *Conservatism*, (London, 1976).
Roger Scruton, *The Meaning of Conservatism*, (Harmondsworth, 1980).

---

[31] C.W. Parkin in David Thomson (ed.), *Political Ideas*, (Harmondsworth, 1969), p. 129.

Chapter Eleven

Paine and the Rights of Man

Norma Marshall

Thomas Paine was born in Norfolk, England in 1737. His formal education was limited as a result both of economic circumstance and his Quaker father's objection to the Latin classics as the basis of the curriculum in the local grammar school. Paine was by no means uneducated in later life, but he was largely self-educated. His adult life until 1774 was in most respects conspicuously unsuccessful, but in that year he made a fresh start, sailing for Britain's north American colonies with a somewhat lukewarm letter of recommendation from Benjamin Franklin, who was then lobbying in London on behalf of the colonists.

Shortly after his arrival in Pennsylvania Paine discovered a talent for political journalism. From his conviction that independence from Britain was the only possible course for the American colonies, then in the early stages of the rebellion which became the War of Independence, sprang his widely read pamphlet *Common Sense*. Its success launched Paine upon a career in journalism and public affairs and brought him into close contact with the most influential figures in the infant United States.

Paine returned to Europe in 1787, largely in order to promote his invention of an iron bridge. In Britain he was welcomed by the Whig circle which included Edmund Burke and which had supported the claims of the American colonists on the grounds that they were seeking only those liberties to which, as free-born Englishmen, they were entitled. This harmony was shattered by the outbreak of the French Revolution. Paine, who regarded himself as an American, welcomed the revolution as the overthrow of an outmoded and unrepresentative government. He was consulted by the moderate revolutionary leaders Lafayette (who had taken part in the American revolution on the side of the colonists) and Condorcet. But Burke was dismayed by the overthrow of established institutions, distinguishing this from the reclamation of ancient liberties by the Americans. He attacked the French revolution in his *Reflections*. Paine's reply in *The Rights of Man* (1792–1793) resulted in his trial and outlawry by the British authorities for sedition.

By the time sentence was passed in December 1792 Paine was beyond British jurisdiction. The French had established a Convention charged with drawing up a constitution for the nation, following the model of the United States. It was possible for constituencies to choose anyone to represent them and Paine was elected by the people of Calais. Paine was seen as a hero representing American liberty; his practical, rather than symbolic, value in the Convention was limited because he could not converse in French. Though he had departed to take up his seat before the British authorities brought him to trial he was by no means out of danger, though from a different source. In the factional turmoil of the French Revolution he was imprisoned in 1793 and narrowly escaped execution during the Terror. Released in 1794 after the fall of Robespierre and the other Jacobins and through the intercession of the American ambassador, Paine continued to publish. He returned to the United States in 1802, but was no longer seen there as a hero. The years of the revolution were past, and his deistic attack upon revealed theistic religion in *The Age of Reason* (1793–1796) had turned American public opinion against him. He spent the years until his death in 1809 in obscurity.

Paine significantly influenced the political events of his time through his best-selling pamphlets, which combined clear and vivacious statements of issues with commonsense solutions, the whole couched in terms which were readily understood by a mass readership. Through his writings and his acquaintance with revolutionary leaders in the United States and France he played a part in events which contributed to the shaping of modern political institutions. There is in addition evidence that Paine's ideas remained influential during the nineteenth century; leaders of the struggle to widen the franchise in Britain acknowledged their debt to him. Evidence of his supposedly wicked influence is provided by continuing attacks from nineteenth century pulpits upon the 'godless' views attributed to him.

But does Paine have any claim to be considered in any but an historical sense? I shall argue that he does, that he transcended the ephemeral pamphlet form to make worthwhile observations upon enduring political questions. Certainly Paine accepted assumptions about human nature, rights and society which could have been examined in a more rigorous fashion, as David Hume had recently done. But the lack of formal training which perhaps stood in the way of such rigour also assisted Paine in expressing in a direct fashion and to a mass audience a view which has become fundamental to modern liberal democracy; the view that each individual possesses equal natural rights which require that he be treated equally before the law and that he be given the same opportunity as every other individual to choose a government. Paine's most important ideas may appear trite and obvious to the modern reader precisely because they are so generally accepted in liberal democratic political culture. But as J.S. Mill pointed out, commonly-held opinions should not simply be accepted on trust, but should be reassessed so as to prevent them sinking to the level of dogma or superstition. It is therefore of value to return to the original statement of these views.

Natural Rights and Civil Rights

In the debate with Paine, Burke argued the propriety of respecting precedent and tradition as a basis for political action. Paine rejected any such appeal to tradition, claiming that it rested only upon the selection of a favoured precedent among the many available. Tradition was often no more than a means of masking the denial of those human rights which Paine regarded as the only proper basis for making decisions about government. The only appeal to authority which he found acceptable was one based on human nature; in his words, on a return 'to the time when man came from the hand of his Maker'.[1]

Paine based his claim on accounts of the creation, arguing that whatever the religious tradition which they represented, all accounts stressed the unity and equality of man. There are some problems with this method of deriving the notion of equality (and later, of rights); it may demonstrate a universal belief in the original equality of humanity, but it does not show that this belief is true. It is, however, a useful means of demonstrating that there is some fundamental similarity about human beings, regardless of their race or culture. Paine argued that since there were originally no distinctions based on class or status, then all individuals must originally have possessed equal rights. Following from this he argued that every new-born child was in the same position as the first human beings; no individual could claim at birth to possess greater natural rights than others, since all possessed rights by virtue of their humanity. These rights included intellectual liberty, which itself included freedom of religious choice, and the right of the individual to secure his own comfort and happiness so long as to do so did not interfere with the rights of others.[2] The importance of this principle of equal rights as part of liberal democratic culture can hardly be

---

[1] Thomas Paine, *The Rights of Man*, Henry Collins (ed.), (Harmondsworth, 1969), p. 87.

[2] ibid, pp. 88–90.

overstressed. It is assumed that every individual is, or ought to be, treated equally; the onus is upon those who would treat people unequally on grounds, say, of race, gender or intelligence, to justify their proposed behaviour.

From natural rights sprang civil rights. Paine had suggested in *Common Sense* that 'The strength of one man is so unequal to his wants, and his mind so unfitted for perpetual solitude, that he is soon obliged to seek assistance and relief of another, who in his turn requires the same.'[3]

In order to live in society individuals had to exchange some of their natural rights for civil rights, defined by Paine as rights founded on natural rights which an individual could not secure for himself. The purpose of organized society, then, was to guarantee the preservation of rights.

> A man, by natural right, has a right to judge in his own cause; and so far as the right of the mind is concerned, he never surrenders it. But what availeth it' him to judge, if he has not power to redress? He therefore deposits this right in the common stock of society, of which he is a part, in preference and in addition to his own. Society *grants* him nothing. Every man is a proprietor in society and draws on the capital as a matter of right.[4]

Civil power was no more than the sum of the natural rights exchanged for civil rights; it should never be used to invade the rights which the individual retained.

Paine's belief in natural rights and a social contract was basically Lockean. He claimed never to have read Locke, but it would be hardly surprising for him to have been influenced by the earlier writer, given the permeation of British political institutions in the eighteenth century by Lockean ideas and arguments. Certainly Paine's justification of independence for the American colonies used the notion that any contract between the free colonists and the British government had been violated by the oppressive nature of British rule. There were, however, some points of difference between Locke and Paine. Paine placed greater stress on the complete equality of all individuals and on the right of all to participate in government or in choosing representatives. Paine also insisted on complete liberty in the exercise of individual rights; where Locke suggested that the State might limit religious freedom in order to preserve harmony and peace, Paine argued that the State had no legitimate power at all over the individual's religious beliefs.

---

[3]   Thomas Paine, *Common Sense*, Isaac Kraminck (ed.), (Harmondsworth, 1976), p. 66.
[4]   *The Rights of Man*, op. cit., pp. 90–1.

Government, in Paine's view, was not a contract between rulers and governed, but between sovereign individuals who agreed to subordinate certain of their individual rights to social order. Any system of government which purported to subordinate some individuals to others could not be legitimate. 'Every citizen is a member of the Sovereignty, and, as such, can acknowledge no personal subjection; and his obedience can be only to the laws.'[5] On these grounds no monarchy, not even that of Britain after 1688, could be a legitimate government, since it subjected citizens to the monarch, whose dynasty had normally been established by force.[6]

Just as all individuals possessed equal rights, so each generation possessed all rights afresh. Posterity could therefore not be bound by any agreement reached by prior generations to accept a particular form of government, since to attempt to bind it would be an invasion of rights.

On this point Paine assailed Burke's appeal to the Revolution Settlement; if citizens who had not taken part in the formation of a contract could not be said to have consented to it, then how could those not born? Paine argued that a nation might choose not to alter the rules which governed it; consent could be assumed when there were no attempts at change. But consent could only properly be given when the rules of society were clear, that is, when there was a written constitution. Moreover, a constitution had always to admit the possibility of change and to provide machinery for it.[7]

> The circumstances of the world are continually changing, and the opinions of men change also; and as government is for the living and not for the dead, it is the living only that has any right in it. That which may be thought right and found convenient in one age, may be thought wrong and found inconvenient in another. In such cases, Who [sic] is to decide, the living or the dead.[8]

Although Paine referred to the notion of individuals of former generations living in an atomistic, pre-social manner, it is clear that he did not envisage this as an actuality. His arguments concerning rights assume that individual rights must always be tempered by civil rights. His view of civil rights entailed the notion of duties, since society could not function unless individuals played their part in making it work through recognition of their duties towards others. But it appeared to Paine that most government placed obstacles between individuals and their rights and duties.

---

5 ibid., p. 165.
6 ibid., p. 92.
7 ibid., pp. 63–6, 219–20.
8 ibid., p. 67.

The duty of man is not a wilderness of turnpike gates, through which he is to pass by tickets from one to the other. It is plain and simple and consists of two points. His duty to God, which every man must feel; and with respect to his neighbour, to do as he would be done by.[9]

There are some obvious problems with Paine's view of rights, not the least of which is the grounds on which he derives them. A person might indeed feel intuitively that there is some form of inalienable human rights; the problem is in justifying them on grounds which would satisfy a sceptic. Paine's justification requires at least the sort of deist belief in a Supreme Being which was common in the eighteenth century. Paine also slides from the rather unclear claim about equality to one of rights, but does not really show that the first entails the second.

Paine's definition of rights is similar to that of the French 'Declaration of the Rights of Man and of Citizens', which he quotes in full. The first two articles of this set out the ambit of rights which he claimed.

I. Men are born, and always continue, free and equal in respect of their rights.
II. The end of all political associations, is, the preservation of the natural and imprescriptible rights of man; and these rights are liberty, property, security, and resistance of oppression.[10]

It is noteworthy that Paine included the right to property, a right which some later theorists omitted from their list of natural rights. More generally, both the declaration and his own discussion of rights conflate individual and social rights, regarding the individual as necessarily part of society. But in this case individual rights must at some point be compromised by social rights and Paine makes no suggestions on how clashes between the two may be resolved. Civil rights are associated with duties to society as a whole and to individuals; if these duties are not fulfilled can rights be curtailed? Paine simply suggests that rights are absolute and inalienable. He does not tackle the problem of rights and duties, nor consider what may happen if two sovereign individual rights come into conflict.

The problem of rights and duties remains an important philosophical and political question. The nature of human rights has become increasingly important in the context of the 'right to life' debate engendered by changing social attitudes to abortion as well as by the growth of medical technology and its implications for dying and defective human beings. It has also been argued that if there is

---

9 ibid., p. 89.
10 ibid., p. 132.

some minimum right to existence then individuals have a right not to starve; this then suggests that there is a consequent duty to provide food. Another important question has been the rights possessed by non-human animals and the implications for the rights of defective humans. These problems are of practical political importance because individuals wish to express their moral concerns through legislation.

Paine's egalitarianism ignored problems which a century later were to trouble J.S. Mill, namely, should lack of education or similar disabilities disqualify a citizen from voting. The essence of the problem posed by Mill remains of considerable importance in determining the actions of liberal democratic governments. The question is: if individuals possess equal rights, are they prevented from properly exercising those rights if they are illiterate, or if they lack adequate access to any activities or facilities deemed by their society to be necessary to ensure minimum conditions of human dignity? Most liberal democratic societies would argue that some degree of government intervention is necessary to ensure the exercise of rights. As an example, most would support compulsory minimum education. Paine did not tackle such questions. His optimistic belief in human rationality led him to believe that if only the false constraints imposed by 'civilization' were removed, the true nature of humanity would prevent clashes over rights.

In setting individuals in society, with rights and corresponding duties, Paine assumed that they could understand the extent of their rights and could accept the legitimacy of curbing individual, in favour of civil, rights. That is, he saw human beings as rational creatures able to perceive the advantages of social order. This quality of rationality was inherent, not something dependent upon education. Indeed, Paine suggested that 'education' and the habits and prejudices which it instilled often stood between individuals and their true humanity. The example of the United States had shown the advantages to be won by a population transplanted from the artificiality of the old world.

> So deeply rooted were all the governments of the old world, and so effectively had the tyranny and the antiquity of habit established itself over the mind, that no beginning could be made in Asia, Africa, or Europe, to reform the political condition of man. Freedom had been hunted around the globe; reason was considered as rebellion; and the slavery of fear had made men afraid to think.

Only when the physical environment stripped away the falseness of 'civilization' could humanity rediscover its true nature. 'In such a situation man becomes what he ought. He sees his species, not with the inhuman idea of a natural enemy, but as kindred; and the example shows to the artificial world, that man must go back to Nature for information.'[11]

Thus Paine, unlike Hobbes, believed that humanity was inherently virtuous and rational, ready to co-operate if the false habits and prejudices of existing society were stripped away. Paine, however, rather too easily accepted the idea that life in the American colonies was a return to nature, for although the physical environment was harsh, the settlers carried with them so much of the customs and habits of Europe that it is difficult to see their lives as a return to nature. Be that as it may, Paine saw the example of the United States as one to influence the world. He believed that if only an example of a better social order were to be placed before the nations of the old world then their people could not fail to see the advantages, even though they were so oppressed as to be unable to see the truth unprompted.

Believing in the inherent rationality and virtue of humanity, Paine suggested that individuals chose the wrong course only because of ignorance; individuals were attached to beliefs and prejudices only because they believed them to be true. If they were shown that their beliefs were false then their opinions would change. For this reason he argued that there must be complete liberty of expression as a right, even if this meant criticism and eventual abolition of existing forms of government. Through free discussion the truth must emerge. Thus, suggested Paine, Burke's urging that he be prosecuted for sedition was no more than the expression of Burke's fear that the truth could not be to the advantage of the existing order.[12]

The best system of government was a republic, in the sense of a government whose sole purpose was the public good. Both monarchical and oligarchical societies were ruled out immediately, since both were directed to the interests of a small part of society, rather than being in the interests of the whole. Additionally, most societies of this type depended upon the principle of hereditary succession. This was obviously a ridiculous principle, since there was no guarantee of inherited ability to govern. Simple democracy, in which all citizens directly participated in government, was clearly a republican form of government, but could not be applied to nations of extensive areas or large population. The solution was to graft the principle of representation upon democracy, as in the United States.[13]

Good government could not exist if either forms or principles were bad; thus no monarchy could be a good government, no matter how virtuous the monarch as an individual, since the principle on

---

[11] ibid., pp. 181–2.
[12] ibid., pp. 178–9.
[13] ibid., pp. 200–2.

which it was founded was wrong. The nation had therefore first to establish the principles of its constitution and so long as these took proper account of rights and duties then the system of government arising from them could not fail to be in the interests of the whole.[14]

On a slightly different tack, admirers of Paine have claimed for him some insights of startling modernity, some of which, with respect to the role of the State, will be discussed below. In the context of the inability of the individual to influence a bad system for good, Paine, in discussing the French monarchy, made an observation worth quoting at length both for its vivacity of expression and its encapsulation of an idea which has become more prominent in the twentieth century, that of the anonymous tyranny of bureaucracy.

> Every office and department has its despotism, founded upon custom and usage. Every place has its Bastille, and every Bastille its despot. The original hereditary despotism resident in the person of the King, divides and subdivides itself into a thousand shapes and forms, till at last the whole of it is acted by deputation. This was the case in France; and against this species of despotism, proceeding on through an endless labyrinth of office till the source of it is scarcely perceptible, there is no mode of redress. It strengthens itself by assuming the appearance of duty, and tyrannizes under the pretence of obeying.[15]

Constitutions could not bind nations forever; we have previously discussed the grounds on which Paine argued this would violate rights. But there was a further reason for permitting change. Lacking experience, it was unlikely that nations would be able immediately to draw up perfect constitutions. Only the experience of living under a constitution would show up any weaknesses. Given experience, human rationality would inevitably lead to further progress. 'If systems of government can be introduced, less expensive and more productive of general happiness, than those which have existed, all attempts to oppose their progress will in the end be fruitless. Reason, like time, will make its own way, and prejudice will fall in a combat with interest.'[16]

Paine's belief in progress and rationality rested principally on the empirical grounds of his experience in the United States. He referred repeatedly to the honest and economical government and the lack of vast inequalities based on wealth and hereditary status in his adopted country. The American Revolution had assured the preservation of rights without radical changes in society and although Paine perceived greater inequities and injustices under the old régime in France than had been the case in north America, he believed that

---

[14] ibid., pp. 89, 203, 208–9.
[15] ibid., p. 70.
[16] ibid., p. 183.

the experiences of the one could be transferred to the other. His sufferings under the Terror point up the fallacy of this belief. While actuated by pure motives, the French revolutionaries moved more and more to the totalitarian notion of ridding society of all elements which marred its perfection. Paine's experiences lend support to Burke's more pessimistic view of society and human nature. Paine successfully assailed the more ridiculous aspects of Burke's rhetoric, as well as some of his important claims, but he did not tackle the central, conservative claim that the risks of radical change are so great that it must be ruled out in favour of gradual and evolutionary change. That he failed to do so must be accounted a major weakness of his argument.

Equality and the Proper Role of Government

The final aspect of Paine's ideas which I shall discuss is the way in which he proposed that equality be fostered, and the view of the State which this entailed. Humanity was naturally fitted for society, for each individual was unable to supply all his needs unaided. Furthermore, human beings desired companionship. Much of what was commonly called government was in fact no more than the natural actions of society; government was necessary only when society and civilization failed. Only too often the social instincts of humanity were subverted by government, particularly by the militaristic nationalism which Paine saw as characteristic of monarchy.[17]

The only legitimate purpose of government was the good of all, a purpose best accomplished by having the least possible interference in the natural course of society. 'Every man wishes to pursue his occupation, and to enjoy the fruits of his labours and the produce of his property in peace and safety, and with the least possible expense. When these things are accomplished, all the objects for which government ought to be established are accomplished.'[18]

This suggests a minimalist view of government. Certainly Paine wrote approvingly of Adam Smith and his theory of the marketplace; he wrote also of the blessings that must flow from allowing trade to be free, with every individual using his talents to the utmost.[19] But Paine's view of minimum standards and of security was more complex than this, for his commitment to the idea of equality led him to believe that in a society where there were very great differences in material standards, there must be some overriding of rights.

---

[17] ibid., pp. 196–7.
[18] ibid., p. 220.
[19] ibid., pp. 234–5.

> When, in countries that are called civilized, we see age going to the workhouse and youth to the gallows, something must be wrong in the system of government... It is inhuman to talk of a million sterling a year, paid out of the public taxes of any country, for the support of any individual, whilst thousands who are forced to contribute thereto, are pining with want and struggling with misery. Government does not consist in a contrast between prisons and palaces, between poverty and pomp; it is not instituted to rob the needy of his mite, and increase the wretchedness of the wretched.[20]

What Paine proposed was that government should create conditions which would bring about equality of opportunity. He attributed much of the poverty in eighteenth century Britain to an excessive burden of taxation, levied largely to pay for the extravagance of the monarch and his court and for an unnecessarily large army. Militarism undermined the creation of new wealth, for it impeded the free flow of commerce. Lack of education perpetuated poverty and crime. It was therefore in the interests of society to attempt to remedy problems such as these.

The means proposed by Paine was an overhaul of the taxation system and the imposition of new taxes on a progressive basis, that is, on the landed aristocracy whom he believed were best able to bear the burden. Rather than having one section of the poor supporting another through taxation, he proposed that taxation should bear most heavily upon the wealthy and that revenue should be applied to increasing minimum standards of living. Paine observed that poverty was most likely to occur within large families and among the old. He urged therefore that pensions be paid to those who could work no longer, or whose earning capacity had declined with the onset of age. Similarly, he suggested various income supplements for families, as well as subsidized education for children whose parents could not otherwise afford schooling for them. Paine's system would in addition have cut down the normal expenses of government through the abolition of costly sinecures; thus the majority of people would be better off, and by having more to spend would stimulate the growth of commerce.[21]

The notions of progressive taxation and welfare spending would appear to place Paine firmly among those who would argue for a large role for government in regulating society. But as we have seen, Paine believed that society was capable of regulating itself so long as it was established on sound principles. Paine believed that in a properly ordered society taxation should be minimal, since the role of government, as opposed to that of society, would be slight. His

---

[20] ibid., pp. 225, 240.
[21] ibid., pp. 242 ff.

welfare proposals were intended to bridge the gap between the old and the new order. Education would enable the new generation to earn and to save, so that within a short period little in the way of welfare payments would be necessary, while the habits of independence fostered by the society based on the recognition of equality would lead all to seek to manage their own lives. His ideas then, are far more attuned to the free market than to those of the welfarists.

This brief discussion of Paine's ideas is based largely upon *The Rights of Man*, a central and readily accessible work. Besides outlining Paine's ideas and some of their implications I have attempted, through quotation, to convey something of the qualities of his prose, since it was the readability of his pamphlets that made them so influential in their time. To conclude, I shall quote the closing sentences of *The Rights of Man* (1792); this passage conveys some of the essential qualities of Paine, notably his optimistic belief in the inevitability of progress as well as the vividness of his writing.

> It is now towards the middle of February. Were I to take a turn into the country, the trees would present a leafless winterly appearance. As people are apt to pluck twigs as they walk along, I perhaps might do the same, and by chance might observe that a *single bud* on that twig had begun to swell. I should reason very unnaturally, or rather not reason at all, to suppose *this* was the *only* bud in England which had this appearance. Instead of deciding thus, I should instantly conclude, that the same appearance was beginning, or about to begin, everywhere; and though the vegetable sleep will continue longer on some trees and plants than on others, and though some of them may not *blossom* for two or three years, all will be in leaf in the summer, except those which are *rotten*. What pace the political summer may keep with the natural, no human foresight can determine. It is, however, not difficult to perceive that the spring is begun.[22]

Further Reading

On Paine:
A.O. Aldridge, *Man of Reason: the Life of Thomas Paine*, (London, 1960).
R.R. Fennessy, *Burke, Paine and the Rights of Man*, (The Hague, 1963).

On rights:
Eugene Kamenka (ed.), *Human Rights*, (Melbourne, 1978). Includes a useful bibliography and index.
H.J. McCloskey, 'Rights – some conceptual issues', *Australasian Journal of Philosophy*, vol. 54, no. 2, August 1976.
Volume I, Issue 2, Spring 1984, *Social Philosophy and Policy* is composed of 13 articles on human rights.

---

[22] ibid., pp. 294–5.

Chapter Twelve

Hegel and the Organic State

W.V. Doniela

Georg Wilhelm Friedrich Hegel (1770 Stuttgart–1831 Berlin) was the most prominent member of the philosophical school known as German Idealism. It is worth noting that despite his subsequent and not always favourable reputation for abstract thought his early reflections were concerned with concrete social, religious and ethical issues. Indeed, as a young man he was clearly affected by the ideals of the French Revolution which took place in 1789 when he was nineteen, and which he, along with some fellow students of the Protestant Seminary at Tübingen, supported with fervent enthusiasm. Although one need not fully concur with Joachim Ritter's verdict that 'there is no other philosophy that is a philosophy of Revolution to such a degree and so profoundly, in its innermost drive, as that of Hegel',[1] Hegel's approval of the event is well documented. To be sure, after a few years he subjected the course of the Revolution to an analytic criticism but even late in his life he recalled that 'this was a magnificent dawn. All thinking beings joined in celebrating this epoch. A sublime feeling ruled that time, an enthusiasm of the spirit thrilled through the world . . .'. Hegel's own contribution to the climate of emancipation consisted of two youthful compositions. While a house tutor in Bern, Switzerland, he translated, annotated and anonymously published in German a small French book attacking the malpractices of the Bernese oligarchy in the canton of Waadt. He followed it up by writing a political pamphlet himself, calling for reforms in his native state of Württemberg.[2]

---

[1] Joachim Ritter, *Hegel and the French Revolution*, (Cambridge, Mass., 1982), p. 43.
[2] These early compositions are not available in English but are discussed by Pelczynski in his Introduction to G.W.F. Hegel, *Political Writings*, T.M. Knox (tr), (Oxford, 1964), pp. 9 ff.

But on the whole Hegel's early endorsement of the French Revolution – though significant as one of the keys to his political thought – was less important in his intellectual development than the several unpublished historical studies, traditionally grouped under the heading of *Early Theological Writings*.[3] This title is not quite appropriate; Hegel was rather concerned with the question of why early Christianity became authoritarian ('positive'). In these essays, while suggesting that the moral insights of Jesus were distorted by the prevailing cultural and religious climate, Hegel also linked authoritarianism with alienation and, more specifically, with the type of life which was entrapped in legalistic regulations and had lost direct human relatedness. These conclusions reflected the contrast that the German Enlightenment was drawing between the idealized harmony of the ancient Greek polis and the ensuing multi-faceted decline. But Hegel was especially anxious to underscore the dissimilarities between the social integration of the citizen of the Greek city-state and the fragmented existence of the modern European. Interest in the defects of socio-political atomism and its possible remedy through organic unity remained embedded in Hegel's thought.

Hegel's Early Ethic of Love

Hegel's early preoccupation with social harmony acquired a permanent philosophical form when in an unfinished essay, entitled 'The Spirit of Christianity and Its Fate', he lifted the problem of fragmentation to the level of an ethical issue. The occasion was the young Hegel's critical rethinking of Kant's moral theory. Kant had already claimed that morality should be freed from external authorities and that the formulation of the correct norms should be left to Reason, in the form of the immanent Moral Law or, in Kantian terms, the Categorical Imperative. But while Kant contended that morality should be autonomous in this sense, he also created an unbridgeable gap between the Moral Law and everyday psychological inclinations. The Moral Law, argued Kant, cannot be derived from experience; the relation between the Moral Law and inclinations is that of a command, for an action becomes moral only if it is done by following moral duty, out of respect for the Moral Law. To the young Hegel, Kant's view of morality was unsatisfactory: while Kant had rejected external authorities, he still retained a master-

---

[3]   The English translation is selective and Richard Kroner's Introduction is at times seriously faulty in the light of recent discoveries about Hegel's youth. However, it contains 'The Spirit of Christianity and its Fate' which is a crucial landmark in Hegel's intellectual development.

slave relationship within the human being himself. Hegel goes further and argues that a certain human disposition does what the right command would have commanded. This disposition is love; Hegel elaborates this by secularizing the Sermon on the Mount and putting forward an ethic of love.

The emphasis on love as that disposition which is itself moral or good was soon replaced by Hegel with the wider concept of Spirit (*Geist*) which remained one of Hegel's basic concepts standing for, roughly, sociality not only in the everyday human but also in the somewhat unusual cosmic sense. But it is clear that the early ethic of love underpins a great deal of Hegel's later writings as well. The specific form of Hegel's Idealist metaphysics, which postulates that the universe, or the Absolute, is an 'identity in difference', also has its roots in the young Hegel's working out of the dynamic of love.

Some aspects of this dynamic are of vital relevance to Hegel's subsequent political theory. First, Hegel sees the operation of love as essentially *egalitarian*. In a fragment edited as 'Love', Hegel writes: 'True union, or love proper, exists only between living beings who are alike in power and thus in one another's eyes living beings from every point of view; in no respect is either dead for the other. This genuine love excludes all oppositions' (*Early Theological Writings*, p. 304). Love is the opposite of the master-slave relation: 'It detracts nothing from love's greatness, it does not degrade it, that its essence is not a domination of something alien to it, ... it is rather love's triumph over these that it lords it over nothing, is without any hostile power over another' (ibid., p. 247). Love is in principle incompatible with authoritarianism: 'Love pronounces no imperative' (ibid., p. 247). Since Hegel sees love as the most intense expression of the unity of life, the emphasis on love as a non-conflicting relationship lays the foundation for the organicist viewpoint of Hegel's subsequent social and political philosophy.

Secondly, love (and expanded terms such as Spirit and Ethical Life) are essentially linked with *freedom*. For the young Hegel, 'love neither restricts nor is restricted; it is not finite at all' (ibid., p. 304). The reference to 'not finite at all' sums up far-reaching implications which may be put as follows: because love is unselfish, it does not take advantage of others; in so far as this attitude does not exert personal or social domination, it does not cause self-defensive attitudes in others. More abstractly, in a society of loves there is no need for protective barriers; instead of possible divisiveness, the resulting psycho-social situation is that of continuity, i.e. free interaction.

Thirdly, the young Hegel sees the operation of love as *rational*. Using the Kantian criterion of what makes actions moral, Hegel claims that since love is not selfish and does not seek privileges and self-exemptions, love is, to use Kant's technical term, universalizable and therefore rational when measured by the standard of Practical Reason. It is significant that while Kant took rationality, like morality, to be a feature that actions *acquire* when they conform to the criteria set by Practical Reason, for Hegel, by contrast, certain actions (or at least dispositions) are themselves rational. One of the consequences of Hegel's early ethic of love is that Reason is no longer an abstract and therefore obscure mental faculty; Reason or rather its manifestations turn out to be real and effective socio-psychological factors. When the later Hegel speaks of the 'role of Reason in History' he has in mind a certain disposition which, in various measures and intensities, is active in personal relationships, in social phenomena, and in political structures. Putting Hegel's contention in present-day terminology, Reason is for him a certain type of mentality, operative and observable in history.

The Divisive Civil Society

Hegel's main contribution to political thought is the *Philosophy of Right* which appeared in 1821, when he occupied the Chair of Philosophy in the University of Berlin. This work is an expanded version of a rather slim section of his entire philosophical system expounded in a summary form in his *Encyclopaedia of the Philosophical Sciences*.[4] Hegel's selection of his political philosophy for a more articulated and definitive statement reflects his life-long interest in practical issues. Apart from the very early compositions that have already been mentioned, he had written several other political articles and indeed his very last publication before he died in 1831 consisted of several instalments of a critical examination of the English Reform Bill.[5]

The *Philosophy of Right* claims to be descriptive rather than prescriptive; instead of 'giving instruction as to what the world ought to be', it contends that the task of philosophy is to understand the world. In any case, says Hegel, philosophy comes on the scene too late to give advice: 'When philosophy paints its grey in grey, then has a shape of life grown old. By philosophy's grey in grey it cannot be rejuvenated but only understood. The owl of Minerva spreads its wings only with the falling of the dusk'. (*Philosophy of Right*, preface, p. 13.)

---

4   Hegel's *Encyclopaedia* was first published in 1817, then revised and repeatedly enlarged in 1827 and 1830. It is available in English in three volumes: *The Logic of Hegel* (tr. by W. Wallace), *Philosophy of Nature* and *Philosophy of Mind* (the latter two tr. by A.V. Miller). All 3 published by OUP, many printings.
5   Translated by T.M. Knox G.W.F. Hegel, *Political Writings*, (Oxford, 1964), together with several other smaller compositions of a political nature.

Hegel is convinced that in this work he is delineating the direction in which the modern states have been travelling. Although the state proper – the philosophical notion of the state as the embodiment of freedom and rationality – has not been fully realized, progress towards that ideal has been rendered inevitable by the actual movement of history. The *Philosophy of Right* is a combination of an empirical description of how modern states tend to be structured and what problems they face, with the conviction that (his) philosophy has arrived at the understanding of what truly constitutes freedom and rationality. These two central phenomena are to be explicated and distinguished from the transient and less substantial manifestations of political life. The italicized statement in the preface, 'what is rational is actual and what is actual is rational', presupposes precisely this distinction between the insubstantial ('the existing') and the enduring ('the actual'), though it also rests on Hegel's belief expressed elsewhere[6] that world history itself displays a discernible progress of rationality; Reason shifts its point of gravity from culture to culture, but each step signifies an advance in some specific respect.

The *Philosophy of Right* also assumes the correlated belief that the modern state represents a definite improvement upon previous political forms. Quite apart from his dictum that in the Oriental World only one person (the autocrat) was free, in the Classical World only a few were free, but that in the Modern World everyone is free, a crucial mark of the modern state is said to be its capacity to do justice to the citizen's individuality. Although the Classical World may, in certain respects, still serve as an ideal, it was nevertheless politically defective because of its collectivism, that is, because of the submergence of the individual in the prevailing customs and traditions. For the Classical World the rise of selfish ('particular') interests – 'the corrupting element' – was still to come, and when it did come the political arrangements were incapable of dealing with it. But the Modern World has experienced it, faced it and, to its credit, has learned or at least is learning how to control it. The society of the Classical World was, metaphorically, a unity, and subsequent upheavals reduced it to its opposite, multiplicity. The greatness of the modern state is that it is beginning to establish a balance, namely, unity in multiplicity. The modern state prevents the citizen from being swallowed up by the crowd and thus protects his individuality and the rights associated with it ('subjectivity'); for example, the modern state recognizes the individual's right of appeal

---

6 Hegel's conviction that history is a progress of reason is expounded in some detail in his *Lectures on the Philosophy of History*, especially in the Introduction. There are several editions and translations: Sibree's is the more widely used, Nisbet's is the more scholarly.

to his conscience. At the same time, while emancipating the citizen
from obsolete conformism, the modern state shows its citizen how to
interact once more with fellow citizens in a harmonious but now also
a *consciously*, 'subjectively', harmonious manner:

> The principle of modern states has prodigious strength and depth
> because it allows the principle of subjectivity to progress to its
> culmination in the extreme of self-subsistent personal particularity,
> and yet at the same time brings it back to the substantive unity and so
> maintains this unity in the principle of subjectivity itself. (*Philosophy
> of Right*, § 260)

The manner in which the modern state subscribes to, and tries to
maintain, the principle of 'identity in difference' is analyzed by
Hegel in the third and longest section of the *Philosophy of Right*,
under the heading of 'Ethical Life' (*Sittlichkeit*). Ethical Life, a
descendant of such cognate concepts as Love and Spirit, is a mode of
interaction whereby at least some common good is obtained. Hegel
distinguishes three levels in the structure of the modern state: 1 The
Family, 2 Civil Society, 3 The State. The Family represents ethical
life based on feeling. Civil Society is a form of social organization in
which persons function as mere individuals or social atoms who
happen to come together to gratify their natural or acquired needs
through some mode of exchange. Civil Society is the antithesis of
The Family, displaying the maximum measure of merely external
relationships. The State reinstates the lost unity, though it effects
this by the cultivation of conscious reflection rather than spon-
taneous emotion, by education rather than compulsion.

In the Family, unity is based on feeling. This feeling is love which
manifests itself in a natural but also an unreflective manner. But it is
precisely because the sociality of the family is based on feeling that it
does not fully recognize the individual *qua* individual and does not
pay adequate attention to individual rights. The uniformity that the
family requires is too intense and therefore the familial ties cannot be
transferred to the society at large.

Hegel sees civil society as a social interaction of individuals who
are essentially autonomous ('self-subsistent'). They do form a social
system but their communality is 'only abstract'. In essence, this type
of social system is based on the members' mutual needs, especially
economic: 'Their association is brought about by their needs, by the
legal system – the means to security of persons and property – and by
an external organization for attaining their particular and common
interests' (§157). But because the satisfaction of needs is pursued
selfishly, civil society resembles the Hobbesian *bellum omnium contra
omnes*. While interaction cannot be avoided – for otherwise needs
will not be satisfied – the ensuing interdependence lacks genuine

co-operation and maintains only a precarious existence, for the system itself may turn into an object of manipulation for partisan aims.

However, 'though in civil society universal and particular have fallen apart, yet both are reciprocally bound together and conditioned' (§184A). Even if the civil society appears like a 'battlefield', one can discern in it the operation of Adam Smith's 'invisible hand':

> When men are thus dependent on one another and reciprocally related to one another in their work and the satisfaction of their needs, subjective self-seeking turns into a contribution to the satisfaction of the needs of everyone else ... with the result that each man in earning, producing, and enjoying on his own account is *eo ipso* producing and earning for the enjoyment of everyone else. (§199)

> If I further my ends, I further the ends of the universal, and this in turn furthers my ends. (§184A)

The System of Needs is the first aspect of civil society but while at times Hegel seems to be fascinated by the presence of the 'invisible hand' which provides underlying social bonds, he does not accept it as a solution. The most that can be said is that the selfish considerations ('the particular') and the common good ('the universal') are not totally separated. An additional, second, level is needed to keep the particular and the universal together: the Administration of Justice. Given the framework of civil society, Hegel takes legal arrangements to be more impartial and therefore more rational than the rather fragile *self*-regulation of the System of Needs. Because of their conscious and articulate universality, right and law are more 'concrete'; the individual ceases to be a mere social atom and becomes a bearer of universal rights. Indeed, law overcomes local and tribal differences of estate and nationality: in the modern state, 'a human counts as a human in virtue of his humanity alone, not because he is a Jew, Catholic, Protestant, German, Italian, etc.' (§209)

To implement the hopefully impartial law, Public Authority (*Polizei*) is needed. This is the third aspect of civil society, which is described by Hegel in its function as an effective supervisory agency. But while laws may be implemented by force, unenforced sociality may be imparted by education. The latter is, of course, a preferable mode of avoiding personal injustices or social conflicts, and is equally superior to blind reliance on the mechanical self-regulation of needs. Education brings about *awareness* of the reasons why ethical life is higher than egoistic conflict and use of force.

When discussing the System of Needs, Hegel referred to the role of estates (*Stände*); while they pursue class interests, the estates also foster co-operation within their own frameworks. Hegel concludes the section on Civil Society by showing that the links that bring together civil society as the realm of the particular interest, and the state as the realm of the universal interest, are reinforced by the activity of the 'corporations' (*Korporationen*). Corporations are hardly to be understood as present-day trade unions; they are more like the less militant guilds that give coherence to a certain trade or industry. To Hegel, the importance of the corporations lies in their natural capacity to reduce the sharp clash of merely selfish interests: 'The implicit likeness of such particulars to one another becomes really existent in an association, as something common to its members. Hence a selfish purpose, directed towards its particular self-interest, apprehends and evinces itself at the same time as a universal.' (§251)

Hegel's emphasis on the corporations reveals his desire to unearth the socially cohesive forces – which in his view are present in any economic system – in order to show that the pessimistic view of the modern society, a society some may see as hopelessly rent by the division of labour, is not the whole truth. Thus although it is an essential part of Hegel's analysis that the modern state is more divisive and atomistic than previous political structures, he is anxious to show that the interest in the common good ('the universal interest') has not vanished altogether. Indeed, Hegel discerns a *revival* of the universal interest, evidenced by a study of history. Though the classical city-state collapsed at least partly through exaggerated preoccupation with the rights of the individual, this very same preoccupation brought about the recognition that a sound system of rights must presuppose equality as was expressed, for example, in the ideals of the French Revolution. Thus the growth and the divisive effects of social atomism have also been redressed by the awareness of their socially negative character. Hegel sees the modern state as a political entity which can differentiate between the forces that are socially cohesive and the forces that are socially disruptive. As a result, the state can take steps to minimize fragmentation and to maximize cohesion.

The Reconciling Realm of the State

The 'universal interest', the concern with the common good, is in Hegel's view being taken care of by the realm of the State. (In this context, the State represents the third stage, after the Family and Civil Society; it is important to distinguish between the everyday meaning of 'the state' and the specifically Hegelian one.) Since, for Hegel, civil society cannot fully regulate itself, this regulation is completed by the state which in its turn consists of three layers: the assembly of estates, the civil service and the monarchy.

The assembly of estates is for Hegel the locus where the relatively specific interests, characteristic of civil society, achieve at least a considerable measure of integration. The assembly is the place where consensus is reached or at least aimed at; in this way civil society tends to arrive at a common political will. As Hegel puts it, 'The Estates have the function of bringing ... into existence the moment of subjective formal freedom, the public consciousness, [now in the form of] an empirical universal' (§301). The universal interest of the assembly of estates is merely 'empirical' because the views expressed by this assembly still reflect some of the specific issues of the everyday grass-and-roots struggles common to civil society. The members of the assembly cannot put the universal interest in the pure form of law because they are still affected, as it were, by the idiosyncracies of particular situations. In this sense, the assembly is more suited to act as a mediator between civil society and the state – and being responsible to both – than as the formulator of the laws themselves.

This task is left to the civil service, the bureaucratic class which stands above any partisan objectives and which is dedicated to the universal interest itself. The bureaucracy is made up of paid civil servants whose essential characteristic is freedom from specific influences and total dedication to the common good. These posts are to be filled on merit, to be understood as *la carrière ouverte aux talents*. Echoing Plato, Hegel declares that 'the *objective* factor in their appointment is knowledge and proof of ability. Such proof guarantees that the state will get what it requires; and since it is the sole condition of appointment, it also guarantees to every citizen the chance of joining the class of civil servants' (§291).

It may seem that the co-operation of the assembly with the bureaucracy should complete the realm of the (specifically Hegelian) State. Hegel, however, adds the office of the monarch. Though the role of the monarch is not substantial, for he is effectively circumscribed by a rational constitution, Hegel's preference for a monarch rests partly on the unusual argument that heredity supplies a 'natural' justification (§280), partly on the more philosophical point that since the political structure is a cohesion of conscious individuals, it should have an individual at the top of the political pyramid as well. The latter argument does not exclusively favour a monarch, and it is possible that Hegel's preference for monarchy had a more serious motivation in his distrust of mob democracy; to link the highest political office with heredity rather than with the swaying opinions of civil society may have appeared to provide a point of some stability and impartiality.

The basic thrust of the *Philosophy of Right* is to see the political structure as an organism: differentiated as it is into its different members, it is also equally pervaded by cohesive links of various intensities. Clashes and their resolution by checks and balances are inevitable; they are part of the 'fate' of the modern world. But it is erroneous, argues Hegel, to make political thought stop at this fact. Political philosophy which treats society in a mechanistic way and reduces political arrangements to an elaborate game of checks and balances not only overlooks higher forms of political community, but is also a false philosophy. Cohesion, not social atomism, is the underlying fact of any society; though Rousseau was wrong in postulating a social contract, Hegel gives him credit[7] for insisting on the existence of the general will which precedes 'abstract' individuals both historically and logically.

But behind Hegel's argument that organic cohesion is a greater truth about human life there also lies the philosophical contention that it is the organism that displays true freedom and rationality. The *Philosophy of Right*, written after Hegel had already published his system, operates with 'freedom' and 'rationality' in a somewhat careless and *prima facie* arbitrary manner; however, his own conviction was based on grounds which were more solid than their presentation in this late publication.

Freedom and Rationality

It has already been mentioned that Hegel's early ethic of love led him to a new view of freedom. A psycho-social attitude which is not selfish cannot cause the setting up of defensive barricades. Given a society of persons displaying such attitudes, there will be no encroachment and no need for self-protection. In this basic sense, Hegel's concept of freedom is radically different from the popular concept of freedom as it is expressed, for example, in Hobbes's classical definition that 'the liberty of man consists in this that he finds no stop, in doing what he has the will, desire or inclination to do'.[8] Hegel's disagreement with the popular concept of freedom is shown, to take but one passage, in his *Lectures on the Philosophy of History*, where he refers to 'the perpetually recurring mis-

---

[7]   Hegel discusses Rousseau repeatedly in a number of passages in various works. Rousseau's influence on Hegel is considerable but he also blames Rousseau for having made an inconsistent concession to social atomism: Rousseau 'reduces the union of the individuals in the state to a contract and therefore to something based on their arbitrary wills ...' (*Philosophy of Right*, §258). However, Hegel's own emphasis on all-pervasive social continuity goes back to his Frankfurt period, 1797–1800, when, influenced by Hölderlin, he was elaborating his notions of Love and Life. See H.S. Haris, *Hegel's Development: Towards the Sunlight*, (Oxford, 1972), chapter IV.

[8]   *Leviathan*, chapter XXI.

apprehension of freedom, (which misapprehension) consists in regarding that term only in its formal, subjective sense; thus a constraint put upon impulse, desire, passion – a limitation of caprice and self-will – is regarded as a fettering of freedom'.[9]

Hegel's point is that in order to grasp what freedom truly is, it is necessary to distinguish between selfish and non-selfish attitudes and motives. The failure to do so vitiates the popular theory of freedom because in it the selfish attitude is also taken to be an equal component of freedom. Consciously (as in the case of Hobbes) or otherwise, the popular theory of freedom tends to start off with the person who is tainted with egoism and thus, while aiming at the conditions of freedom, it is soon confronted with the *paradox of freedom*. If everyone does what he likes, before long one's own freedom will be encroached upon and restricted, that is, one will become unfree. The freedom of one easily leads to the unfreedom of another one.

Hegel's notion of freedom, being based upon a distinction between what is selfish (in Kantian terms, what is not universalizable) and what is not selfish (what is universalizable) can avoid the paradox of freedom, for under certain conditions – that is, absence of selfishness, self-exemption, privilege-seeking – unjust encroachment and the resulting loss of freedom do not take place. Moreover, it is Hegel's view that the non-selfish attitude is compatible with a *variety* of views, interests, talents. Rousseau had erroneously thought that in order to achieve freedom people would have to be moulded according to a uniform pattern; for Hegel this view was an unfortunate misconception (resulting, among other things, in the terror of the French Revolution). By contrast, freedom is a certain type of mentality. Given this fact:

> Concrete freedom consists in this – that personal individuality and its particular interests may not only achieve their complete development and gain explicit recognition for their right ... but, for one thing, they also pass of their own accord into the interest of the universal, and, for another thing, they know and will the universal; they even recognise it as their own substantive mind; they take it as their end and aim and are active in its pursuit. (§260)

The concluding lines reveal the typical Hegelian stress on *awareness*; while certain types of mentality will be free and will produce free social interaction, it is the task of the theorist to *grasp* this fact – and in so far as he is engaged in politics, to apply this insight to the matters of the state as well.

It is this distinction between types of mentality that renders Hegel

---

[9] Sibree's tr., Dover ed., p. 41.

critical of popular notions of democracy and liberalism. Since democratic theorists and proponents of liberalism do not make the distinctions that Hegel thinks are essential for the correct grasp of freedom, democracy cannot rise above some division between the rulers and the ruled, and liberalism cannot eliminate the danger of letting freedom turn into oppression and exploitation. Putting it differently, in the liberal-democratic theory everyone is right, which means that selfishness is given the same standing as its absence. Thus the liberal-democratic theory has to solve problems by the quantitative method of vote counting, and run the risk, more often than not, of solving problems in a manner which may redress a particular grievance at the cost of causing a new one.

Hegel's criticism of democracy and liberalism does not lead him (as many have supposed that it does) to authoritarianism or worship of the state. The state as a political totality is for Hegel a free interaction among citizens who possess not only different interests and talents but a certain type of mentality as well. Hegel's metaphysical principle of 'identity in difference' stipulates the organic balance or harmony between the particular and the universal interest. The individual is not to be subordinated to the state; rather:

> The state is actual only when its members have a feeling of their own selfhood and it is stable only when public and private ends are identical. It has often been said that the end of the state is the happiness of its citizens. That is perfectly true. If all is not well with them, if their subjective aims are not satisfied, if they do not find that the state as such is the means to their satisfaction, then the footing of the state itself is insecure. (§265A)

Indeed, in the organic state the relation of subordination has no room. For Hegel, 'this relation of end and means is not at all appropriate in the present context. For the state is not an abstraction which stands in opposition to the citizens; on the contrary, they are distinct moments like those of organic life, in which no one member is either a means or an end'.[10]

The concrete content of freedom is, then, a certain mentality, which Hegel calls Spirit. But just as 'the substance of Spirit is Freedom',[11] so for Hegel Spirit is Reason. Does it mean that what is free is rational, and what is rational is free?

The answer is in the affirmative, though its explication is more complicated and necessitates a return to Kant's moral theory. As already mentioned, Kant had postulated the existence of the Categorical Imperative according to which 'I ought never to act except in such a way that I can also will that my maxim should become a

---

[10] *Lectures on the Philosophy of World History*, (Cambridge, 1975), Nisbet's tr., p. 95.
[11] This contention is developed especially in the opening sections of the *Lectures*.

universal law'. This law, according to Kant, is a sufficient guide for moral action in any situation. But, significantly, Kant derives the 'rule of universalizability' from Practical Reason; a universalizable action is therefore not only moral but *rational* as well. Similarly, an action which contradicts the rule is immoral and irrational.

By and large, Hegel accepts Kant's line of argument and differentiates between the willing which is rational and the willing which is not rational. The willing which is not rational will be self-seeking, insistent on privilege and self-exemption; it may be encroaching and exploitative. Rational willing, by contrast, is of the opposite nature: it is also *genuinely* social in the sense of being productive of smooth social continuity. To put it differently, rational willing enables *organic* co-existence.

Since the willing which is rational is also free or freedom-producing, freedom and reason turn out to be correlated. A social or political structure which is pervaded by a certain mentality, Spirit, will be both free and rational. It is in this sense that Hegel, having ascribed to his notion of the state certain desirable attributes, can call it rational as well. Conversely, it is only the rational type of willing that can bring about and maintain the rational state. When Hegel says that (translated literally) 'it is the walk of God in the world that the state is' (§258A), he is saying metaphorically that the unalienated political condition is the highest thing imaginable.[12]

Concluding Remarks

Hegel thought that his (model of the) state was superior to any other. But as history has since shown, he was too optimistic in his predictions and not clear enough in his semantics. The subsequent course of world politics was to prove that it was not the organic state but its opposite, unconcealable economically-influenced clashes, that would become the order of the day. Marx's pluralism rather than Hegel's harmony came to provide a more fitting account of modern

---

[12] The first substantial rehabilitation of Hegel's political thought in this century occurred in France. Though the existentialists were interested in other aspects as well, great impact was made by Alexandre Kojève's claim that Hegel's political theory was pervaded by radical rejection of the master-slave relation:

Man can be truly 'satisfied', History can end, only in and by the formation of a Society, of a State in which the strictly particular, personal, individual value of each is recognised as such, in its very particularity, by *all*, by Universality incarnated in the State as such; and in which the universal value of the State is recognised and realised by the Particulars as such, by *all* the Particulars. Now such a State, such a synthesis of Particularity and Universality, is possible only after the 'overcoming' of the opposition between the Master and the Slave . . .' (*Introduction to the Reading of Hegel*, (New York, 1969), p. 58).

political life. But Hegel was also too optimistic about the rationality of political actors: he did not take adequate note of the danger that Rousseau's 'Legislators', intent on the enforcement of social cohesion in the name of co-operation, might translate the desirable freedom of the organically self-regulating community into the unfreedom of the distinctly authoritarian state.

At the theoretical level, Hegel's language turned out to be singularly open to misconstruals. It was easy to accept the praise accorded by Hegel to his philosophical notion of the state and apply it wholesale to the actual Prussian state of Friedrich Wilhelm III, though, as Avineri has argued, 'the reformed, enlightened Prussia of von Stein and Hardenberg' was far more liberal than the Prussia of Friedrich Wilhelm IV and his Divine Right of Kings. Indeed, under the latter – a fact not noticed by Hegel's critics – Hegelian heritage was being stamped out root and branch.[13] Even more open to misunderstanding was Hegel's critique of incipient liberalism: whereas Hegel attacked the liberal principle for its failure to differentiate between selfish and non-selfish actions, he was erroneously taken to reject individual freedom altogether. This very serious confusion snowballed: Hegel was said not only to glorify the state but to advocate a state which was narrowly nationalist as well; he was supposed to regard war as ethical and thus to bless militarism. This image of Hegel the reactionary was initially fostered, among others, by the contemporary Schopenhauer for reasons of personal animosity, a few decades later it was reinforced as a virtue by those who looked for support for their nationalist and militarist policies, and was eventually enshrined by historians who needed clear-cut prototypes. The Hegel-legend reached its climax in Karl Popper's passionate charge that Hegel was most consciously pitting New Tribalism against the Open Society.[14]

After the old and more recent controversies have subsided, and with the benefit of greater access to Hegel's own words, it is now possible to see the structure and effects of his political thought with greater clarity. However mistaken he was in his predictions and however short-sighted he was with respect to the feasibility of the organic state, the power of Hegel's political thought may be said to reside rather in his systematic reflections on freedom and rationality. He was right to point out that the traditional notion of freedom, so fashionable not only in everyday life but in theoretical treatises as well, is a defective theory resulting in the paradox of freedom.

---

[13] See Shlomo Avineri's articles reprinted in Walter Kaufmann (ed.), *Hegel's Political Philosophy*, (New York, 1970). This volume contains several debates on Hegel's alleged worship of the state, nationalism, militarism, anti-liberalism, etc.

[14] See Karl Popper, *The Open Society and Its Enemies*, (London, second ed., 1952) vol. II, pp. 27–80.

Hegel's own analysis in which he commences not with the desirability of being able to do what one likes, but with the mentality ('the will') which may be egoistic or non-egoistic, social or non-social, has given a much clearer explanation of what does and what does not promote freedom, what maintains and what hinders organic co-operation.

Similarly, Hegel's view of what is rational dethroned abstract Reason and placed it among other facts of everyday life. Hegel's account of rationality is more solid than those theories which equate rationality with efficiency or success and which may then have to admit that the very same action which is rational with regard to one aim may be irrational with regard to a different aim. Hegel's account removes the essential relativity of such theories and recognizes rationality as something qualitative or substantial, a disposition which retains its distinctive nature regardless of circumstances. Even if nothing else were to survive from Hegel's political philosophy, his analyses of freedom and reason are still incisive and challenging.

Further Reading

Hegel, G.W.F. *Philosophy of Right*, tr. with notes by T.M. Knox, (Oxford, 1942).

Hegel, G.W.F. *Political Writings*, tr. by T.M. Knox, with an Introductory Essay by Z.A. Pelczynski, (Oxford, 1964).

Hegel, G.W.F. *Natural Law*, tr. by T.M. Knox, with an Introduction by H.B. Acton, (Pennsylvania, 1975).

Hegel, G.W.F. *System of Ethical Life and First Philosophy of Spirit*, ed. and tr. by H.S. Harris and T.M. Knox, (New York, 1979).

Shlomo Avineri, *Hegel's Theory of the Modern State*, (Cambridge, 1972). An excellent exposition and commentary.

Bernard Cullen, *Hegel's Social and Political Thought*, (Dublin, 1979). Very useful, though stresses the development of Hegel's thought.

Michael B. Foster, *The Political Philosophies of Plato and Hegel*, 1935, (repr. New York, 1965). An early but intelligent comparative work.

L.T. Hobhouse, *The Metaphysical Theory of the State: A Criticism*, (London, 1918). An indicting appraisal of Hegel and the British Idealists.

Walter Kaufmann (ed.), *Hegel's Political Philosophy*, (New York, 1970). A lively collection of journal controversies.

George A. Kelly, *Idealism, Politics and History: Sources of Hegelian Thought*, (Cambridge, 1969). Includes material on Rousseau, Kant, Fichte.

Herbert Marcuse, *Reason and Revolution: Hegel and the Rise of Social Theory*, (New York, 1954). Sympathetic, with an analytic exposition of related nineteenth century social theorists.

Z.A. Pelczynski (ed.), *Hegel's Political Philosophy: Problems and Perspectives*, (Cambridge, 1971). A memorial collection of articles on important themes.

Raymond Plant, *Hegel*, (London, 1973). Solid, with some emphasis on Hegel's development.

Manfred Riedel, *Between Tradition and Revolution: The Hegelian Transformation of Political Philosophy*, (Cambridge, 1984). Competent and instructive.

Joachim Ritter, *Hegel and the French Revolution*, (Cambridge, Mass., 1982). Includes essays on Hegel's ethics and theory of property.

Judith N. Shklar, *Freedom and Independence: A Study of the Political Ideas of Hegel's Phenomenology of Mind*, (Cambridge, 1976). A vivid presentation.

Charles Taylor, *Hegel*, (Cambridge, 1975). A comprehensive treatment with a useful chapter on Hegel's political thought.

Charles Taylor, *Hegel and the Modern Society*, (Cambridge, 1979). Reflections on political and social themes.

Chapter Thirteen
Mill's Liberalism
H.J. McCloskey

J.S. Mill was born in 1806 and died in 1873. He made significant contributions which were recognized as such during his lifetime in most areas of philosophy, logic, epistemology, philosophy of religion, ethics and political theory as well as in areas outside philosophy, most notably economics. Today his writings in ethics and political philosophy receive the most serious attention, *Utilitarianism* and *On Liberty* being extensively studied by professional philosophers, undergraduates and non-philosophers throughout the world. Increasingly his other philosophical writings are becoming matters of interest largely to scholars and historians of ideas.

Mill was no mere academic philosopher although he wrote at a time at which it had become possible to make a career of being a philosopher. He was an active public figure concerned to make contributions to public life and to public debates about matters of national and general concern, this largely through articles, letters, speeches and also through a brief period of office (1865–1868) as a member of the House of Commons. Until the company was wound up in 1858, from the age of seventeen Mill worked as an employee of the East-India Company (initially under his father's supervision), combining that work with his very considerable other activities. Much has been written by Mill himself in the *Autobiography* and by many others of the extraordinary intense yet comprehensive education, compressed as it was into his pre-teen years, to which he was subjected by his father James Mill aided by Bentham and his father's Benthamite friends. Mill at the age of twelve studied Plato's major dialogues, having the previous year been required to help his father in the correction of the proofs of his *History of India*. This education led to his contributions to moral and political philosophy being either determined or coloured by the Benthamite utilitarianism with which his father sought to indoctrinate him, albeit with only partial success. His strange relationship of adoration and subservience, even to an important degree concerning philosophical matters, to Mrs Harriet Taylor whom he first met in 1830 and whom he married in 1851, gave rise to important questions for Mill scholars, and has itself occasioned a rich literature.

Mill's major writings include: *A System of Logic*, *Essays on Some Unsettled Questions of Political Economy*, *Principles of Political Economy*, *On Liberty*, *Dissertations and Discussions*, *Considerations on Representative Government*, *Utilitarianism*, *An Examination of Sir William Hamilton's Philosophy*, *Auguste Comte and Positivism*, *Inaugural Address at the University of St Andrews*, *The Subjection of Women*, *Autobiography*, *Three Essays on Religion*, and *Chapters on Socialism*. Besides the major works on political philosophy, very many essays are of importance. Further the *Memorandum of the Improvements in the Administration of India During the Last Thirty Years, and the Petition of the East-India Company to Parliament* written by Mill is also of interest. The letters especially those to and from Harriet Taylor are also essential reading for scholars.[1]

Mill's Contribution to Political Philosophy

Mill is not in the first rank of political philosophers. Indeed, although his contributions in respect of liberty and the state, democracy, socialism and communism and the equality of women were significant contributions when they were written, only the contributions concerning liberty and the individual remain of real contemporary significance, and this notwithstanding the increasing attention being paid to *The Subjection of Women*. The defence of liberty is of continuing importance even though much of the respect and deference accorded it is simply lip-service to the saint of *liberalism*. Most contemporary liberals today, including those who profess great loyalty to Mill's liberalism, lack Mill's unlimited optimism about the future progress of mankind and favour considerable curtailments of freedom of expression and action for the sake of values such as justice, privacy, truth, well-being and happiness that Mill would not have entertained. As these comments indicate, Mill's concerns in his political writings related to a relatively small range of problems. He sought to state and defend a liberal democratic view of the state and society.

Mill's approach was that of defining the legitimate limits to the state's and society's right to interfere with liberty, and then qualifying his principles with unsystematic, *ad hoc* exceptions, the implications of which are nowhere carefully worked out. Equally

---

[1] Unless otherwise stated, all page references are to the University of Toronto Press, Routledge and Kegan Paul edition of Mill's works.

important, he failed fully to examine the arguments for the opposed views of such notable exponents as Plato, Aristotle, St Thomas Aquinas, Hobbes and Hegel. This and his total unawareness of the writings of his contemporary Karl Marx (who was fully aware of Mill's writings on political economy) greatly coloured Mill's limited coverage. There are important arguments and deep insights; many valuable lines of inquiry are suggested, but the final result falls short of being a carefully worked out political philosophy. Today Mill's defence of liberty has an air of unreality completely separated as it is from a consideration of other rights which are of current concern, those to life, justice and equality, privacy, respect, and the like. The discussion of democracy is very dated and fails to anticipate the major developments in democracy such as the increasing remoteness from the people of government, the strengthening of political parties and the party system, the growth and vast increase in power of the bureaucracy and the development of powerful organized pressure groups including the trade unions that have so concerned political theorists such as J.A. Schumpeter, R.A. Dahl and others.[2]

Mill was a rationalist and a utilitarian who believed that it was possible to plan society, political and social arrangements, social changes and institutions on the basis of values and ideals, chiefly but not exclusively utilitarian. Scholars disagree concerning the version of utilitarianism, hedonistic or ideal, act or rule, that colours his theory; and there is now even a questioning as to whether Mill applied his utilitarianism directly or indirectly, as well as concerning the extent to which he compromised his utilitarianism by reference to other values including justice seen as something distinct from utility.[3] The most plausible interpretation is that Mill was a sophisticated ideal-act utilitarian whose values included knowledge, rational and true belief and self-development, and not simply pleasure and happiness, but that he was prepared to be an inconsistent utilitarian as required by the realities of social life. Although he believed in the possibility of rationalistic planning, he generally favoured a cautious, careful, non-doctrinaire, flexible approach, one given more to compromise and modification on the basis of facts as they are found in the world, than was Bentham's. Consider here his support for a free society and its qualifications, his case for political and full legal equality for women, his more general support for universal franchise, albeit introduced in a cautious, qualified, weighted way, and his insistence that the state plan colonization rather than leave it to

---

[2]   J.A. Schumpeter, *Capitalism, Socialism and Democracy*, (London, 1950), 3rd edn; R.A. Dahl, *A Preface to Democratic Theory*, (Chicago, 1956).

[3]   See J. Gray, *Mill on Liberty: A Defence*, (London, 1983); C.L. Ten, *Mill On Liberty*, (Oxford, 1980), M. Strasser 'Mill and the Utility of Liberty', *Philosophical Quarterly*, 34, 1984.

be developed by individuals. Increasingly, the problems enountered by utilitarian rationalism in practical morality are being appreciated. Those encountered by political utilitarians are even greater. Yet it was as a rationalistic utilitarian that Mill approached the problems of defining the proper sphere of government and the principles defining the rights to liberty of thought, expression, discussion and of action, and what are illegitimate invasions of these rights.

A good deal has been made in recent years of Mill's discussion of the art of life in the *Logic* (Book VI, ch. xii) where he claims that the principle of utility is the ultimate principle of the whole of the art of life, where morality is seen simply to be one branch, with other branches such as prudence and aesthetics.[4] This raises the problem as to the principle(s) that inform morality over and above the principle of utility which informs the whole art of living. It also bears on the issue of state concern for and promotion of morals, as Mill clearly did not see it to be proper for the state to seek to make people lead prudent and noble, admirable lives. Yet in terms of utilitarian ethics, harmful imprudence is immorality, immorality which ought to be prevented by whatever agency, the state or other, that can best prevent it with least cost.

The State and the Individual

On the basis of his ideal utilitarianism Mill argued that the state ought so to act as to maximize good. His general approach is well expressed in the statement in *On Liberty*: 'I regard utility as the ultimate appeal on all ethical questions; but it must be utility in the largest sense, grounded in the permanent interest of man as a progressive being' (p. 224). It is utility in the largest sense that comes to underlie the defence of liberty. He believed that there was a prima facie presumption in favour of the *laissez-faire* view of the role of the state, greater good commonly resulting if the state left the promotion of good to other agencies. Nonetheless, as a matter of principle, Mill claimed that the state was entitled to do whatever was expedient, where the expedient was to be determined by reference to a wide range of goods including the cultivation of self – including moral development, individuality, happiness and liberty as a condition thereof. Hence it was that he observed in the *Political Economy*, after noting the very varied, legitimate (necessary and optional) activities of government, involving as they do authoritative and non-authoritative interference:

> There is a multitude of cases in which governments, with general approbation, assume powers and execute functions for which no

---

[4]   See for example, A. Ryan, *J.S. Mill*, (London, 1974), pp. 104–6.

reason can be assigned except the simple one, that they conduce to general convenience... But enough has been said to show that the admitted functions of government embrace a much wider field than can easily be included within the ring-fence of any restrictive definition, and that it is hardly possible to find any ground or justification common to them all, except the comprehensive one of general expediency; nor to limit the interference of government by any universal rule, save the simple and vague one, that it should never be admitted but when the case of expediency is strong. (*Political Economy*, Book V, ch. i, sn 2, pp. 803–4.)

This view is set out in Mill's other writings, most notably *Representative Government*, *Bentham*, *The Utility of Religion*, and *On Liberty*. Thus he wrote:

A government is to be judged by its actions upon men, and by its action upon things; by what it makes of the citizens, and what it does with them; its tendency to improve or deteriorate the people themselves, and the goodness or badness of the work it performs for them, and by means of them. Government is at once a great influence acting on the human mind, and a set of organized arrangements for public business: in the first capacity its beneficial action is chiefly indirect, but not therefore less vital, while its mischievous action may be direct. (*Representative Government*, ch. 2, p. 392).

Liberty and the Limits to Interference

Mill professed to argue for the fullest freedom of expression but allowed some significant limitations which render this statement far from clear. 'Fullest' is intended to be interpreted by way of contrast with the less full freedom to be accorded to freedom of action. There his position is explained in terms of general principles, that it is never right to coerce a person for his or her own good (the anti-paternalist principle), and that it is never right to interfere with an individual's self-regarding actions, only with harmful other-regarding actions, and then not always (the immunities, self-regarding, other-regarding, prevention of harm principle). (See *Liberty* ch. I, pp. 223–5, ch. V, pp. 292–3; also *Political Economy* V, xi, 2.)

Mill wished to extend a fuller freedom to thought, discussion, and expression of opinion than would be permitted in terms of the self-regarding other-regarding, harm prevention principle, given that expression of opinion is typically other-regarding and that much of the cherished use of free expression is harmful to the interests and well-being of others. However Mill nowhere explicitly sought to explain why expression of opinion did not come under the prevention of harm principle, nor did he offer a clear principle defining legitimate and illegitimate interferences with speech parallel to those he offered concerning action.

Mill's discussion of freedom of action is made difficult because the accounts he offered in terms of the above principles were not in fact those with which he operated. He modified or abandoned the principles whenever greater utility so dictated. Further the accounts of the nature of liberty he explicitly gave in terms of pursuing our own good in our own way (p. 226) and doing what one desires (p. 294) were not that with which he operated, his operational definition being that of self-determination. We are free, when we are capable of being self-determining, where for Mill, self-determination is explained by contrast with coercion, external constraints and interferences, not with absence of internal compulsions and external lacks of facilities and conditions. Thus, in modern parlance, his concept of liberty is the negative concept made more definite than it commonly is. It is that of the tradition of John Locke, Wilhelm von Humboldt, Herbert Spencer.[5] Hence it was that so much that exponents of positive liberty such as D.G. Ritchie, T.H. Green and L.T. Hobhouse seek to justify as enlarging liberty – compulsory education, welfare measures and institutions based on coercive tax, and the like – Mill saw as involving interferences with liberty which are to be justified by reference to their utility in terms of the promotion of other goods.[6]

Freedom of Thought, Expression, Discussion
Although Mill claimed to be defending the right to the fullest freedom of expression he explicitly allowed that 'even opinions lose their immunity, when the circumstances in which they are expressed are such as to constitute their expression a positive instigation to some mischievous act... The liberty of the individual must thus far be limited; he must not make himself a nuisance to other people'. (*Liberty*, ch. III, p. 260.) This statement is commonly interpreted as qualifying free expression by reference to incitement to riot. However, Mill did not confine what he saw as permissible limitations to speech that incited riots. He allowed intolerance of indecent expressions, and, by his acceptance without protest most of his adult life of defamation and libel laws, he seems to have accepted the limitations they impose as also legitimate. Similarly with respect to matters which are *sub judice*.

---

5   See for example John Locke, *Second Treatise of Civil Government*, (1690); Wilhelm von Humboldt, *The Sphere and Duties of Government*, J. Coulthard (trs), (London, 1854), reprinted and published as *The Limits of State Action*, J.W. Burrow (trs and ed.), (Cambridge, 1969); Herbert Spencer, *Social Statics; Man Versus the State*, (London, 1982).

6   D.G. Ritchie, *Natural Rights*, (London, 1894); T.H. Green, *Lectures on the Principles of Political Obligation*, (1882) reprinted with introduction by A.D. Lindsay, (London, 1941); L.T. Hobhouse, *Liberalism*, (London, 1911).

In *On Liberty* Mill bases his case for such a freedom of expression on arguments set out in Chapter 2, namely the infallibility argument, or that from human uncertainty, the argument from rational belief, and that from the value of vital belief. D. H. Monro has argued that Mill rests his case even more heavily on an argument from self-development.[7] Certainly an important argument may be developed from self-development, and it may plausibly be claimed to be implicit in the latter part of *On Liberty*. However, it is nowhere made explicit. These arguments are claimed to hold also in respect of freedom of action but with more qualifications. They will be examined and assessed when treating of freedom in general.

Lovers of liberty of recent times have favoured as legitimate a significant range of limitations to free expression – libel and defamation laws, *sub judice* laws, restrictions by way of wartime censorship for the sake of national security, and, with less general agreement, censorship of pornographic and obscene material. Increasingly liberals have come to favour many more restrictions on free speech. They favour bans on incitement to racial hatred and violence, and in Australia it is presently being urged that it be made a crime even so to speak or write as to cause racist attitudes and actions to occur (and similarly with sexist attitudes and actions by way of discrimination). Advertising that misleads or which simply fosters to an undesired degree harmful self-regarding behaviour is increasingly under control or scrutiny, with proposals to limit even true speech by way of extension of the tort of defamation being seriously canvassed by self-professed Australian liberals. Further controls for the sake of protection of privacy are widely being demanded by self-professed 'Millean' liberals even though such controls constitute very serious incursions into free speech. Such far-reaching controls as are now coming into being would not have been countenanced by J.S. Mill. In assessing his position and the arguments he advances in its support, it is vital to determine whether or not such new restrictions are genuinely defensible, where these restrictions are directed at preventing harm to others and/or protecting the individual from him or her self. The dangers inherent in such far-reaching, all-encompassing harm-prevention and paternalistic controls are very considerable, not least to liberty and the free society.

Freedom of Action

Mill sought to set out what are illegitimate interferences with freedom of action by reference to the anti-paternalist and prevention of harm principles. This attempt has resulted in a good deal of

---

[7]   See D.H. Monro, 'Liberty of Expression: Its Grounds and Limits II', *Inquiry*, 13, 1970.

critical discussion of the meaningfulness of the latter principle, it commonly being argued that no or very few and then only relatively trivial actions are purely self-regarding. Reinterpretations of that principle in terms of legitimate interference being restricted to other-regarding actions which harmfully affect the interests of others as expounded by J.C. Rees and others have been advanced as devices for making Mill's position less implausible.[8] There seems little to be gained by exploring new, more plausible interpretations of the principles if we are to be faithful to Mill's thought or if we are seeking through a study of Mill's writings to formulate a coherent, defensible liberalism. This is because Mill himself saw that a tenable liberalism admits of a great deal of interference with action of kinds not allowed in terms of his principles. Thus Mill allowed significant interferences for the sake of both weak and strong paternalistic protection of the individual against his or her own ignorance, stupidity and weakness, also authoritarian including moral authoritarian interference to make the individual do what is right and be a morally better person, specifically by way of enforcing performance of utilitarian morality, by way of preventing harm and by way of enforcing the carrying out of social obligations based on utilitarian considerations.

Mill's anti-paternalist stance is qualified in a large variety of cases where the individual is either not the best guardian or not the best judge of his own interests. Hence he allowed the legitimacy of coercion to prevent an ignorant person cross an unsafe bridge, coercion of the uneducated, coercion to ensure thoughtfulness about long-term and irrevocable contracts, and coercion to prohibit slave contracts even though the latter may be what individuals rationally wish to enter and also the coercion of social pressure in respect of divorce. The restrictions Mill entertained on the sale of liquor, the operation of gaming houses and of brothels are similarly paternalistic, Mill being concerned that the state protect weak persons where others make it their business to prey on and profit from the weakness of others. His approval of the ban on religious suicides in India is less clear as many such 'suicides' were in fact a result of strong pressure by relatives of the deceased.

A vast range of interferences are deemed legitimate by Mill to prevent harm and thereby to impose utilitarian morality. Harm is widely construed so as to include the causing of suffering to sentient animals, Mill however did not spell out this restriction in any detail in respect of cruel sports nor did he think it through in respect of vegetarianism, legally enforced or otherwise. Bans on offensive, indecent conduct come under the prevention of harm characteriza-

---

8   See J.C. Rees, 'A Re-reading of Mill on *Liberty*', *Political Studies*, VIII, 1960, pp. 113–29 and J.C. Rees, *Mill and his Early Critics*, (Leicester, 1956).

tion, as does the proposal that provided they have no harmful effects means tests be permissible to prevent marriage among the poor who could not support their children, such controls preventing the harm of the mischievous act of having children one cannot support. (This proposal is obviously relevant today where there is overpopulation.) On the other hand, a good deal of harmful conduct is exempt from interference or control, namely the harm that comes from successful, fair competition in examinations, business, and the like, as well as the harm that comes from one's bad example being copied.

Many restrictions on freedom to act as one pleases are specifically noted by Mill as being legitimate, some being tendentiously described as harmful acts of omission. Hence it is that Mill permits the curtailment of liberty to enforce the carrying out of what he calls 'assignable duties', his example suggesting that these are determinate social, morally-based duties such as that of the policeman, of parents to children, and children to aged parents. Coercion to enforce the rendering of specific services to the community, military, jury service, service as a witness, etc. is allowed in this way. For Mill, coercive taxation for the sake of welfare services, culture and other valued goods and not simply for the sake of law and order, constitutes a further legitimate ground for interfering with freedom of action.

Mill's moral paternalism is evident in his protection of the weak against those who prey on their weakness in respect of drink, gambling, fornication with prostitutes, and in his being prepared to deny the vote to the immoral, among whom he included the idle and intemperate. It is also inherent in his imposition of utilitarianism – as shown in the prevention of cruelty to animals and more generally in respect of so-called harmful acts and in his acceptance in *An Examination of Sir William Hamilton's Philosophy* of utilitarian punishment which is designed morally to reform the criminal. What is notably absent from Mill's discussion is any claim that purely private immorality – which for the utilitarian would consist not in homosexuality or the like, but in self-neglect, self-stultifying, self-harming activities such as intemperance and drug taking leading to addiction – should be rendered illegal, Mill seeming to believe such promotion of purely private morality would lack utility. However Mill was not adverse to social pressure operating here. Sympathizers with Mill's liberalism seek to construe such conduct not as immoral but simply as unaesthetic or imprudent on the basis of the comments in the *Logic* about the art of life.

Various of these interferences allowed by Mill as legitimate would violate religious freedom, for example some bans on cruelty to animals, the enforcement of parental assignable duties, compulsory military service. Mill did not explore the problems for liberalism raised by this fact.

Mill's Arguments for Legal and Social Rights to Liberty
The bulk of the utilitarian case for liberalism comes in Mill's detailed
arguments for the state and society according mature and civilized
persons the right to liberty. However the utilitarian defence is either
supplemented by appeal to non-utilitarian ethics including a moral
rights ethics or it needs to be underpinned by way of appeal to a
basic moral right to access to goods. What Mill is concerned to
establish by way of his arguments is not that we have a moral right to
liberty but simply that there are good moral reasons, largely of an
ideal act utilitarian character, for according the social and legal right
to liberty to mature civilized people. The arguments relate to the
goods that will come from the according of liberty, but they seem
also to assume a right to access of basic goods. If Mill is to be
interpreted as seeking to establish the more radical thesis that
there is a moral right to liberty, his argument would be seriously
incomplete without appeal to a more basic moral right of access to
intrinsic goods. Mill's arguments for liberty appeal to the fact that
liberty is a means to, condition or ingredient of goods, and perhaps
also to the claim that it is an intrinsic good in its own right, where the
goods pointed to are true, rational and lively belief, individuality,
self-development, happiness, progress. The arguments set out a
strong presumptive case for liberty but are not as strong as Mill and
his followers suppose them to be.

The infallibility argument, the argument from human fallibility
and uncertainty, that intolerance involves an unjustified claim to
infallible knowledge and hence may deprive mankind of access to
true knowledge, is without doubt Mill's most important argument
for liberty of speech. (See *On Liberty*, ch. 2 especially pp. 229–30.)
Yet the argument is subject to many qualifications. It bears on
religion, politics and morality – the main areas of intolerance – only
if statements in those areas are truly cognitive and such as to admit of
truth and falsity. It rests on a very high evaluation of truth *vis-à-vis*
other goods. Intolerance does not deprive mankind nor even all
members of a community of access to the truth. The argument is a
much more qualified defence of liberty than Mill and his followers
have supposed. Acknowledgement of such qualifications makes
nonsense of Mill's claim that *On Liberty* sets out and vindicates a
single truth. The argument from partial truths is simply an application of this general argument. The argument that freedom of
expression (and action) is necessary for rational belief rests on a
valuing of rationality and rational belief, liberty being claimed to be
an essential condition for this. It too is subject to many qualifications
as is the argument that freedom of expression (and action) is
necessary for vital belief, that without such freedom, beliefs will be
held as dead dogmas.

Mill rightly noted that both freedom of speech and action are

necessary for self-development. However he realized that the people
to whom he wished to accord the fullest freedom of expression were
imperfectly rational, that 'The prospect of the future depends on the
degree in which [the labouring classes] can be made rational beings'.
Mill saw freedom of action in particular as a condition and ingredient
of individuality and self-development. It was in this context that he
stressed the value of what he called experiments in living. And,
although the argument that each is the best judge and guardian of his
own interests was urged in support of related conclusions rather
more than in respect of self-development, it is relevant there also. Of
course the so-called experiments in living are not genuine experiments. The conclusions that can legitimately be drawn from them
are highly tentative and qualified. Similarly, only tentative conclusions can be drawn in respect of the claim that each is the best
judge and guardian of his own interest – Mill acknowledged in the
Political Economy that it is subject to very many qualifications.
Mill's appeal to the educative value of liberty – as in the *Political
Economy*, *On Liberty*, *Representative Government*, and *Subjection of
Women* – holds as Mill himself saw only of civilized adults and then
not always. His claim that liberty contributes to progress and
improvement has always been questionable. Today, given the less
optimistic view about the desirability of what is called progress and
improvement, it would be more widely questioned.

Mill made the strange, indefensible claim that all restraint *qua*
restraint is intrinsically evil, seemingly as the corollary of the view
that liberty is of intrinsic value. Liberty viewed as negative liberty
as it was by Mill, as the absence of interferences with self-
determination, cannot always be of intrinsic value. Nor can that
individuality which exists in a context of negative liberty be seen as
always of intrinsic worth. Mill's claim would have been less indefensible, although still not sound, had he grasped the concept of
positive liberty and had he pressed the value of that individuality
that sprang from the possession and exercise of positive liberty. That
was to be left to be done by later liberals including socialist liberals.

In brief, Mill's arguments collectively constitute an important
group of considerations in support of liberty, albeit that the case they
make out for liberty is one that is even more qualified than Mill and
his followers have supposed. They do not establish that authoritarian
moral legislation, weak and strong paternalistic legislation, legislation to uphold values and to prevent evils, and the use of social
pressure towards these ends may not on occasion be justified if such
measures overall have a utilitarian justification. More important,
unless supplemented by other arguments such as those relating to
respect for persons and for human autonomy, they do not provide an
adequate liberal basis for repulsing the assaults on liberty of the new
human rights moralists, who today seek to have the state impose

their moral preferences under the characterization of protecting human rights, and this by violating that very basic right, the right to free expression and free action. This need for Mill's liberalism to be supplemented by acknowledging the worth of persons and the importance of respect for personal autonomy by reference to the Kantian liberal tradition is all the more essential because of the contemporary disillusionment with liberalism, associated as is that disillusionment with Marxian attacks on the superficiality of liberal theory.

Equality: Mill's Contributions Concerning Democracy, Women and Socialism

Although he was far more egalitarian than the bulk of his contemporaries, by today's standards Mill was a very qualified egalitarian. He was an élitist who believed that natural and moral superiorities should be acknowledged where it was useful that they be acknowledged. At the same time it is clear that he would have had no time for the contemporary egalitarianism of outcome, nor the coercively achieved equal representation of groups in work, education, and elsewhere sought by exponents of affirmative action and reverse discrimination today and even less for equality of wealth. For Mill equality had to be a subordinate value, given the priority he gave to utility and through it to liberty.

Democracy
Mill's approach to democracy was a utilitarian one. For him it was one of a number of possible, equally legitimate constitutions, but one which admitted of being the ideal form of government if the necessary conditions for its flourishing could be brought about. (*Representative Government*, ch. II.) He did not believe these conditions could always prevail, hence he could not favour democracy as a desirable and the only desirable form of government no matter what the conditions. Mill favoured democracy because and in so far as it made for greater self-dependence greater individuality and self-development than did other practicable forms of government, that is, in so far as it improved its citizens, and because under it the individual's and the general interest can better be protected. (*Representative Government*, p. 208.) There is a suggestion of a non-utilitarian argument from justice, that it is unjust to withhold the suffrage unless there are grounds for so doing in terms of prevention of greater evils. (*Representative Government*, p. 469.)

Just as in *On Liberty* Mill saw each person's liberty as deserving of respect when it should be respected on utilitarian grounds, so in his discussion of democracy he sees each person's individuality, self-development and interests as equally deserving of consideration where the desert is cashed in terms of the utility of so respecting such. Hence it was that Mill gave qualified support for democracy, the qualifications being directed at avoiding misgovernment. He saw dangers to good government would come from class legislation (in a pre-Marxist sense of class) and stupidity as well as from pressures that threatened liberty and diversity. He supported gradualism in introducing the franchise, the élitist view that the educated and well-informed should have more than one vote, proportional representation, and no voting rights for the illiterate and immoral. Of these matters, only that concerning proportional representation occasions serious consideration in liberal democracies today. Similarly, today, his concern about sinister interests and class legislation as being likely to result in excessive power coming to the working class reads as naive and pre-Marxian.

A utilitarian approaching democratic theory as did Mill would today be concerned with very different issues. He would be concerned with the way democracies are much less aptly to be called popular governments, with the immense power of the bureaucracy, with the role of political parties, and with the great influence exercised by pressure groups of which trade unions are but one important kind. Not the least problem facing democracies today is that of making elected governments responsive to and responsible to the electors.

Women

At the time Mill was writing, the political, legal and social status of women was grossly inferior to that of men, and it was to combat this that he wrote. His writings in this area are those which met with least favour in his day. Until today they have been viewed rightly as philosophically minor works, notwithstanding their social importance. *The Subjection of Women* reads as a laboured defence of the obvious on a much narrower front than many feminists today deem it important to develop their case. Mill's arguments are a mixed bag, some being *ad hominem*, others of more interesting kinds, some being from liberty and equal liberty, others from justice, and others again from utility *simpliciter*. Mill rejected the argument for inequality in marriage from the need for a head in any community, noting that in ordinary business partnerships there is equality not subordination. Mill's most severe critic James Fitzjames Stephen nowhere met this contention.[9] Mill rejected the claim that the rule of

---

[9] See James Fitzjames Stephen, *Liberty, Equality, Fraternity*, (London, 1873) reprinted Cambridge, 1967.

men over women is not like slavery since women consent to their role, pointing out that many women do not freely consent to it. More interestingly, he argued that the burden of proof lay with opponents of equality, there being an *a priori* presumption in favour of freedom and impartiality. Here he presumably meant to draw on his arguments for liberty which he saw as applying equally to women as to men.

Other significant arguments relate to the claims of justice and not simply utility. Thus the appeal 'Each is the best judge and guardian of his own interest' is pressed not simply as part of the argument from liberty and self-development but also as an argument from justice, the suppressed premiss being that it is unjust to regulate the affairs of others contrary to their interests. (Everyman edition, p. 234.) This is advanced as the fruit of 1,000 years experience. What truth the argument possesses springs from the fact stressed in the Speech, Admission of Women to Electoral Franchise, 1867, that women are not (natural) servants, nor are they to be classed with children, fools and lunatics, they being in a significant sense equal with men. However, the key arguments from justice rest on the premiss, accepted also by Mill's opponents, that equals ought to be treated equally, unequals unequally in relevant respects, this premiss being explicitly accepted in *Thoughts on Parliamentary Reform*, 1859 thus:

> If it is asserted that all persons ought to be equal in every description of right recognized by society, I answer, not until all are equal in worth as human beings. It is a fact, that one person is *not* as good as another; and it is reversing all the rules of rational conduct, to attempt to raise a political fabric on a supposition which is at variance with fact. (p. 323.)

This in turn rests on appeals to claims that women, some women at least, are equally intelligent and able as men (p. 235), that women are naturally equal with men, the differences that are observable being due to education and circumstances (p. 269), that they are suited to different jobs but that some women are fit for duties of political office (pp. 267–9). Mill observes that 'As long therefore as it is acknowledged that even a few women may be fit for these duties, the laws which shut the door on those exceptions cannot be justified by any opinion which can be held respecting the capacities of women in general'. That is, it is illicit to argue from averages – even if true – to conclusions about all women. These and other arguments from justice are important being, as they are, arguments from the possession of relevant capacities, mental ability, temperament, physical abilities, and the like, to a demand for equality of recognition and treatment in respect of legal and political opportunities and status.

They parallel Plato's argument for fully opening the guardian and auxiliary classes to women.

Thus Mill's more impressive arguments for equalities for women are by no means thorough-going egalitarian arguments. If applied on the basis of a recognition of human differences they would dictate inequalities, not inequalities based on sex, race or creed, but inequalities based on relevant capacities and abilities. This is relevant to how Mill would react to today's affirmative action, reverse discrimination programmes and to the ethics underlying equality of outcome ideologies. Mill clearly attributed great importance to the socialization of women as women as relevant to their actual and likely achievement, and he favoured changes so that women were not to be 'deformed', disadvantaged by their education, although he acknowledged that we could not know what was the true nature of women. On the other hand, he did not and could not favour the coercion and denial of opportunities to some that are favoured by exponents both of weaker affirmative action and reverse discrimination programmes in terms of targets and quotas for representation of disadvantaged groups. All Mill argued for was that women should not be disadvantaged by their socialization. It is relevant to note here that unlike later liberals such as Hobson, Tawney and Laski, Mill did not see poverty and lack of education and the socialization that went with both as disadvantaging in ways that made it the business of the state to interfere to bring about something nearer to real as distinct from mere legal equality of opportunity.[10] Similarly, he did not and would not opt for coercive action to counter the disadvantaging caused by the socialization of women, even less would he deny liberty to many to bring about the desired quotas or proportional representation of women in work and education.

Socialism

Mill was never a socialist although in the *Autobiography* he claimed to have become one. He took seriously socialist and communist theories most notably Owenism, Fourierism, Saint-Simonianism but not Marxism, (he being unaware of Marx's writings) observing in the *Political Economy* that socialism had now become irrevocably one of the leading elements in European politics (IV, vii, 5). His writings therefore probably contributed towards advancing the cause of socialism and making it more acceptable among liberal thinkers. Given Mill's rationalism and utilitarianism this response to socialist theories is not surprising. Like the socialists Mill rejected all idea of

---

[10] See J.A. Hobson, *The Crisis of Liberalism*, (London, 1909), H.J. Laski, *A Grammar of Politics*, (London, 1925), and R.H. Tawney, *Equality*, (London, 1931).

a natural right to private property and believed that property rights must be assessed in terms of their overall utility. In estimating utility Mill stressed the value of liberty, individuality, self-development and the goods they make possible. He feared the oppressiveness of public opinion under communism and seemingly to a lesser degree, socialism, asking whether 'there would be any asylum left for individuality of character; whether public opinion would not be a tyrannical yoke; whether the absolute dependence of each on all, and surveillance of each by all, would not grind all down into a tame uniformity of thoughts, feelings, and actions'. (*Political Economy*, II, i, 3, p. 209.) On this basis, and on the basis of the claim that the principle of private property had never yet been given a fair trial in any country (*Political Economy*, II, i, 3, p. 207), Mill opted for private property and hence for capitalism. However he did not accept uncritically the gross inequalities of wealth of his day but proposed controls on rights of inheritance which he hoped would eliminate extremes of wealth.

Whilst Mill's discussion of socialism contains a good deal of worthwhile material the overall argument is quite inadequately thought out and even more inadequately researched. Mill completely failed to appreciate the insights that have made Marxism an influence on political and economic thinking since his day, there being scant understanding of the importance of economic power and of class in the Marxist sense in Mill's works. This, in spite of the formal noting of the evils of capitalism in *Political Economy*, Book II, ch. i, is associated with a complacency verging on insensitivity for the sufferings wrought by capitalism, which contrasts sharply with his passionate espousal of the cause of liberty and equality for women on the one hand, and on the other hand with the deep concern and compassion for the victims of capitalism so evident in the writings of such contemporaries as Charles Dickens and Karl Marx.

Further Reading

Works by Mill Reprinted by University of Toronto Press and Routledge Kegan Paul

Volume I	*Autobiography* and Literary Essays
Volumes II, III	*Principles of Political Economy*
Volumes IV, V	Essays on Economics and Society
Volumes VII, VIII	*A System of Logic*
Volume IX	*An Examination of Sir William Hamilton's Philosophy*
Volume X	Essays on Ethics, Religion and Society (contains *Utilitarianism*)
Volume XI	Essays on Philosophy and the Classics

Volumes XII, XIII   The Earlier Letters 1812 to 1848
Volumes XIV, XV,   The Later Letters 1849 to 1873
  XVI, XVII
Volumes XVIII, XIX   Essays on Politics and Society (contains *On Liberty*,
                     and *Representative Government*)

Major Writings about J.S. Mill's Philosophy

Anschutz, P., *The Philosophy of J.S. Mill*, Oxford, 1953.
Britton, K., *John Stuart Mill*, London, 1953 reprinted, New York, 1969.
Cowling, M., *Mill and Liberalism*, Cambridge, 1963.
Gray, J., *Mill On Liberty: A Defence*, London, 1983.
Himmelfarb, G., *On Liberty and Liberalism*, New York, 1974.
McCloskey, H.J., *J.S. Mill: A Critical Study*, London, 1971.
Ryan, A., *J.S. Mill*, London, 1974.
Ten, C.L., *Mill On Liberty*, Oxford, 1980.

Chapter Fourteen

Marx, Communism and Anarchism

Eugene Kamenka

Socialism has been presented as an age-old yearning, movement or theory, a protest against inequality and injustice, a longing for rational co-operation and the brotherhood and sisterhood of all human beings, an elevation of the common social good over sectional interest and the individual avarice and self-seeking of rulers and ruled alike. People have looked back to a golden age of peace and perfect co-operation; they have constructed recipes for a perfect moral commonwealth and sketched laws that would produce utopian societies and utopian human beings; they have believed that the Second Coming of Christ and/or the Rule of the Saints would introduce the Millennial Society in which all men and women would be selfless and just.

Nineteenth and twentieth century socialists and communists look back on these earlier yearnings, movements and projects with qualified approval, as inadequate and often unrealistic adumbrations of their own later views. Nevertheless, we can understand socialism and communism clearly and properly only if we realize that they are specific historical movements developing in the first half of the nineteenth century in Europe as a critique of the new European industrial society in the light of the ideals of rationality and human emancipation preached by the eighteenth century European Enlightenment and by the French Revolution through its slogan 'Liberty, Equality, Fraternity'. The eighteenth century, which invented the concept of happiness as the end of human government and human society, also invented the concept of progress. Its leading radical thinkers came to believe that education, science and reason enabled people to cast off the shackles of political, religious and legal superstition and bondage, to become free and to develop human capacities in a spirit of rational cooperation in which the common happiness would replace private gain and the maintenance of coercive power as the end of government. Saint-Simon and his followers, indeed, believed that the new scientific age of industrial production would see the end of coercion by human beings against other human beings; the government of men would be replaced by the administration of things.

The French Revolution consummated and symbolized the political birth of the modern era. It gave the world the very idea of Revolution as a natural and inescapable part of social progress. The world that followed the French upheaval of 1789 stood, as Hegel saw, under the category of the *Incomplete*. Countries and kingdoms were entering upon a new *Becoming*. The French Revolution was the seedbed of most of the important *isms* of the nineteenth and twentieth centuries – of liberalism and democracy, of nationalism, socialism and communism – the last two developing out of the extreme radical wings of French revolutionary clubs and societies. For the implications of the slogan 'Liberty, Equality, Fraternity' went beyond the political and legal liberty and equality that the French Revolution had proclaimed: they raised sharply and urgently the question of social, especially economic, equality and justice.

As Marx was later to argue in his contributions to the *Deutsch-französische Jahrbücher* of 1844 (see E. Kamenka, ed., *The Portable Karl Marx*, Harmondsworth, 1983, pp. 96–124 or other translations), the political liberation brought about by the French Revolution also consummated the economic liberation of an actual or nascent class of industrial property owners and financial investors and speculators from the social (political, moral, religious and legal) restraints of the feudal order; it divided society even more sharply into those who labour and those who live off that labour without working themselves. It abstracted and atomized human beings in society, converted them into buyers and sellers in a market and made their very labour power a commodity. It tore an increasing number of people out of the bondage but also the security of the village community and herded them into the impersonalized life, the appalling social conditions, the barracks of the new industrialized towns in which people lived in increasingly sharp competition with each other, gaining their livelihood at other people's expense or going to the wall. To these people, individual legal and political freedom in the end meant very little unless it was accompanied by a chance to attain that ownership of property which alone could guarantee independence and economic security.

Socialism, therefore, emerges in the 1820s and 1830s – especially in England and France – as a critique of the new industrial society with its new forms of economic inequality and increased economic power of some people over others. It insists that the problem of the new society is not only a problem of abstract legal and political equality but a problem of economic organization and of *class* and rights. It proclaims that the social ramifications of property have become so great that property should no longer be seen as a private function or right. It must be subordinated to a concept of the common social good. Socialists defined themselves as people who pursued and stood for that common social good in the conditions of modern industrial society against private property and economic individualism. Communists, until Karl Marx gave the term a new and more specific meaning in *The Communist Manifesto*, which he wrote with Friedrich Engels in 1848, were defined by their more frank and open identification with the proletariat, with the vast mass of society who labour and have nothing. Where the socialists talked about the common social good, the communists, arising out of Babeuf's Conspiracy of Equals in the closing phases of the French Revolution, spoke and acted – often violently – on behalf of the interests of the poorest sections of society.

Karl Marx (1818–83) was the greatest thinker in the history of socialism. He gave socialism its intellectual respectability and its theoretical self-confidence. From diverse sources and materials, from phrases in radical pamphlets and slogans at socialist meetings, from German philosophy, French politics, and English economics, he created a socialist system of thought, a total socialist critique of modern society. He refined and systematized the language of socialism; he explained and expounded the place of socialism in history; he reconciled, or seemed to reconcile, its conflicting hopes and theoretical contradictions. His work – itself a process of self-clarification – set the seal upon the transition from the romantic revolutionism of the 1840s to the working-class movement of the 1860s, 70s, and 80s. It fused into a single body of connected doctrine moral criticism and economic analysis, revolutionary activism and social science, the longing for community and the acceptance of economic rationality and industrial progress. It clothed the interests and demands of a still largely nascent and despised working class in the dignity of a categorical imperative pronounced by history itself. It laid the foundations for a critical account of the birth and development of modern society. Marx correctly recognized the world-historical importance of the French Revolution and the Industrial Revolution. He saw that, in Europe at least, they were part and parcel of one development. He realized that they had inaugurated a new era in history, an era in which civil society – the world of industry and trade – had moved to the centre of the stage and was being driven by violent internal compulsions to ever more rapid change and expansion. Marx recognized more clearly than others the birth of modern society and the tensions and conflicts involved in its internal dynamic. Since the Napoleonic wars set the seal of destruction upon the old order and the old regime in Europe, we have been living through a continuing crisis which has spread outward from Europe until it engulfs the world. Marx was the first and in many respects the greatest student of that crisis. His predictions have proved at least partly false; his presentation of the issues may now seem far too simple; but he saw where many of the issues lay, not only of his time but of ours. The study of modern society still cannot bypass the work of Karl Marx.

Marxism as social theory is one thing and Marxism as ideology another, though the two are, of course, related in a variety of interesting ways. The great success of Marxism, it has often been claimed, came when armed workers burst into the streets of Petrograd in October/November 1917 and established the first Marxist government in the world. That government has since grown from strength to strength and Communist states now govern half the population of the world. Yet only some – and probably a minority of – socialists have seen this as a realization of Marx's predictions and a vindication of his hopes. The Communist revolutions took place at first sight in defiance of Marx's theory of history and not in accordance with it. The practical actions and theoretical proclamations of the governments that were brought into being have seemed to many a far cry indeed from Marx's vision of a free co-operative and ultimately stateless workers' community, in which class-division, alienation and all forms of coercion would be totally overcome. If Marxism is one of the most important theories of the birth, inner tensions and future development of modern society, it is also one of the most controversial. It is attacked from without, and significantly amended from within. Like Christianity, it has many conflicting tendencies, spokesmen and sects that quarrel bitterly with each other.

'My writings, whatever shortcomings they may have, have one characteristic: they form an artistic whole', Marx wrote to Engels as he was preparing the first volume of *Capital* for publication. This is true not only of Marx's writing taken individually; it is true of his creative output taken in its entirety. The outstanding thing about Marx's career as a thinker was the powerful logical thrust lying at the centre of his work, the way in which he expanded and developed his views, assimilating the most diverse materials and remoulding them to suit his system and his purposes.

In the early 1840s Marx was under the influence of Rousseau, Feuerbach and the Left Hegelians. He stood for a rational society, in which man would be free and self-determined as a *social* being, co-operating rationally and spontaneously with his fellows, mastering nature and social life instead of being mastered by them. In 1843, on becoming more seriously aware of (French) socialism and of Moses Hess's work on money, Marx proclaimed that such a transformation of society had for its prime targets the two fundamental conditions (and expressions) of human *alienation*: money and the state. The struggle against these required not only philosophy but also 'a material weapon' – the proletariat – the class outside existing society and its existing system of property which was fitted by its very deprivation to overcome the whole apparatus of social and economic coercion and to inaugurate the society of freedom.

In his *Economic and Philosophical Manuscripts of 1844*, and somewhat more concretely and less philosophically in the *German Ideology* a few years later, Marx spelled out his view that the division of labour, accompanied by private property, made men the slaves of a social system of production instead of being its master; it forced each man to play out a certain role, to subordinate himself to his needs and to the abstract economic role of money necessary to satisfy those needs; it brought man into conflict with other men, forced men to live at each other's expense. This alienation was monstrous and dehumanizing, but it was also a necessary step in the history of mankind. If the division of labour made men slaves to the process of production, it also enabled them to realize and perfect their powers. The process of production, developing by its own logic, was the great moulder and educator of mankind. The 'material' life of men, Marx discovered between the spring and autumn of 1845, shaped their political institutions, ideas, conceptions, and legal systems. The history or 'pre-history' of man in the period of alienation and consequent class struggle was to be understood through economic history or, at least, through the history of material production.

By 1848 when Marx and Engels published the *Communist Manifesto*, Marx had worked out the outlines of a general view that has come to be almost inextricably linked with his name. The introduction of tools, the division of labour, and the rise of private property divide men into social classes, primarily into the class of exploiters, who own and administer means of production, and the class or classes of the exploited, who actually work and produce. Each class of exploiters – slave owners, feudal lords, capitalist merchants and manufacturers – comes upon the arena of history as the bearer of economic enterprise, as a class developing new techniques of production and increasing human capacities. But the class relationships in a social system tend to be rigid, whereas the productive forces are constantly developing. There comes a time, at each stage, when the class that inaugurated and developed a given mode of production becomes a fetter upon further development and is swept aside by revolutionary change. Thus slave owners give way to feudal landlords and feudal landlords give way to the bourgeoisie. The state that pretends to represent the *general* social interest is in fact representing a *sectional* interest, safeguarding the social and political conditions congenial to the ruling class.

The alienation and 'contradiction' expressed in the class struggles of history is oppressive and dehumanizing, but it is nevertheless necessary for the development of economic and human potentialities, for progress. Thus, in the *Communist Manifesto*, Marx and Engels recognize fully the historic role of the bourgeoisie in developing human productivity and capacities, in tearing down privileges, superstitions, and national barriers:

> The bourgeoisie, by the rapid improvement of all instruments of production, by the immensely facilitated means of communication, draws all, even the most barbarian, nations into civilisation. The cheap prices of its commodities are the heavy artillery with which it batters down all Chinese walls, with which it forces the barbarians' intensely obstinate hatred of foreigners to capitulate. It compels all nations, on pain of extinction, to adopt the bourgeois mode of production; it compels them to introduce what it calls civilisation into their midst, i.e., to become bourgeois themselves. In one word, it creates a world after its own image...
>
> The bourgeoisie, during its rule of scarce one hundred years, has created more massive and more colossal productive forces than have all preceding generations together. Subjection of nature's forces to man, machinery, application of chemistry to industry and agriculture, steam navigation, railways, electric telegraphs, clearing of whole continents for cultivation, canalisation of rivers, whole populations conjured out of the ground – what earlier century had even a presentiment that such productive forces slumbered in the lap of social labour?[1]

The bourgeoisie, however, is also doomed. The 'inner logic of capitalism' – economic forces independent of the will of man – will produce the breakdown of the whole system of private property and production for a market; it will raise in its stead the socialist-communist society of conscious co-operation and rational planning. Then production will be *socially* controlled and directed toward use instead of profit. Man will cease to be the *object* of history, the slave of a productive process that he himself created, and will become master of himself, society, and nature. Human relations, instead of being determined by forces beyond man's individual control, will assume the aspect of rational and intelligible relations; they will no longer be 'mystified' – concealed from the consciousness of the actors involved through their abstraction from their real context and their real purpose. Men will act as conscious and co-operative members of a *community* and will cease to live and act as individuals existing at each other's expense.

The process by which the collapse of capitalism would come about was sketched by Marx in a number of earlier works – in the

---

[1] Eugene Kamenka (ed.), *The Portable Marx*, (Harmondsworth, 1983), p. 208.

Communist Manifesto, in *Wage-Labour and Capital*, and in the *Contribution to the Critique of Political Economy* – but it was in the first volume of *Capital* that Marx presented what seemed to many to be the *scientific proof* that capitalism must collapse. Economic systems have their own laws; those who participate in them must play out their allotted roles or perish. The function of the capitalist is to make a profit; if he ceases to make a profit, he ceases to be a capitalist and is replaced by another. But the capitalist can make profit only out of the exploitation of labour, and Marx thought he could show, from Ricardo's labour theory of value, that this search for profit, in capitalist conditions, would lead to collapse.

Value, Marx argued, was congealed labour. The capitalist's profit – surplus value – therefore could only be created by the labour he employed. The worker in capitalist society does not sell the *product* of his labour, but his *capacity* to work. What the labourer produces belongs to his master; what he is paid for is his *labour* and that alone. The capitalist therefore does not pay the worker the value of what he produces; he pays the worker only what is needed to keep the worker alive to produce. The difference between the subsistence wage paid to the worker and the values produced by him is surplus value, on which the capitalist's profit depends. If in a ten-hour day the worker works for six hours to produce the equivalent of his subsistence, then in the remaining four hours he produces surplus value, profit for the capitalist. The fierce competition of capitalism and what Marx believed to be a falling rate of profit due to the increased use of machinery will force the capitalist to exploit the worker even more viciously, to bring his wages nearer and nearer to the level of bare subsistence. The capitalist will be able to do this because the increased use of machines and the increasing proletarianization of middle-men and artisans create a growing reserve army of the unemployed – a miserably dependent potential labour pool that helps to depress wages and to prevent palliative action by trade unions. Meanwhile, however, capitalist competition leads to the concentration of capital in fewer and fewer hands through the bankruptcy of the weaker, less ruthless, and less efficient. Society is split and simplified into two classes, each recognizing its interests with increasing clarity:

> Along with the steady decrease in the number of capitalist magnates who usurp and monopolize all the advantages of this development, there grows the extent of misery, oppression, servitude, degradation and exploitation, but at the same time, there arises the rebellious indignation of the working class which is steadily growing in number, and which is being disciplined, unified, and organized by the very mechanism of the capitalist method of production. Ultimately, the monopoly of capital becomes a fetter upon the mode of production which has flourished with it, and under it. Both the centralization in a

few hands of the means of production, and the social organization of labour, reach a point where their capitalist cloak becomes a strait-jacket. It bursts asunder. The hour of capitalist private property has struck. The expropriators are expropriated.[2]

The collapse of capitalism, Marx appeared to be saying, was inevitable. The very steps that capitalists took to overcome their difficulties only deepened and intensified the crisis. As the rate of profit falls, the capitalist attempts to overcome his difficulties by extending the scope of production and by making ever-increasing use of machinery. He squeezes out the middle-man and reduces the number of workers in his employment; he thus extends production at the same time as he contracts the market. The upshot is overproduction and underconsumption – crisis, the paralysis of productive forces, and the wastage of capital. It becomes evident that the bourgeoisie can no longer produce the goods and can no longer feed its slaves. Revolution – the seizure of the means of production by the workers themselves and the placing of production under social control – ensues.

The immediate motive force of all this, in Marx's mature system, is the class struggle. The concept of class moved to the forefront of Marx's work in 1843–44 and remained there to the end of his life.

Marx, in the Victorian tradition, had universal aspirations. In fact, he never completed a careful and systematic exposition of any major aspect of his theory. His main work on the economic foundations, structure and tendencies of capitalism and their ramifications was planned to occupy six large volumes. Only one was completed in his lifetime and it was sent to the printer before Marx was fully persuaded that it was ready. The other two volumes of *Capital* were constructed out of Marx's notes and drafts after Marx's death by his life-long collaborator, Friedrich Engels, who was a nicer, more practical and in many ways very gifted man, but who stood to Marx in the relationship of a senior and respected disciple who did not always fully grasp the subtlety and complexity of the Master's thought. Most of Marx's writings were polemical; much of the work that has aroused most interest in recent years, from the *Economic and Philosophical Manuscripts* of 1844 to the *Outline Draft of the Critique of Political Economy* (the *Grundrisse*) of 1857–58 are incomplete drafts and notes, published long after his death and not known to Marx's earlier disciples. A careful study of Marx's work reveals some fundamental shifts in approach, from the philosophical to the political to the economic, though the underlying thrust toward a society of human self-determination and rational co-operation is constant. It also reveals tensions and 'contradictions' that result from

---

[2]   Eugene Kamenka (ed.), *The Portable Marx*, op. cit., pp. 492–3.

elaborations and departures that seem to contradict his general theory. Historically, these tensions and contradictions have expressed themselves in many Marxisms, some emphasizing one side of the Master's work, others emphasizing another. Recent Marx scholarship and even Marxist thinking are becoming increasingly aware of the tensions, complexities and contradictions in his thought. Many of those in the West today who call themselves his followers have elevated attitudes and concerns not based in Marx but derived from contemporary sociology, historiography, philosophy, moral theory and even economics and then try to reconcile them with Marxism. The 'philosophy' of Marxism was based for a long time on philosophical works published by Engels in the last years of Marx's life and after Marx's death. Their authority, long elevated into dogma by Soviet Marxism and the international communist movement, has declined sharply in recent years, when competing interpretations of Marx outside communist countries are not so sharply denounced and persecuted as heresies.

Despite the complexity and varied character of Marx's writing, certain conclusions and methodologies to be found in them have been seen as central to Marxism.

The *stage theory of history* was long seen to provide the basis for and the guarantee of success for socialist revolutions and the socialist movement. The constant expansion of human production and productive capacities led by its internal logic and internal requirements to the necessary and inevitable passage from primitive communism to slave-owning society, from slave-owning society to feudalism, from feudalism to capitalism, then from capitalism to socialism. Within socialism, there would be two stages: an initial stage in which the dictatorship of the proletariat would exercise coercive power to expropriate and repress the former exploiters and in which state law and state administration would be used to place all the means of production, distribution and exchange under 'social' control, in which labour would be made compulsory and in which the distribution of goods would be organized according to the principle 'From each according to his capacity, to each according to his contribution'. When such a system had been firmly established, when the moral consciousness of socialist society had become a habit, the ultimate communist stage would have been reached. The dictatorship of the proletariat and the state would have withered away and so would law. Decisions would now be reached collectively in working groups and communities; labour would have become a habit and would be consciously engaged in for the good of society. Distribution would be organized on the communist principle 'From each according to his capacity, to each according to his needs'.

Marx's stage theory has been criticized and by some Marxists amended from many points of view. Marx himself speaks not only of slave-owning society but also of the Asiatic mode of production, based, according to him on the need for large-scale irrigation in what he believed to be arid and initially sparsely settled areas such as India and China. Here the organizational and administrative power of the state was necessary to make agriculture possible; private property in land became unimportant, independent economic classes failed to develop. So did real cities, as opposed to military camps and centres that moved with the court and were dependent on it. A vast state bureaucracy administered a system of public slavery, of labour for the state. This concept of Asiatic despotism or the Asiatic mode of production stands in contradiction with Marx's more usual view of the state as representing the ruling class rather than constituting it. It has been a powerful weapon in the hands of those who see present-day communist societies as closer to Asiatic despotism and the Asiatic mode of production than to Marx's vision of a socialism in which the proletariat had come to organize society in its own interest and in that of the vast majority of mankind. It also highlights the role of geographical determinism in some of Marx's thought and brings out the fact that he himself, in his detailed work, did not portray the whole of mankind as passing through the same inevitable and internally determined sequence of stages. It brings out the extent to which Marx saw war as affecting human development – ancient private slavery, as represented by the Roman empire, collapsed directly not only as a result of internal contradictions but through the Frankish conquests which imposed a feudalism arising out of the very early development of private property in north-western Europe, where slavery was never economically important. Similarly, Marx sees Asiatic despotism in Russia as produced by geographical conditions and the Mongol-Tartar conquest as destroying an earlier feudalism. Again, according to Marx, the Asiatic despotisms of India and China are being destroyed by bourgeois penetration, not by internal contradictions. It was the bourgeoisie which created, for the first time, a universal history. Side by side with Marx's unilinear view of human development presented in the *Communist Manifesto*, we find in other works a much more complex multi-linear view in which geography, conquest, population density and even customs and traditions play an important causal role and in which history is no longer dominated everywhere and at all times solely by the development of internal contradictions, or the struggle of classes, within a mode of production.

All this is part of a renewed questioning, even within Marxist circles, of what was long taken to be the foundation of all Marxist theory and practice – the materialist interpretation of history. It has been seen both as a method for studying the general trend of historical events and as a summation of the most general conclusions to be derived from such studies. Critics have complained that it is vague and that Marx's own writings show that it must be constantly modified or ignored in practice. The method begins with the proposition that social being, the material productive life of men lived in relation with each other in society, determines social consciousness, i.e., ideologies and forms of state and social organization. Marx therefore divides social life into an economic or material base, seeing society as an organization for production and reproduction, and an ideological superstructure which 'reflects' that base. The economic base consists of productive forces and relations of production. The productive forces are the tools and skills, including knowledge, all of them socially conditioned, which are available at any given period for the purposes of material production. The relations of production are the manner in which factors of production, tools, and the social product are owned and distributed in any given mode of production. A principal line in Marx's writing suggests that the state of productive forces at a given stage of development determines the relations of production at that stage – a particular form of relations being the most economically efficient for the utilization of the productive forces available. Productive forces, however, develop steadily, incrementally, while relations of production are comparatively fixed at any given stage. This produces the possibility and reality of a growing time lag between the stage of development of productive forces and the relations of production or class-structure of a given society. The irresistible growth of the productive forces then bursts through the integument of the relations of production which have become a fetter on the productive forces. Social and political revolution takes place and a new set of relations of production, a new mode of production, is born.

The superstructure, in Marx's principal line of reasoning, is entirely derivative, to be explained in terms of the economic base. It consists of political and legal forms of state and, at a level still further removed from the material, of political, legal, philosophical, ethical, aesthetic, etc., ideologies. The state and its political and legal structure, according to Marx, represent the will of the ruling class and its method of organizing and securing the relations of production advantageous to it. The state is born with the division of society into classes as a result of the appropriation of tools by one section of society which forces another section to labour and secures a disproportionate part of the return – a line of thought developed by Engels in his *Origin of the Family, Private Property and the State* rather than by Marx. Ideologies, according to Marx, reflect the outlook and interest of specific classes of society, often with a certain time lag. The ruling or dominant ideology of any social period is the ideology of its ruling class.

The language Marx uses in setting out the materialist conception of history as a historical method is not precise and his work contains many concessions and admissions of countervailing influences. Marx speaks of the economic base 'determining' or 'conditioning' the superstructure. Some read this to assert causal determination, others a functional relationship of concomitant variability between super-structure and base without any claim of temporal or causal priority. Yet a third view, allied with structuralism, sees the causality involved as not mechanistic but structural, the causality of a whole determining the nature of its parts. There is further disagreement whether, on the mechanistic causal view, the productive forces determine relations of production which in turn determine the superstructure, or whether the productive forces and the relations of production must be taken together as causal factors. Critics suggest that Marx cannot maintain a one-way determinism from productive forces through relations of production to superstructure, but that his and Engels' conceiving a reaction back (i.e., in a two-way determin-ism) destroys the long-run predictability or inevitability that his theory requires. At the logical level, critics have argued further that superstructural elements – for example, scientific knowledge in the case of productive forces and legal provisions in the case of relations of production – are required for the very definition and characteriza-tion of elements in the base, thus destroying Marx's attempt to separate these elements for the purpose of causal relationships.

The materialist interpretation of history has generated an enor-mous literature and very different interpretations. A general difficul-ty might be expressed this way. Marx, like many nineteenth century theorists, often writes as though a cause produces an effect: water, for example, or oxygen, produces rust. But this is not true. Causal relationships are not relationships between two terms but between three: a cause has to act on something, in a field, to produce an effect. Water produces rust in iron, but not in copper or plastic. We usually single out as *the* cause the new or unexpected element in a situation; there are no causes that are always causes and never effects and no causes that produce effects by themselves without interac-tion. The notion of *the* cause is convention – or theory – laden. If someone throws a bedstead into a swimming pool, we would say that the bedstead, not the water, produces the rust in the water because we do not expect bedsteads to be put into swimming pools, just as we do not expect water to permeate bedrooms. Precisely the same point applies to the origin of feudalism or capitalism, to 'the cause' of a revolution, to the origin of the state or to the reasons for economic backwardness. At least two factors will be necessary; no one will be sufficient. Marxists, in talking about the cause of this or that, constantly smuggle in other factors under the guise of describing or naming the situation in which the change takes place and in the process implicitly admit that many non-economic factors are neces-sary for this development or change. Thus, the separation of powers

in Europe between church, barons and king, the existence of a legal
system which protected rights and grants, even against the king, and
an earlier tradition of private property and the individual were as
important to the development of capitalism as the influx of gold
from the New World or the development of trade and commodity
production. Considerations of this sort have led many Marxists to
deny that the materialist interpretation of history is properly understood as a causal economic determinism; instead of elevating productive forces, determining relations of production, they turn to the
concept of a mode of production, as a systematic structure, in which
constituent processes – political, cultural as well as economic – are
determined or discarded according to the requirements of the system
as a whole. But this, too, raises many problems. Do societies really
form a single system and are all tensions within them to be
understood as consequences of the system as a whole? Is it possible
to claim, as Marxists do claim, that the economic process of
production and reproduction is dominant in the system and that
other structures have only relative autonomy, without falling back
into causal economic determinism? Some recent Marxists have
argued – I would say have conceded to a long-standing criticism of
Marx's theory – that the economic becomes primary only in the
capitalist mode of production and that political and legal arrangements rather than economic ones constituted the definition of
feudalism, just as the political and managerial functions of the state
constituted the defining characteristics of the Asiatic mode of
production.

The ramifications of such criticisms and amendments of Marx's
theory are very great. They throw into question Marx's view that the
state is merely the executive committee of the ruling class, serving its
economic interest. They throw into question the Marxist definition
of classes in terms of their relationship to the means of production
and the neglect of race, sex, nationality, and the intense suspicion of
the peasantry as forming a class only in the sense that a sack of
potatoes constitute a sack. They have led to widespread rejection by
more intelligent Marxists of the reduction of cultural phenomena –
political thought, philosophy, literature and even religion – to crude
notions of class interest and class point of view. Recently, Marxists
have begun to see similar difficulties in treating law as simply the will
of the ruling class. In the process, the systematic coherence of
'Marxism' that was supposed to distinguish Marxist doctrine from
other socialist ideologies is coming unstuck.

Historically, the most important problems of Marxism arose with
the failure of Marx's prediction concerning the fate of capitalism.
The most advanced industrialized countries have not been the most
revolutionary. The proletariat has grown increasingly prosperous
and not poorer; class tensions have not sharpened to the point of

revolution; the 'system' has not proved incapable of feeding its 'slaves'. The state has become ever more significant in modern industrial societies and is not plausibly treated as the executive committee of the bourgeoisie. The fiercest labour conflicts in modern industrial and post-industrial societies are increasingly between unions and the state rather than with private employers. Public ownership has not proved an instant panacea guaranteeing economic efficiency and good labour relations. Further, the proletariat as an industrial working class is becoming a smaller and smaller segment of the society. Service industries, totally neglected by Marx, are becoming more and more prominent, creating new moralities and new attitudes to work. All this has weakened the relevance of classical Marxism to the problems of modern post-industrial societies, leading many 'Marxists' to revert to an earlier conception of socialism as a coalition of the deprived, the scorned and the oppressed, from unskilled labourers to homosexuals, from racial minorities to feminists, or of those who identify Marxism with the growth of the public sector and the increasing power of teachers, public servants, social workers, etc. Certainly, the industrial proletariat, which was to be the vehicle of Marxist revolution and whose competence, collective labour discipline and capacity for rational and increasingly scientific co-operation was to be the foundation of socialist organization, socialist egalitarianism and socialist morality, has failed to play the role Marx predicted and shows no signs of doing so. Some Marxist concepts – the concepts of exploitation and surplus value, the concept of alienation, the emphasis on class conflicts in society (even if classes are now often defined very differently), the notion of internal 'contradictions' in the economic system of uncontrolled capitalism – continue to have some relevance and bite. The Marxist belief that industrial societies will lead the way to socialism, that a planned society based on public ownership will be more egalitarian, more free and more prosperous, and that the state, external coercion and law will wither away once socialism has been firmly established and secured, no longer carries much conviction. For historians, too, nationalism – perhaps the most significant force dominating nineteenth and twentieth century historical and political developments – remains largely ignored (in theory) and not convincingly explained by the Marxian interpretation of history with its primary emphasis on the role of an international class struggle.

The actual influence of Marx and Marxism on the labour movement in advanced industrial societies is a matter of dispute but, by the 1890s, the most Marxist of Western labour movements – German Social Democracy – while proclaiming Marxist orthodoxy was recognizing more and more clearly that the democratic state and the universal ballot provided opportunities for continual improvement in the position of the working masses and an evolutionary path to socialism. Even the orthodox version, represented by Karl Kautsky, emphasized that the development of capitalist society was a natural and necessary process, which would almost automatically end in the collapse of the capitalist system and the coming of socialism. Socialism could not come about until the economic potentialities and cultural progress created by capitalism had been fully exhausted.

While the labour movement in the West, even the Marxist sections of it, increasingly turned to parliamentary activity, economic demands and the socialization of capitalism from within, not preaching direct and immediate revolution, the situation in Russia was gaining more and more revolutionary potential. A momentous development in Marxism was inaugurated by V.I. Lenin (1870–1924). Disgusted with the increasingly unrevolutionary attitudes of Western European Social Democracy and their Russian Social Democratic followers, appalled by the break-up of the Second International as socialist parties voted support for their governments in the 1914 war, convinced that the time for revolution in Russia was ripe if only Russian Marxists would will it and that workers by themselves would never surmount the trade union 'consciousness' that seeks immediate material benefits, he set Marxism on a new course not envisaged by Marx. He did so in two ways: first, he elaborated the theory of consciousness, the belief that the working classes must be led to revolution by a disciplined and in most conditions conspiratorial party of professional revolutionaries, bringing (Marxist) consciousness to the proletariat and the peasantry and making it possible to preach revolution in developing countries such as Russia. Secondly, he argued that the failure of the proletariat in industrialized countries to become poorer or more and more revolutionary was due to the fact that capitalism had entered an imperialist stage and that the super-profits derived from colonial exploitation had made it possible to bribe the proletariat of advanced industrial societies, but only by intensifying exploitation in the colonies and creating great revolutionary potentials there. From then on, in the theory of the Communist International founded by Lenin after the Russian Revolution or Bolshevik seizure of power of October 1917, and in the practice of the Soviet Union and other communist states, the capture of state power and the subsequent transformation of society into an industrialized and state-managed economy has been seen as the principal goal of Marxist endeavour. All communist parties on gaining power have insisted on the primacy of Marxist doctrine and of the Communist Party in guiding state and society and have created systems in which both individuals and institutions are powerless to claim or gain independence from the pervasive control of state and party organs.

The split in Russian Social Democracy between gradualists and more democratic factions that placed their hope on the natural evolution of capitalism, on the growth and increasing consciousness of the proletariat, and on political persuasion (the Mensheviks), and the Lenin-led Bolshevik faction that preached discipline within the party, determined activity to create a single 'revolutionary situation' and make possible a seizure of power, and a strong dictatorship of the proletariat afterward, was paralleled by similar splits in Marxist–socialist movements throughout the world. Since the Russian Revolution, the term communist has described those who accepted Lenin's interpretation of Marxism and the primacy of the Soviet Union as the first 'workers' state', the inevitability of revolution as opposed to evolution and – until the late 1950s – the authority of the Communist Party of the Soviet Union in interpreting Marxist theory and proper political tactics for the world communist movement. The term socialist covered those who believed in a democratic, evolutionary path to socialism, made possible by workers' power at the ballot box and the resultant possibility of legislation to protect workers and promote socialism being passed with widespread popular support. Some socialists claim to be nearer Marx's original vision and concerns than communists whose theory and practice they see as a perversion of Marxism, resulting in a dictatorship over the workers and completely neglecting Marx's concern with freedom and even equality. The split in the world-wide communist movement in the 1950s and the development of a Maoist ideology in the People's Republic of China – reaching its apogee in the Great Proletarian Cultural Revolution inaugurated in 1966 but now repudiated in China – as well as Khrushchev's revelations about the horrors and misuse of personal power in the Soviet Union under Stalin, have led to various more democratic interpretations of Marxism in Western communist parties and among dissidents in communist countries, though they have also greatly weakened the appeal of any kind of Marxist orthodoxy. One principal shift in these developments is a shift from the earlier Marxist belief that public ownership of the means of production, distribution and exchange in modern conditions as a result of revolution by or for the working class would inevitably bring about the socialist/communist commonwealth of freedom and equality, to the recognition (by Italian Marxists, for instance) that such public ownership was a necessary but not sufficient condition. It had to be accompanied by a genuine political and cultural basis for socialist democracy. While Marxists see in the new complex and structural problems of advanced industrial societies a chance for a revitalization of Marxist doctrines that admittedly need some emendation, non-Marxists see as a result of all these developments a disintegration of Marxism. It has proved crude and seriously mistaken as a theory of the future development of the modern industrial society. Its great success, in its communist version, has been as an ideology of revolution and subsequent labour discipline in the interests of industrialization in 'economically backward' societies where only state power can carry through the economic transformation needed for national independence and the modern world. There is no more significant development in this respect than the recognition in some communist societies – notably China – that public ownership, in practice state ownership and control, can be economically stultifying and counter-productive. Marxism, a penetrating analysis of aspects of nineteenth century society in the advanced capitalist world of the time, is now seen by the Chinese and by many other developing countries as not a good guide to the problems of twentieth century economic management and development. At the same time, it might be argued that socialist sentiment, belief in state provision of services and a concern for substantive social equality, are most developed in advanced Western societies.

Anarchism is a movement that became prominent, especially under the leadership of Mikhail Bakunin (1814–76), who knew Marx and first admired then criticized him, at the same time as Marxism. The term is usually used to describe those socio-philosophical and political doctrines whose purpose is to establish justice, equality and fraternity in the whole of society by eliminating all state and social means of coercion. The ultimate communist society portrayed by Marx, in which the state and law would have withered away, differed in no way from the anarchist ideal, except that Marx, perhaps, put greater emphasis on industrial production, while anarchist movements have generally appealed more to peasants and workers of peasant background, caught up in the early stages of industrialization, or to individual workers. The primary difference between communist and anarchist movements lay in the Marxist belief that the future society of communism could only be created by seizing and then using state power and in the Marxist emphasis on stages of economic development, on the necessity of making revolution only when the conditions are ripe. Anarchists, on the contrary, tended to elevate the innate goodness and co-operativeness of mankind, to argue that only the system, or property, or bad education made human beings coerce each other and that this could be righted any time with one blow. Generally, anarchists have been divided into individualist anarchists, who see the anarchist community as an association of free and independent individuals, and collectivist anarchists and anarcho-syndicalists, who share the Marxist emphasis on mass movements and collective ownership, but who reject political activity aimed at capturing the state and often elevate violence as a way of wiping the slate and starting society afresh. English-speaking anarchists such as William Godwin, Josiah Warren, Lysander Spooner, Benjamin Tucker and more recently Herbert Read, have been distinguished from continental anarchists by standing for reform rather than revolution, by stressing the importance and equality of education and by seeking to make room for diversity in personal conviction including religious conviction. Pierre-Joseph Proudhon (1809–65) – of whom Marx was sharply critical – inaugurated continental anarchism as a political movement; he sought the social and economic emancipation of the working man through the establishment of an exchange bank which would purchase commodities from producers against credit notes and supply free credit on the basis of goods put up as security, thus eliminating money and the unjust distribution of income. Mutualism or reciprocal assistance would supplant state coercion and the only compulsory legal norm would be the fulfilment of contractual obligations voluntarily entered into. Prince Kropotkin (1842–1921), and Leo Tolstoy (1829–1910), though less individualistic than Godwin or Proudhon, put a similar stress on voluntary associations and on moral regeneration.

Bakunin, insisting that man achieves consciousness as a human being only through labour in the collective and is personally and intellectually prone to violence, proclaimed that the state must be 'extirpated' together with its ecclesiastic, bureaucratic, military and economic institutions through violent revolution, that marriage and the right of inheritance must be abolished, that children must be educated collectively and the means of production transferred to communes and workingmen's associations.

While Marxists and anarchists shared a rejection of private property and an emphasis on revolution, they began to quarrel bitterly in the First International and the Bakuninists were expelled from the International in 1872. Since then, anarchism has been important for a limited period in Russia and in those countries where Romance languages are spoken, especially France, Italy and Spain, where the anarcho-syndicalist movement spread in conjunction with trade unionism and played a significant role in the Spanish Civil War. The doctrines of the French syndicalist Georges Sorel, with their emphasis on working-class violence, have a certain independent interest, especially in his perceptive criticism of Marxism, but anarchism has always been stronger as a critique of alternative paths to freedom, justice and equality than as a realistic promoter of these on any scale larger than those of utopian colonies.

Further Reading

On Marxism:
S. Avineri, *The Social and Political Thought of Karl Marx*, (Cambridge, 1968). A careful study of Marx's thought as a whole.

G.A. Cohen, *Karl Marx's Theory of History: A Defence*, (Oxford, 1978). The most intelligent though controversial attempt to restate Marx's theory and amend it to met the requirements of modern analytic precision.

A. Jordan, *The Evolution of Dialetical Materialism: A Philosophical and Sociological Analysis*, (London, 1967).

E. Kamenka, *Marxism and Ethics*, (London, 1969).

E. Kamenka (ed.), *The Portable Karl Marx*, (Harmondsworth, 1983). A one-volume selection portraying Marx the man through his letters and contemporary reminiscences and presenting the range and intellectual development of his writings from 1841 to 1882, with a long introduction, chronologies of his life and works and editorial notes, comments and a Reader's Guide.

L. Kolakowski, *Main Currents of Marxism: Its Rise, Growth and Dissolution*, 3 vols, (Oxford, 1978).

G. Lichtheim, *Marxism – An Historical and Critical Study*, 2nd edn, (London, 1971) and subsequently. The best general introduction to the development of Marxism in Europe.

A.G. Mayer, *Marxism: The Unity of Theory and Practice*, (Michigan, 1954), (New York, 1963).

J. Plamenatz, *Karl Marx's Philosophy of Man*, (Oxford, 1975).

J. Plamenatz, *Man and Society: A Critical Examination of Some Important Social and Political Theories from Machiavelli to Marx*, 2 vols, (London, 1963), vol. 2, pp 216ff.

William H. Shaw, *Marx's Theory of History*, (London, 1978). A simpler, more descriptive account that owes something to Cohen.

A. Ulam, *The Unfinished Revolution*, (New York, 1960).

There are numerous editions and translations of Marx's chief works for the student wishing to go beyond a one-volume selection. The *Penguin* Marx Library has reissued in new translation the whole of *Capital*, the *Grundrisse* and multi-volume collections of Marx's philosophical and political writings. Progress Publishers, Moscow, have a three-volume selection of the writings of Marx and Engels.

On Anarchism:

S. Edwards (ed.), *Selected Writings of Pierre Joseph Proudhon*, (Garden City, N.J., 1969).

G.P. Maximoff, *The Political Philosophy of Bakunin*, (London, 1964). A wide-ranging one-volume selection from his writings.

J.R. Pennock and J.W. Chapman, *Nomos XIX: Anarchism*, (New York, 1978). Yearbook of the American Society of Political and Legal Philosophy; the eighteen articles range widely, but put emphasis on contemporary philosophical anarchism and the relationship of anarchism to law and authority.

Chapter Fifteen

Modern Political Ideas: A Dialogue

D.H.Monro

Democrat:
Hobbes was right about one thing: that the State is at bottom a device for enabling each individual citizen to gratify his own desires without interference from other people. This means that there has to be a set of rules or laws which everyone accepts, and some kind of central authority to enforce them.

Liberal:
But surely Hobbes was in favour of dictatorship?

Democrat:
I didn't say he was right about everything. He saw that there had to be some final authority, and he thought that government was more efficient when that authority was in the hands of one man. We have since come to realize that he was wrong about that. Representative democracy makes it possible for the people as a whole to be sovereign.

Left Wing Anarchist:
Hogwash! The sovereign is supposed to be the 'uncommanded commander' in the State. Do *you* feel like an uncommanded commander? I know I don't. How can you, or Hobbes, or anyone else possibly say that the State is a device for satisfying the desires of the ordinary man? A device for frustrating them would be more like it!

Democrat:
When you share your sovereignty with all your fellow citizens, of course you can't be free to do absolutely everything you might like to

do. You have to suppress those of your desires that cannot be satisfied except at the expense of other people. We are inclined to think that people outside society – that is, in Hobbes' state of nature – are absolutely free, have no restraints whatsoever. But of course that isn't true. They have no legal restraints: that is true enough. But they are not free from the restraints imposed by their weakness. In the words of T.H. Green:

> In one sense no man is so well able to do as he likes as the wandering savage. He has no master. There is no one to say him nay. Yet we do not count him really free, because the freedom of savagery is not strength but weakness. The actual powers of the noblest savage do not admit of comparison with those of the humblest citizen of a law-abiding state. He is not the slave of man, but he is the slave of nature. Of compulsion by natural necessity he has plenty of experience, though of restraint by society none at all. Nor can he deliver himself of that compulsion except by submitting to that restraint.[1]

Left Wing Anarchist:
I don't admit that the choice between these two types of freedom (freedom from natural compulsion and freedom from social restraint) exhausts the alternatives. I'll come back to that later, if I may. But let's suppose that it does, that no other possibility is open. It is still not obvious that man will be more free if he chooses submission to the sovereign State. Rousseau, you will remember, at least in his *Discourse on the Origin of Inequality*, thought that the choice between the two was a cruel dilemma. And he was not at all sure that our ancestors made the right choice. Perhaps, he thought, it would have been better to choose freedom from social restraint and sacrifice freedom for natural compulsion.

Conservative:
If Rousseau really did believe that (as distinct from merely saying it in a prize essay in order to attract the attention of the judges by putting forward something outrageously original), he changed his mind when he wrote *The Social Contract*. There he finds a different solution. In submitting to the requirements of the State, he suggests, the individual may lose some independence, but he gains something else infinitely more valuable, morality. He becomes a different person, with different aims and aspirations. And that shows up the absurdity of saying that the State is merely a device for satisfying the desires of its members. The truth is that the desires the citizen has

---

[1]   T.H. Green, 'Liberal Legislation and Freedom of Contract', in *Works*, R.L. Nettleship (ed.), (1885), v. 3, p. 371.

will depend on the type of society he belongs to. If you had been born in the Middle Ages, your desires and aspirations would be very different from those you now have. And different again if you had been born in Ancient Greece. And different in another way if you had been born, even in modern times, in Central Africa. And so on. The individual is moulded by the State. That being so, how can the State possibly be merely an instrument to serve his desires?

Left Wing Anarchist:
Moralized? The citizen is moralized by the State? Don't you mean brain-washed?

Conservative:
That is just cheap abuse. The truth is that without the State the individual would not develop at all. People often talk as if the State were some kind of Proscrustean bed, crippling and cramping its citizens and stopping them from realizing their most heart-felt aspirations. The truth is that the aspiration the individual has (whether it is to become a millionaire, a saint, an Olympic champion, or a Field Marshal) will depend on the kind of community he has been brought up in. An entirely solitary individual, if he managed to survive, would be limited to the purely animal wants: food, shelter, sex.

Liberal:
Aren't you confusing the State with the society, the community? They aren't at all the same thing. You may be right about the solitary individual, but we are moulded by other associations as well as the State. First the family, and then the school, the peer group, the University, the church and so on. Any of these individually, and certainly all of them collectively, may be more influential than the State.

Conservative:
I don't deny that they are important. But when you talk about all of them collectively, you forget that they may pull the individual in different directions. The ideals they foster need to be harmonized. It is through the State that this is done. The State reconciles the conflicting claims, not only of individuals, but also of associations.

Liberal:
I'm not sure that the State does that very efficiently, unless its powers are limited. But I grant your other point, about the individual being moulded by society. It does not follow, though, that the State cannot be judged by its success in satisfying individual desires.

Conservative:
But surely that would be meaningless, when the State creates those desires in first place?

Liberal:
It is the society that creates them, not the State. But quite apart from that, it is perfectly possible for a society or a State to create desires it then frustrates. For example, the society may make each individual want to be richer than his neighbours. Just as a matter of logic, that is a desire which is bound to be thwarted more often than not.

Left Wing Anarchist:
In any case, it's not true that all the individual's desires are created by the State, or even by society. You spoke slightingly of the merely animal wants. You can afford to spurn them, because you have no real fear of not being able to satisfy them. If you were starving and homeless, you would think differently about them. These desires are not created by the State, and certainly one can judge a State, or a society, by its success in satisfying them. Most States fail that test, for at least some of their citizens; sometimes for a very large number of them.

Liberal:
Well, that gives us a fairly clear criterion for judging a State, or a community. It must provide its members with a reasonable chance of satisfying both the basic material needs of its members and the higher-level aspirations which its own institutions generate. So we can admit that the State, together with the rest of the community's institutions, creates a good many of the individual's desires and we can still regard it, quite consistently, as a device to enable him to satisfy them.

Conservative:
I can't accept that.

Liberal:
Are you saying, then, that, because the individual is moulded by the State, he must just accept that mould, however it may shape him? Is the State always right, whatever form it takes?

Conservative:
No, I don't say that, though actually there is rather more to be said for that position than you are admitting. The metaphor of the mould is a useful one, but it can be misleading. You can, of course, make a mould in any shape you like. The point about the State, at least when it genuinely harmonizes the various institutions within it, is

that it is bound to mould its members in a particular way. As I said before, it moralizes them.

Left Wing Anarchist:
You mean, I suppose, that suffering is good for the soul? That might make Nero, or Genghis Khan, or Napoleon, or Hitler, or Idi Amin, or President Marcos, great moralizing agents. But I don't see how else you could make that out.

Conservative:
There's nothing paradoxical about it. Living with other people does involve some sacrifice of freedom, as Rousseau pointed out. You can no longer do exactly what you like; you have to consider their desires as well as your own. Consideration for other people is after all the foundation of morality. The customs and practices of any institution evolve as the result of an infinite number of small compromises made over the years (often the centuries) as people have learned to live and work harmoniously together. The legal institutions, the domain of the State, embody a similar series of compromises between the interests of those other institutions, as they too have learned to co-exist in harmony. In adapting himself to those customs and practices the individual citizen becomes a moral being. Or, if you prefer it, a social being, a civilized being. It amounts to the same thing. This applies to the rulers as much as to the other citizens. You mentioned Napoleon a moment ago. Listen to what T.H. Green said about him:

> With all his egotism, his individuality was so far governed by the action of the national spirit in and upon him, that he could only glorify himself in the greatness of France; and though the national spirit expressed itself in an effort after greatness which was in many ways of a mischievous and delusive kind, yet it again had so much of what may be called the spirit of humanity in it, that it required satisfaction in the belief that it was serving mankind. Hence the aggrandisement of France, in which Napoleon's passion for glory satisfied itself, had to take at least the semblance of a deliverance of oppressed peoples, and in taking the semblance it to a great extent performed the reality; at any rate in western Germany and northern Italy, wherever the Code Napoleon was introduced. It is thus that actions of men, whom in themselves we reckon bad, are 'overruled' for good. There is nothing mysterious or unintelligible in such 'overruling'.[2]

---

2   T.H. Green, 'Lectures on the Principles of Political Obligation', ibid., v. 2, p. 440, paras, 128–9.

Liberal:
Let me get this quite straight. You are saying that even an ambitious and unscrupulous ruler can succeed only if he adapts himself to the national spirit. And, since the national spirit has evolved as a means of reconciling the varied interests of all the citizens, this means that the ruler's measures, whatever they are, must also satisfy those interests, at least to some extent. Is that it?

Conservative:
Ye-e-e-s. Of course, in practice there will always be complicating factors, as well. So the 'to some extent' is important.

Liberal:
But that would apply to Hitler, or Stalin, or any of the other people Left Wing Anarchist mentioned, as much as to Napoleon. So you do seem to be saying, after all, that there are no bad States.

Conservative:
No. Remember that I am talking about nations in which the citizens are firmly attached to the traditional customs and institutions which have slowly evolved to suit their peculiar circumstances and by which they themselves, in their turn, have also been modified: moulded, if you like. This interaction should result in something like a perfect fit. But there are also peoples whose traditional institutions have been destroyed, perhaps by foreign conquest. The Australian aborigine is one tragic example. More insidious than, but just as destructive as, conquest is the belief in Reason.

Liberal:
What's wrong with that? Surely you wouldn't want us all to be irrational?

Conservative:
Burke wasn't being irrational when he said that in this matter prejudice is a safer guide than reason. What he meant by 'prejudice', of course, is the almost instinctive belief that is arrived at, not by reason, but simply by being immersed in a tradition. Since that, as I have tried to explain, will be the result of a million fine adjustments brought about by actual practice, it is not at all surprising that it should be a safer guide than someone's blueprint for a brave new world, an *a priori* paradise untested and untried. When it is tried and doesn't work, its misguided supporters will try to impose it by force. That is how your bad States, your tyrannies and dictatorships, came into existence.

Liberal:
If that is meant as a historical thesis and is not itself an a priori

hypothesis, I doubt if it will stand examination. I would have thought that the tyrants are just as likely to appeal to traditional prejudices as to rational plans for reform. Hitler, for example, invoked the emotions surrounding patriotism, pride of race, imperialism and militarism, all of which can claim long traditions. By comparison with the leader principle, democracy was new-fangled. But in any case, aren't you now changing your ground? You began by saying that the State is not an instrument for gratifying the desires of its citizens. Now you seem to be saying, on the contrary, that its nature is such that it can hardly help satisfying these desires.

Conservative:
It is not really a question of satisfying desires, but of self-development, which is a different thing. In the process of becoming a citizen, the individual will have to suppress some old desires and develop some new ones. As a result he becomes a moral being, or, if you prefer it, a civilized one. In particular, he comes to see that his own petty desires are quite insignificant in comparison with the welfare of the whole community. He is happy to submerge himself in something much larger and greater than he is. How ignoble to regard one's native land as a mere instrument for self-gratification!

Liberal:
'Who dies if England lives', eh? But isn't that a piece of rhetorical nonsense? Dangerous and delusive nonsense, too? If it means that some individual Englishmen may be prepared to die in order to save the lives, or the happiness, of other individual Englishmen, then it may be unobjectionable. But if it means that there is something called England or the English Way of Life which has value in itself quite apart from the welfare of individual Englishmen, and whose survival justifies the destruction of any number of those Englishmen, then it is the most appalling bilge! Unfortunately, lost of people have swallowed it.

Conservative:
The State has rather a bad name nowadays, partly because of those bad States I mentioned a moment ago. Let's take another institution: the University. The University has an end or purpose: broadly, the advancement of learning. Any individual member of the University may have other purposes as well as, or even instead of, that one: if he is a student, he may simply want a professional qualification; if he is a lecturer, he too may want professional advancement or perhaps the modest fame which comes from making scholarly discoveries. So it makes sense to say that the University has a purpose which is not simply the sum of the purposes of its members. The purposes of the members *may* further the purpose of the University: for example,

one way to gain fame and fortune may be to make a genuine contribution to learning. But there may also be other ways; in which case those other ways may actually hinder the purpose of the University. It may well be, of course, that every member of the University does genuinely want to advance learning as well as to attain other, private ends: in Rousseau's terminology, as well as having particular wills they participate in the general will. But it is dangerously misleading to say that the University is a device to gratify the desires of its members. That suggests that their particular wills are all that matters. The opposite is true: it is up to the University's members to subordinate their private ambitions to the purpose of the University: the advancement of learning. In that way they become better scholars and better men. They also contribute to something of lasting value to humanity, something that is vastly more important than the gratification of transient desires. It is the same with the citizen who subordinates his private good to the good of his country.

Liberal:
It does of course make sense to say that the advancement of learning is in some sense the purpose of the University, but we don't need to draw the mystical conclusion that the University is a kind of superperson having purposes in precisely the sense that we lesser persons have them. A corporate purpose is after all only a purpose which a number of individuals share and which they hope to promote by means of a corporate body. It is true that some members may have joined because they have other purposes in mind. Some members of a University may be interested only in professional advancement, some church members may be interested only in respectability and not at all in religion. But if this were true of all its members, and particularly of those responsible for organizing its activities, then the institution would have changed its purpose. So that it is not, after all, that there is something larger and more important than mere individuals which has its own ends, to which individuals may make their humble contribution; it is merely that individuals have a variety of ends, some of which they pursue conjointly with other individuals.

Left Wing Anarchist:
It isn't true, either, that those joint ends are always the more valuable ones. No doubt the corporate purpose of the University does happen to be more valuable than the purely individual purposes of its members. But is it of more value *because* it is a corporate purpose? Corporations exist for all sorts of purposes. It is by no means obvious that the corporate purpose of the Ku Klux Klan, for example, should prevail over the particular purposes of its members,

which might occasionally lead them to compassion for its victims. The University is not typical of all corporate bodies. The State is far more like the Ku Klux Klan.

Conservative:
Oh, come! That's going much too far. I have conceded that there can be bad States. They turn bad when they are taken over by individuals who use them to further their private wills. They almost always have to use ruthless suppression to keep in power, which proves that what they are doing does not really represent the general will. But these are exceptions. In general, Green's point about the ambitious ruler being overruled for good does hold. If it is allowed to develop naturally, by a multiplicity of gradual, unforced adjustments, the general will is necessarily a good will.

Left Wing Anarchist:
Poppycock! I don't deny that living together with other people, especially in a small community, may help an individual to develop sympathy and understanding. Even that needs qualifying. The family, for example, can often be cramping. But a large involuntary association, like the State, isn't a moralizing agent at all. Exactly the opposite is true. The State corrupts.

Conservative:
How can it possibly do that?

Left Wing Anarchist:
In at least three different ways. First of all, by relieving the individual of responsibility for his actions. It is a commonplace that people often behave much worse as members of a corporate body, pursuing the corporate purpose, than they ever would as private individuals. The most notorious example is of course war, in which quite normal, kindly people can be induced to perform acts of unspeakable cruelty, like blowing other people to pieces with bombs. There is hardly any limit to what people will do, without the slightest twinge of conscience, if they know that public opinion (the general will, if you like) approves. Quite tender-hearted people, who would never ill-treat a cat or a dog, take pleasure in shooting and fishing, without any qualms, because this kind of cruelty is acceptable in our culture. It is almost universally accepted that killing is justified provided that it is initiated on a large scale by the official rulers, and that its object is at least ostensibly an impersonal one. (Though this need not prevent it from being something like gaining a disproportionate share of the planet's mineral wealth.) Recently some dissidents have not unnaturally asked why this licence to kill should not be extended to groups other than nations who are also

pursuing what they regard as impersonal and patriotic aims, so that various minority groups have taken to behaving like States, planting bombs, commandeering aeroplanes and so on. So much for the State as a moralizing influence! Private individuals who follow its example are rightly regarded as assassins and terrorists.

Conservative:
Patriotism may sometimes be perverted, no doubt, but you must admit that there is something noble about being willing to sacrifice one's life for an impersonal cause.

Left Wing Anarchist:
Remember the Private of the Buffs? Unlike the Sepoys who were captured with him, he was prepared to die rather than make obeisance to an Emperor with a yellow skin. Sir Francis Doyle wrote a poem about him:
'Let whining Indians cringe and kneel, an English lad must die!'
Was that nobility? Or arrogant stupidity?

Liberal:
Let's not get side-tracked into a discussion of war. The first way that the State corrupts, according to you, is by freeing the individual of personal responsibility for his actions. What are the other two ways you spoke of?

Left Wing Anarchist:
It is a defining characteristic of the State that it has, within a given area, a monopoly of organized violence. The State disintegrates if a private army, not under its authority, seizes control in part of that area. Coercion and violence are bound to corrupt, for more reasons than one. They corrupt both those who use them and those against whom they are used. If you are completely free and uncoerced you have to work out for yourself what is the best thing to do. But if you are under coercion there is no question of that: you must learn the rules and follow them, whatever they are. Even if the rules are good ones, you don't obey them because you recognize that and understand why they are necessary, but because you have to obey them or else.

Liberal:
But mightn't you do both?

Left Wing Anarchist:
There is no real point in racking your brains over the justice and morality of the rule, since you have to obey it anyway.

Democrat:
Surely that doesn't apply in a democratic State, where the citizens make the rules themselves?

Left Wing Anarchist:
That is largely a fiction. Any given citizen may disagree profoundly with a particular law, may even have worked hard to stop it from being enacted. He will still be told that it is his duty to obey it. It is his duty, that is to say, to sink his own judgment in that of the majority. Since this is an overriding principle, which transcends any personal convictions he may have, conformity to the general opinion becomes in practice the sole virtue. This is a peculiarly subtle form of corruption. It results in an even more thorough-going irresponsibility than the kind I mentioned a moment ago. My point then was that the conscripted soldier (for example) dropping bombs on innocent non-combatants could tell himself that the action was not really his, but that of his superiors, since they had ordered him to do it on pain of imprisonment or worse. My present point is that the citizen, at a further stage of corruption, becomes genuinely incapable of distinguishing between morality and legality. You can see this in the attitude of many people towards tax avoidance. They think that any scheme, however obviously contrived to enable them to get out of paying their fair share of the national expenditure, is permissible if it can, by some ingenious subterfuge, be brought within the letter of the law.

In our society, even people in positions of minor and temporary authority can issue the most horrifyingly inhuman orders and get them obeyed. Stanley Milgram demonstrated that by getting people to take part in an experiment in which they believed that they were administering electric shocks of increasing severity to other subjects in the next room. The object (unknown, of course, to the subjects) was to find out at what point they would protest and refuse to go on. When do you think that would be?

Democrat:
I suppose, as soon as the shocks they thought they were giving got at all painful.

Left Wing Anarchist:
That is what the experimenters had expected. They were horrified to find that all the subjects went on beyond the point at which the shocks were labelled 'very strong', and sixty-five per cent of them obeyed orders to the very end, where the shock they thought they were administering was 125 volts stronger than what had been labelled the danger point, and the supposed recipient, after frantical-

ly pounding on the wall between them, had long since fallen silent.
These subjects were quite ordinary, humane people, like you and
me. Like us, and all other 'civilized' people, they had been conditioned to ignore their own judgment when it ran counter to any
kind of 'authority'.[3]

Democrat:
Aren't you exaggerating? In a democracy, the citizens choose for
themselves the kind of authority they want to submit to.

Left Wing Anarchist:
Not really. Whichever party is in power, the actual decisions are
made by a few politicians and bureaucrats. The ordinary citizen has
no real say. As Rousseau said, the English people are free only at
general elections. The use they then make of their freedom shows
how richly they deserve to lose it.[4]

Democrat:
It is true that in a modern State laws will be framed and administered
by a relatively small body of experts. But the ordinary man still has a
real say, provided that there are alternative sets of experts, with
differing policies, for him to choose from; and provided, too, that
anyone is free to lobby for particular reforms.

Left Wing Anarchist:
What is the use of that, when the individual's judgment has been
subtly corrupted in the ways I have been describing?

Liberal:
So far you have only told us about two of your three ways. What is
the third?

Left Wing Anarchist:
That is the most subtle of all. As a citizen of a large State, or even of
what passes as a small State, the individual necessarily lacks intimate
knowledge of most of his fellow citizens. Consequently he thinks of
them merely as representatives of this or that group: as bloated
capitalists or trade union stirrers, as male chauvinist pigs or unsexed
women's libbers, as long-haired ratbags or hidebound proto-
Fascists, as wops or boongs or ockers. These stereotypes become
jaundice-tinted spectacles which distort our view of the actual

---

[3] See S. Milgram, *Obedience to Authority*, (1974).
[4] J.J. Rousseau, *The Social Contract*, (1762), ch. 15.

human beings who surround us, and turn them into cartoonist's caricatures.

Conservative:
You can hardly blame that on the State, surely? No doubt all generalizations distort a little, but language and indeed thought would be impossible without them.

Left Wing Anarchist:
I am told that there are no absolutely straight lines in nature. Actual individuals, of any kind, never conform exactly to what we think of as the ideal type: they are always mixtures of many different types. This applies particularly to human beings. Every individual is unique.

Conservative:
But you can't have a separate law for every individual.

Left Wing Anarchist:
That is why you shouldn't have laws at all. You do need to regard each individual as a separate case: to get close enough to him to understand his motives and sympathize with his aspirations. In a large State that is impossible, but it can occur in a small community. Circuit judges have been known to complain that it is difficult to get juries in small country towns to convict, even when the man being tried is obviously guilty. That illustrates my point perfectly. To the judge the prisoner is just one more petty thief or whatever, who 'deserves' to be punished: to his fellow citizens he is old So-and-so, whose little failings are well known to them. Because they do not see him through the generalizing spectacles, they can ask themselves: what would be the point of shutting him up in prison? If you merely ask yourself: should thieves be imprisoned? you may get one answer; if you ask the same question about old Bill, whom you know very well, you may very well get a different one.

Conservative:
I am not at all sure that small communities really are more tolerant and understanding than large ones. Many people from small towns feel liberated when they move to large cities. But are you seriously suggesting that we could manage without any laws at all?

Left Wing Anarchist:
Without any penal laws, yes. There might need to be some rules, like keeping to the left on the highway. But people would not be coerced into obeying them. They would obey them because they understood the reasons for them and agreed with the purpose behind them.

Conservative:
People don't always obey the rules of the road even when they are backed with penal sanctions. Why should they obey them when they are not?

Left Wing Anarchist:
Tell me, to which of these exhortations would you be more likely to respond: (a) Please do this, or a lot of innocent people may get hurt! (b) Do this, or I'll knock you down!

Conservative:
To the first, I suppose, But –

Left Wing Anarchist:
Exactly. The second one rouses antagonism, makes you look for excuses for not agreeing. And in a society full of social inequality, in which one section thinks of the laws not simply as ways of behaving which they impose upon themselves, because that is the way they want to behave, but as arbitrary rules forced on them by 'the bosses', that reaction is exacerbated.

Conservative:
That is all very well, but in any community there will always be some unscrupulous people who will cheat and steal if they can get away with it. Without penalties of some kind you would have chaos. Aggrieved people would take the law into their own hands. Isn't it much better to have clearly stated laws and properly organized penalties for those who disobey them?

Left Wing Anarchist:
Prevention is better than cure. Crime is the product of social conditions, and it is much better to alter those conditions than to punish the criminal. In a society in which a large number of people feel that the cards are stacked against them, that they will never really be given a fair go, and that the laws are framed and enforced by the privileged class it is true that there always will be law-breakers. In a smaller community, such as the family, in which it is easier to appreciate the effect of your actions on other people, things are different.

Conservative:
Even in a family, some sanctions, some pains and penalties are needed to get children to behave well.

Left Wing Anarchist:
The most effective sanction is public approval: the knowledge that

certain behaviour will make one disliked. When you have a disaffected group, who don't really believe that the laws are in their
interest, that sanction won't work, because the law-breaker will have
the approval, and perhaps even the admiration, of others in the
group. In effect, they form a society within the larger society.

But in a small community without social or economic inequalities,
where people identify themselves with the community rules and
understand the inconvenience they cause other people by breaking
them, there is no need for coercion. The desire to be liked and
thought well of by one's neighbours is a very strong motive.

Conservative:
That is Utopian. Abolish all penal laws and we would revert at once
to something like Hobbes' State of Nature.

Left Wing Anarchist:
In our society, if they were abolished overnight, you are of course
right. We need to create the right social conditions first: in particular, social and economic equality. That won't be brought about
overnight. But what I am suggesting is not as Utopian as you think.
After all, you and I don't refrain from theft and murder just because
we are afraid of the police. And that is true of most of our fellow
citizens, even in this society. In a more obviously just society it
might be true of all of them. The thing to grasp is that the structure
of society, and its coercive laws, cause far more crime than they
prevent.

Conservative:
Nonsense! You have far too rosy a view of human nature.

Left Wing Anarchist:
It was you who insisted that what we call human nature is very
largely a product of the social environment. We are all moulded by
society, and by the State. It follows that, if we can create the right
conditions, a society of free and independent individuals, under no
coercion whatever, but helping and co-operating with one another
simply because they see that that is the best thing to do, is perfectly
possible, at least if communities are fairly small.

Liberal:
I doubt if it is possible, but it does give us an ideal to aim at.

Conservative:
That is exactly where all you starry-eyed reformers go wrong. You
aim at an impossible ideal, and then when it can't be achieved you
try to impose it by force. Whenever Utopian dreamers seize power
they end up as totalitarians and tyrants.

Left Wing Anarchist:
Abolishing the State could conceivably bring about Hobbes' war of each against all, though I think that can be avoided, but it obviously produces the exact opposite of a totalitarian State.

Conservative:
Except by way of reaction, later on.

Liberal:
Anyway, all I meant was that existing States can be judged by how nearly they approach Left Wing Anarchist's ideal. He agreed that it couldn't be brought about overnight. We can work towards it by limiting the State's power as much as possible. I am sure that we will always need criminal laws and a police force, but at least we should follow Mill's rule of penalizing only actions which cause actual harm to other people. Otherwise each citizen should be free to go his own way without any interference from the State.

Socialist:
Does that apply to his economic activities as well? Complete *laissez-faire*, with no holds barred?

Liberal:
Economic activities do affect other people's interests, as Mill himself realized. At the same time, they are an important part of everybody's life. A forced labourer can hardly be said to have any freedom worth having. The difficulty is that the State is not the only body that may use force. Cartels of manufacturers, for example, may cut off supplies to any retailer who tries to lower prices. Trade unions may cut off the supply of labour to firms which have offended them in any way. There are all sorts of commercial and industrial practices which impede freedom far more than they further it. That may justify State interference. The general principle is that the State should act as a referee who doesn't play the game himself, but sees to it that everybody else has a fair chance to play. That applies to economic games as well as to all the other kinds.

Socialist:
That doesn't go nearly far enough. The trouble with the theory of *laissez-faire* is that it is inherently self-contradictory. The theory is that if everyone is free to pursue his own interest, the net result will be in the general interest. Free competition will ensure that. For example, if someone charges an extortionate price for his goods or his services it will be in someone else's interest to set up in competition and undersell him. In that way a just price will be arrived at simply by the operation of the market. And this applies

quite generally: for example, to wages as well as prices. That is the theory. One trouble with it is that, as you have just admitted, self-interest will lead the suppliers of goods and services to band together to stifle free competition. So the State has to intervene to stop what are called 'unfair practices'. But the difficulty doesn't end there. The theory of *laissez-faire* really presupposes equal bargaining power. According to the theory the operation of the market will ensure that the most urgent needs of the community are satisfied before the unimportant ones, because people will be prepared to pay more for the things they need more. But when incomes are unequal the rich man may well be prepared to pay more for a quite trivial luxury than the poor man can afford for something he urgently needs. This applies, too, to trade between rich and poor nations. If incomes were equal, *laissez-faire* might work as it is supposed to – for a time. But only for a time, because the operation of the market, with free competition, is bound to lead to inequality before very long.

Liberal:
Well, what is the alternative?

Socialist:
One solution would be the ownership by the State of production, distribution and exchange. Socialists used to advocate that. Some still do.

Liberal:
Why should a State monopoly be better than a private monopoly.?

Socialist:
The people in control have different aims. The aim of the private capitalist is to make a profit through the operation of the market. His doing that is supposed to lead, automatically though indirectly, to the public benefit, but I have just been arguing that that belief is false. The politician, on the other hand, aims at gaining the votes of the electors. That means that he has to consider the public interest directly, and allow that to override the making of profits. With the private capitalist it is the other way round.

Liberal:
But what will happen to the national economy if all industry and commerce are in the hands of people whose primary concern is not running them efficiently but buying votes?

Socialist:
'Buying votes' is a tendentious and misleading way of putting it, but

I accept that expression if all you mean by it is that it is in the interest of a goverment in a democracy to try to win the confidence of the citizens by making them, as far as possible, prosperous, happy and free. For that you need a flourishing economy. It will, then, be in the interest of the government to ensure that the State enterprises are efficiently run.

Liberal:
But it would no longer be possible for someone with a bright idea just to go ahead and set up a factory or whatever (no doubt with a bank loan) and try it out. He would have to submit it instead to a government department, and there would be endless red tape and frustration. The community would lose enterprise and initiative, and individuals would lose at least some freedom.

Socialist:
That freedom has been lost anyway, in these days of huge multi-national firms and cannabalistic mergers. The day of the small independent craftsman is over. But I agree that complete State ownership might mean a lack of enterprise and flexibility. Many Socialists now (and I am one of them) would settle for increased State control. You have admitted that some control is necessary. But we need to go further than just preventing what are called 'practices in restraint of trade' (that is, businessmen getting together to cheat the rest of us) or stopping little boys from having to sweep chimneys for a pittance. The State needs to see that commercial practices really do work for the public good. It can do that by doing something to increase the bargaining power of those who have least of it, by providing competition itself where monopolies have cornered the market and are exploiting the public, by subsidizing activities, such as the arts, which are unprofitable but of value to the community, and by using taxation to mitigate the inequality of incomes which *laissez-faire* always tends towards.

Liberal:
Won't the last of these measures, and perhaps some of the others as well, lessen the incentive to make profits and so damage the economy?

Socialist:
Now, now! No Communist propaganda, please!

Liberal:
What do you mean?

Socialist:
Communists contend that capitalism won't work unless the workers

are paid only a bare subsistence wage, or something approaching it. You seem to be agreeing with them.

Liberal:
Most Australian workers are a long way from a subsistence wage.

Socialist:
Yes, but even the very mild steps taken by Labor Governments to bring about a more equal distribution ruin the economy, according to their opponents. If that is right, then the Communists are at least partly right. These days it is apparently only socialists who believe that capitalism is compatible with social justice. But only, of course, if it is a tamed and carefully controlled capitalism.

Communist:
Of course capitalism and social justice are not compatible! What none of you seem to understand is that political power inevitably springs from economic power. That is why attempts to control capitalism are bound to fail, and why the democracy you boast about is just a sham.

Socialist:
The fact remains that the worst excesses of the industrial revolution and unrestricted *laissez-faire* have been got rid of. To that extent capitalism has been tamed, at least in democratic countries. Of course there is still a lot to be done, but even now the ordinary working man or woman is better off in capitalist democracies than in Communist countries. Better off economically, and certainly better off in personal freedom. Marx's prediction that the lot of the workers would get steadily worse has simply turned out to be false.

Communist:
All the same, the real power always remains with big business, which is always able to ruin the economy by withdrawing capital. Your so-called socialist democratic governments will never be allowed to do more than throw a few sops to the workers to keep them quiet. As for Marx's prediction, there are signs that it may be coming true after all.

Socialist:
How do you make that out?

Communist:
Marx's main contention is that power changes in a society are caused by changes in the mode of production.

Socialist:
Well?

Communist:
A new industrial revolution is taking place under our noses, with the invention of computers and the micro-chip. For the first time, both the unskilled and the semi-skilled workers are becoming superfluous. This creates a new dispossessed class, the unemployed. As they become more numerous and more discontented, the time may well come when they will revolt and take over control of the new machines so that they may be used for the good of the whole community and not just the wealthy few.

Socialist:
That would still be very different from what Marx foresaw. Instead of being indispensable, and the real producers of wealth, the workers, according to your prediction, are becoming unnecessary. All the same, I agree that this is a very serious problem indeed, and one that won't be solved without a quite radical social change. We have to realize that the traditional method of distributing income just won't work under the changed conditions. We can no longer allow the individual's share of the community's wealth to depend on his contribution to the making of that wealth.

Communist:
It never did depend on that, really. And doesn't now.

Socialist:
Only in a rough and ready way, I agree. Some sections of the community get less than they deserve, on that criterion, and some more. But the point is that up till now the individual's income has depended on the job he does, using 'job' in an extended sense in which it would apply to the contribution to the economy made by the landed proprietor, the investor and the like as well as to the wage and salary earner. I don't dispute that some such jobs have been overpaid and others underpaid. What I am saying now is that, if a significant number of people have become, or are about to become, unnecessary (redundant, to use the current euphemism) then we need to sever the link between job and income altogether. And that is a very profound social change, which will need to be thought out very carefully, and which no one at the moment seems to be facing.

Communist:
So we do need a revolution after all?

Socialist:
In our attitudes, certainly. A bloodless revolution. The other kind

doesn't really achieve anything, except a lot of hatred and bitterness. People still have to sit down afterwards and think hard about what needs to be done.

Communist:
Revolutions get rid of the privileged people who stand in the way of necessary changes.

Socialist:
There is no need to suppose that the people who are good at fomenting successful revolution are also the best at solving this kind of problem. It will need a lot of hard thought and a lot of goodwill, and the whole community needs to be involved, at least to the extent of accepting the changes and understanding the need for them. That can only be achieved by democratic processes.

Left Wing Anarchist:
You are quite right to say that revolution doesn't solve anything, but democratic processes don't either. The person who is good at winning elections is no more likely to be a profound political thinker than the one who is good at fomenting revolutions. All he needs is charm, and the ability to pander to the unthinking prejudices of the electors. A champion tennis player or footballer or film star is a much better prospect, electorally, than a professor of politics. Every Australian Prime Minister has to be a known supporter of some football team or other; he can't afford not to be among the spectators at every important match. You might think that he would have better things to do. As for bringing about any really fundamental changes, he wouldn't dare do that. He knows that he has to stick to the familiar clichés.

Conservative:
That is the great strength of democracy. If radical changes are really needed, they will come about slowly, as people gradually adapt themselves to changing conditions. It is important that the government should be in tune with people's attitudes at any given moment. It should not try to force changes on them before they are ready.

Socialist:
They never will be ready unless there is some determined leadership. I agree that change should not be forced on people before they are ready, but it is possible to educate people so that they come to see the need for change. *Your* ideal statesman seems to be the man who said: 'Where is that crowd going? I must follow them and see, for I am their leader!' After all, it shouldn't be too hard to get people to agree that something must be done about unemployment. The difficulty is

to know what. Anyone who can find a coherent solution shouldn't have too much difficulty in getting people to accept it.

Conservative:
If it involves a fundamental change in the whole social structure, as would a change in the way income is distributed, people won't accept it readily. It needs to come about slowly, bit by bit. That way the changes will be adapted to people, and not the other way round. That is what you reformers, with your ready-made blueprints, never seem to understand.

Socialist:
I don't think the school leaver with nothing to look forward to but a lifetime as one of the dispossessed, with no job and no accepted position in the community, dependent for his existence on a skinflint dole grudgingly and contemptuously given, can be expected to wait for a slow change in community attitudes which might well take the whole of that lifetime.

Conservative:
You are assuming, like any rationalist reformer, that the only solution for this particular problem is to turn the whole social system upside down. It would be more sensible to try less radical measures first. Granted that computers will take over many of the jobs now done by men and women, surely there are other jobs, not now done by anybody, which would be of value to the community and which could be taken over by the people thrown out of work because of computers? No doubt the community will adapt itself to the coming of computers in some such way, in the normal course of social evolution. Provided it doesn't interfere too much with the community mores, the government might well hasten the process along a little, perhaps by subsidizing promising new industries.

Liberal:
Perhaps the best thing the government could do would be to abolish all the existing restraints on free enterprise, both those it imposes itself and those imposed by cartels or trade unions. One hears, for example of unemployed youngsters trying to set up a pie-cart in a shopping centre and doing quite well until they are stopped by some inspector enforcing a bureaucratic regulation. If all restrictions of that sort were done away with, and initiative and enterprise given free play, perhaps the unemployed would be able to solve the problem themselves.

Socialist:
If all restrictions of that sort were done away with, we would be back in the worst conditions at the beginning of the industrial revolution.

Liberal:
When I said 'restrictions of that sort', I meant a quite specific sort. Those which interfere with freedom. If you make a law prohibiting child labour, or starvation wages, you are not really interfering with the freedom of the child or the low-paid working man. You are merely making on his behalf the bargain he would have made for himself, if he had had equal bargaining power with the employer. You *are* interfering with the employer's freedom, but only in the interest of the more important freedom of someone else. I don't object to that. But regulations which prevent both parties from doing what they genuinely want to do are very different.

Socialist:
What prevents most people from doing what they genuinely want to do is lack of money. So long as you have vast inequalities of income, it is absurd to talk of people being equally free. The State needs to intervene much more directly than you suggest if it is really interested in freedom. It is mockery to tell the pauper that he and the millionaire are equally free to sleep in a luxury hotel or on a park bench, just as they choose.

Communist:
It may well be that only the millionaire is free to do either. There is a convenient charge called being without visible means of support which would require the police to arrest the pauper but not the millionaire if, by some odd chance, they should be found slumbering on adjacent benches.

Liberal:
It is precisely that sort of oppressive law that I am objecting to.

Socialist:
Yes, but do you think it enough that they should be equally free only to do what neither would choose to do?

Liberal:
I think that there should be equality of opportunity. And that may well mean that the State should ensure that education is free (perhaps up to the very highest levels) and that all careers should be open to those with the appropriate talents, without any artificial barriers because of race, sex or family background. Perhaps it also means the provision of free libraries, museums and the like. Certainly no one should be so grindingly poor that he lacks the energy to develop his talents and make the most of them. But I don't see how you can go much further than equality of opportunity without quite intolerable interference with personal freedom.

Socialist:
Why? I have already pointed out that a relative equality of income would make capitalism more efficient, not less. I don't mean complete equality. But great wealth and genuine poverty could both be eliminated without seriously affecting incentive. And that would do something to prevent the whims of the rich from outweighing the needs of the poor.

Liberal:
That is an admirable objective, no doubt. What I am afraid of is that it might lead you to ignore a quite fundamental principle.

Socialist:
What principle?

Liberal:
In a nutshell, the Rule of Law.

Socialist:
I am talking about ordinary democratic measures. Graduated income tax, for example.

Liberal:
As I understand it, the Rule of Law goes beyond that. It means that the State should confine itself to laying down very general rules which it then applies quite impartially to everybody.

Socialist:
Of course! I have no quarrel with that.

Liberal:
But, since people are themselves unequal, to treat everybody equally is to end up with different results. As Hayek points out: 'To produce the same result for different people it is necessary to treat them differently.'[5] Any thorough-going attempt to equalize incomes would mean making *ad hoc* decisions about particular people.

Socialist:
There is nothing inconsistent about treating different people differently and applying the same general rule impartially. Quite the contrary. If the difference between persons dictates a corresponding difference in treatment, then you *are* applying a general rule, and applying it impartially. 'All passengers over twelve years of age will

_____
[5]   F.A. Hayek, *The Road to Serfdom*, (1944), p. 59.

be charged the full fare.' 'That portion of income over thirty thousand dollars will be taxed at a higher rate.' There is nothing contrary to the Rule of Law in either of those.

Liberal:
Hayek has a more general point to make. In a free society everyone should be free to pursue his own ends, whatever they may be, subject only to very general rules of just conduct, rules, one might say, that give everyone a fair go. That means that the State has no specific ends of its own. And that rules out economic planning by the State. All the Government should do is to determine the conditions under which the available resources may be used, leaving to the individual the decision for what ends they are to be used. But, as Hayek puts it:

> When the government has to decide how many pigs are to be reared or how many buses are to be run, which coal mines are to operate, or at what prices boots are to be sold, these decisions cannot be deduced from formal principles, or settled for long periods in advance. They depend inevitably on the circumstances of the moment, and in making such decisions it will always be necessary to balance one against the other in the interests of various persons and groups. In the end somebody's views will have to decide whose interests are the most important; and these views must become part of the law of the land, a new distinction of rank which the coercive apparatus of government imposes upon the people.[6]

Socialist:
Of course it would be better if every individual could get exactly what he wanted, and everybody's views about whose interests are the most important could be acceded to. Hayek seems to be implying that is what will happen if there is no government control. But of course that can't be true. These matters have to be settled somehow, and if there are conflicting interests someone is going to be disappointed. It is surely better that the decisions should be made by a democratically elected government, able to call on the most expert advice and answerable to the people if it makes mistakes, than that they should be left to the operation of the market, which may very well produce quite unjust results which nobody would have voted for.

Liberal:
Hayek also says somewhere that it is nonsensical to say that the results of the market can be either just or unjust. Justice can be

---

[6] ibid., p. 55.

meaningfully attributed only to human action. The results of the
market are essentially unpredictable. Consequently the concept of
justice does not apply to them.[7]

Socialist:
But the decision to abide by those results is a human action. If
you fire a gun at random in a crowded street the results may be
unpredictable, but your action, whether or not we would call it
unjust, is certainly reprehensible.

Liberal:
Hayek's point is that the distribution of incomes under a market
system is not the sort of thing that can be either just or unjust,
though capitalism as a whole can be. In fact it is just, because it is
beneficial to society in the long run.

Socialist:
That is a very rough sort of justice indeed. I prefer John Rawls'
criterion. He says that inequalities are not justified merely by
making the whole society wealthier than it would otherwise be; to be
just the inequality must also improve the position of those members
of the community who are worst off.

Liberal:
The fact remains that control of the economy does mean imposing
the values of one section of the community on the rest, whether they
share them or not.

Socialist:
So does capitalism, but the imposition is less open, and so harder to
counter.

Liberal:
You mean that there is a secret conclave of financiers somewhere –
probably in Switzerland – deciding to enrich this nation and ruin
that one? That is fantasy.

Socialist:
I don't mean anything like that. But under capitalism anything that
yields a profit will be given precedence over things that are merely of
general social value, like unpolluted air.

---

7   F.A. Hayek, 'The Principles of a Liberal Social Order', in A. De Crespigny and
     J. Cronin (eds), *Ideologies of Politics*, (1975), pp. 62–3 and 67.

Liberal:
I don't deny (nor does Hayek) that government control may be justified there. But the fact remains that individual liberty is better preserved, on the whole, under a market system, because there is more scope for different individuals to make different choices. To quote Hayek once again:

> In a competitive society the prices we have to pay for a thing, the rate at which we can get one thing for another, depend on the quantities of other things of which, by taking one, we deprive the other members of society. This price is not determined by the conscious will of anybody. The obstacles in our path are not due to somebody disapproving of our ends, but to the fact that the same means are also wanted elsewhere. In a directed economy, where the authority watches over the ends pursued, it is certain that it would use its powers to assist some ends and prevent the realisation of others. Not our own view, but somebody else's, of what we ought to like or dislike would determine what we should get.[8]

Socialist:
That argument might be sound if there were equal incomes. Then my inability to buy something might really mean that it was wanted more badly elsewhere. As things are, the rich man has, as it were, many hundreds of votes to the poor man's one. You admit that it is necessary to control capitalism in order to prevent cartels and monopolies keeping prices artificially high. It is only going one step further to add controls that will prevent incomes from getting too unequal. That step is just as important if capitalism is to work in the way you claim that it does.

Right Wing Anarchist:
In other words, Liberal, you've already sold the pass. Socialist is right about that, though he's wrong about everything else. It's true about capitalism what some Christians say about Christianity: far from having been tried and proved a failure, it hasn't really been tried at all. There has always been State interference. The only way to safeguard individual liberty is to leave absolutely everything to the market. And that means abolishing the State.

Left Wing Anarchist:
That would mean replacing one tyranny by an even worse one. The unremitting pursuit of personal profit is even more corrupting than submission to arbitrary power.

---

[8]   F.A. Hayek, *The Road to Serfdom*, (1944), p. 70.

Liberal:
Leaving everything to the operation of the market? The police force,
for example? The law courts?

Right Wing Anarchist:
Why not? Hobbes' State-of-Nature men were really a servile and
submissive lot to invent the sovereign State. It is far more likely that
some entrepeneur would have arisen to offer protection against theft
or violence for a suitable fee.

Socialist:
And how would he protect his clients?

Right Wing Anarchist:
In exactly the way that the police force protects you now – when it
does. The thief (for example) would be ferreted out and made to
restore your property, plus a substantial fine. Other offenders would
be made to pay compensation.

Socialist:
In other words, a protection racket?

Right Wing Anarchist:
Call it that if you like. A protective agency, certainly. The only
difference between that and what the State does now is that you
wouldn't be compelled to subscribe to it.

Liberal:
Wouldn't you though? What is to prevent the agency from treating
non-subscribers the way it treats criminals?

Right Wing Anarchist:
In practice I suppose nearly everybody would find it necessary to
subscribe to an agency, just as everybody now belongs to some State
or other. But at least you would be free to opt out if you thought you
could manage without it. And there would be competing agencies to
choose from.

Socialist:
What you are describing sounds like a community terrorized by rival
gangs of so-called protectors.

Right Wing Anarchist:
If the Hobbes men could realize that they would be better off under
a sovereign than in the state of nature, my agencies would soon see
that they would be better off agreeing to submit disputes between

them to an arbitrator. As I imagine it, each pair of agencies would agree in advance on which professional arbitrator they would use. Each firm of arbitrators would have its own code of laws. It would be in the interest of the arbitrators to get a reputation for giving fair decisions and in the interest of the agencies to be known to employ such firms.

Socialist:
The Hobbes men were relatively helpless individuals. Your agencies are organized and have strong-arm men at their disposal. They are much more like nations than like individual citizens. It is not easy to get nations to agree to submit their disputes to arbitration, or to international law.

Right Wing Anarchist:
You forget that my agencies are business concerns. Business men would realize that arbitration is cheaper than war.

Socialist:
And what if one agency refused to accept the arbitrator's decision on behalf of its client?

Right Wing Anarchist:
Presumably it would be blacklisted by all the other agencies. Consequently it would lose its clients, who would realize that they now had no guarantee, if they had a case against the client of another agency, of getting satisfaction.

Liberal:
I think you underestimate what a determined gang of well-armed thugs can do. But, in any case, the State has other functions as well as maintaining law and order. What about roads, for example?

Right Wing Anarchist:
Residential streets would be the property of the residents. One might expect the householder to take the same pride in the condition of his part of the street as he now takes in his garden. Both of these will affect the value of his property. At present, he pays for the upkeep of his street through rates and taxes, but has very little say in how it is kept. Main highways would charge tolls. They would be better kept than at present, because alternative routes would be owned by different firms competing against one another. One might expect them, too, to charge less at non-peak hours and do other things of that sort to attract custom by making driving less of a strain.

Liberal:

I agree with you that leaving things to the operation of the market is often the best way of making it possible for each individual to make his own choice. But what you seem to overlook is the need of some control to ensure that the market will work as it is supposed to. At the very least, monopolies and cartels must be eliminated. And also, I think, exploitation, whether by employers or by trade unions.

Socialist:

You are overlooking something else as well. What about the poor? Are the men and women who can't afford the fees of your protective agencies to be left to the mercies of any thug who chooses to ill-treat them? Are the unemployed to be left to starve?

Right Wing Anarchist:

That is where *you* are overlooking something – and it is something fundamental to my whole argument. To the extent that these people are looked after by the State, is it at the taxpayer's expense?

Socialist:

Of course.

Right Wing Anarchist:

And the taxpayer either consents to this or he doesn't?

Socialist:

That would seem to be true, as a matter of logic.

Right Wing Anarchist:

Well, if he really consents to it, he will give the same amount to private charities, and the poor will be no worse off. If he doesn't consent to it, then he is being coerced into supporting other people against his will. That is clearly an infringement of liberty. If the welfare state really has widespread approval, it is unnecessary. If it does not have that approval, it is oppressive. Anyone who thinks that the State should do this or that (provide free libraries, museums, meals, education) is at liberty to try to raise money for the purpose. If enough people agree with him, he will succeed. If he doesn't raise enough money, that proves that he was really asking the State to commandeer other people's money for *his* pet projects.

Liberal:

I know many employers who are strongly in favour of legislation about basic wages, award rates and the like simply because it saves them from having to worry about such things. They want to do what is fair, and they are happy to leave it to the experts to decide what is fair in each particular case. I think that applies to social welfare generally. I am, of course, very much in favour of individual freedom and the removal of all restrictions which genuinely interfere with it. But after all, an important part of personal freedom is being able to leave to other people decisions about things outside your immediate concern in the confidence that they will be made pretty much in the way you would wish. A good many social arrangements can be left to the automatic workings of the market, but not all of them.

Socialist:
There is a much more fundamental objection than that to our friend's anarcho-capitalist theories. Left to itself, capitalism results in a society that is basically unjust. It needs to be controlled, not merely to ensure that competition will be genuinely free, not merely to ensure that the owner of property benefits from all the useful services rendered by that property and suffers from all the damage caused to others by its use, not merely to provide those necessary services which cannot be left to the operation of the market, but also to remedy that basic injustice, or at least to prevent it from going too far.

Right Wing Anarchist:
I am sure that you are both quite wrong, but I don't suppose there is much point in going on arguing about it. These discussions always remind me of those lines of Omar Khayyam's:

> Myself when young did eagerly frequent
> Doctor and Saint, and heard great argument
> About it and about, but evermore
> Came out by the same door where in I went.

I'm sure none of us will change his mind.

Socialist:
People sometimes do. But even if they don't, arguing like this helps one to clarify one's own views.

Liberal:
Yes, and to realize what is really at issue. Whether the argument is about ends or means, for example. All of us here agree in wanting a free, just and prosperous society. We differ only about how that can be achieved. Left Wing Anarchist thinks that it can be done by abolishing the State and having a kind of co-operative commune on a large scale, Right Wing Anarchist says that we need to abolish the State and have unrestricted *laissez-faire* capitalism, Communist says

that the only way is to abolish both capitalism and democracy as we know it, and to substitute a one-party State run on Marxist-Leninist principles. Socialists like you think that we can attain it by retaining democracy but restraining capitalism quite severely. I agree up to a point but want the restrictions to be minimal. The differences between us are about a question of fact, not of theory: which of these methods will produce a free, just and prosperous community? Perhaps it is really a problem for the economists to solve, not the political scientists.

Socialist:
That is not quite true. Even if we do all want a just, prosperous and free community, we may differ about which of these three goals is most important; freedom, justice or prosperity? And we certainly differ on the even trickier question of what precisely it is to be just, or free, or prosperous. And these are matters of value, not of fact. To solve them, even to talk about them coherently and with sensitivity, we certainly need philosophers as well as economists.

Further Reading

Communism
Cornforth, Maurice, *Communism and Human Values*, London, 1972.
Daniels, Robert V., *The Nature of Communism*, New York, 1962.
Harrington, Michael, *The Twilight of Capitalism*, New York, 1976.
Hunt, R.N. Carew, *The Theory and Practice of Communism*, 5th edition, Harmondsworth, 1963.

Conservatism
Harbour, William R., *The Foundations of Conservative Thought*, Notre Dame, 1982.
Kirk, Russell, *The Conservative Mind*, London, 1954.
Oakeshott, Michael, *Rationalism in Politics and Other Essays*, London, 1962.
Smith, N.A., *The New Enlightenment*, London, 1976.
White, R.J., *The Conservative Tradition*, London, 1950.

Democracy
Holden, Barry, *The Nature of Democracy*, London, 1974.
Lindsay, A.D., *The Essentials of Democracy*, 2nd edition, Oxford, 1935.
Macpherson, C.B., *The Life and Times of Liberal Democracy*, Oxford, 1977.
Mayo, Henry B., *An Introduction to Democratic Theory*, New York, 1960.
Plamenatz, John., *Democracy and Illusion*, London, 1973.

Left Wing Anarchism
Carter, April, *The Political Theory of Anarchism*, London, 1971.
Krimerman, L.I. & Perry, C., eds., *Patterns of Anarchy: A Collection of Writings in the Anarchist Tradition*, New York, 1966.
Monro, D.H., *Godwin's Moral Philosophy*, Oxford, 1953.
Read, Herbert, *Anarchy and Order*, London, 1954.

Ritter, Alan, *Anarchism; a theoretical analysis*, Cambridge, 1980.
Taylor, Michael, *Community, Anarchy and Liberty*, Cambridge, 1982.
Wolff, Paul, *In Defense of Anarchism*, New York, 1970.

Liberalism
Bartley, Robert and others, *The Relevance of Liberalism*, Research Institute
   on International Change, Boulder, 1978.
Feinberg, Joel, *Social Philosophy*, New York, 1971.
Hayek, F.A., *The Road to Serfdom*, London, 1944.
Hobhouse, L.T., *Liberalism*, Oxford, 1964. (First published 1911)
Popper, Karl, *The Open Society and its Enemies*, 5th edition, London, 1966.
Rawls, John, *A Theory of Justice*, Oxford, 1972.

Right Wing Anarchism
Friedman, David, *The Machinery of Freedom: Guide to a Radical Capital-
   ism*, 2nd edition, New York, 1978.
Hiskes, Richard P., *Community Without Coercion*, Newark, 1982.
Hospers, John, *Libertarianism*, Los Angeles, 1971.
Nozick, Robert, *Anarchy, State and Utopia*, New York, 1974.
Rothbard, Murray, *For a New Liberty*, 2nd edition, New York, 1978.

Socialism
Cole, G.D.H., *Fabian Socialism*, London, 1943.
Crosland, C.A.R., *The Future of Socialism*, London, 1956.
Crossman, R.H.S., ed., *New Fabian Essays*, London, 1952.
Jay, Douglas, *The Socialist Case*, 2nd edition, London, 1946.
Shaw, G. Bernard, *The Road to Equality: ten unpublished lectures and essays,
   1884–1918*, Boston, 1971.
Von Mises, Ludwig, *Socialism*, 2nd edition, London, 1951.

Glossary

ad hoc
(Latin: for this.)
A phrase used to signify 'arranged for this purpose' and which often carries with it criticism that the matter has been insufficiently planned.

a fortiori
(Latin: from the stronger.)
A term used to express 'even more certainly' or 'all the more likely'. It may be used of necessary propositions (q.v.), thus: 'she is entitled to vote, then *a fortiori* she must be a citizen' and of contingent (q.v.) propositions, thus 'he bats last in the team, so *a fortiori* he isn't as skilful as the players we've already dismissed'.

analytic and synthetic
A proposition is said to be analytic if the concept of the subject is contained in the concept of the predicate, thus 'All bachelors are unmarried people' is analytic, it must be true and its negation is contradictory. Analytic propositions are contrasted with synthetic propositions which are expressions about matters which happen to be true (or false), thus 'All bachelors are unhappy people' is synthetic, it might be true but its negation is not contradictory (though it might be false).

a posteriori and a priori
(Latin: from what comes after and from what comes before, respectively.)
Both these terms are applied to concepts and to propositions and to arguments. An a posteriori proposition is one whose truth or falsity may be known only after certain sorts of observation and experimentation. An a priori proposition is one whose truth or falsity can be known without observation and experimentation. 'Many forms of illness are caused by smoking cigarettes' is an a posteriori proposition; and 'everything which is coloured is extended' is an a priori proposition.

contingent and necessary	A quality of a term, thus 'red' of 'rose', or of a proposition whose truth value could have been different from what it in fact was. 'Tom, my cat, is on the mat' is a contingent proposition. By contrast, a necessary proposition is one whose truth values could not have been different; it logically must be the case. 'The angles of an equilateral triangle are equal' is a necessary proposition.
contradiction	A proposition which is false on logical, not factual, grounds. Thus, and pace Hobbes (see chapter 6), 'this circle is square' is a contradiction.
defining and accompanying characteristics	A characteristic is the defining of a term if its presence is essential for that that to be that rather than something else. A characteristic is the accompanying of a term if its presence (even if in fact invariable) is not essential to the that being a that. Thus: being a plane figure is a defining characteristic of being a triangle; having sides of equal lengths is an accompanying characteristic. (See also 'analytic and synthetic' and 'contingent and necessary'.)
empirical	A statement is empirical if its truth or falsity can be established only by observation, measurement or experiment. Often called factual statements, they are sometimes also called descriptive statements and are to be contrasted with analytic, a priori and necessary propositions on the one hand and with evaluative, for example personal preference, aesthetic and moral, judgements on the other.
epistemology	Philosophical enquiry into the nature of knowledge and the grounds for making claims to knowledge and, more widely, experience and belief.
hedonism	Ethical hedonism is the view that pleasure is the highest good. It is neutral on the question whose pleasure should be promoted and it must be distinguished from psychological hedonism, the view that as a matter of fact every person always aims at maximizing his or her own pleasure.
metaphysical	A statement is metaphysical if it is claimed to be factual but is not establishable as true or false by experimental tests: e.g. 'substance is the that to which qualities (like colour, shape, weight etc.) are attached'. (Verificationists deny that there can be factual but non-empirical propositions and argue that metaphysical remarks are literally nonsense.)
mutatis mutandis	With due alteration of details (Latin).
natural	A notoriously malleable notion, much used in political and social contentions and conclusions, as fecund of fallacies as a magician's hat of scarves, flags, doves and

copulating rabbits. When one hears or reads the word nature, one should usually reach if not for one's revolver at least for one's sceptical scalpel or perhaps for one's dictionary or Encyclopaedia of philosophy. A thing to say (one of very many) is that not all things said to be natural (e.g. earthquakes and malaria) are good, not all things said to be unnatural (e.g. ships and clothing) are bad.

naturalistic fallacy	The alleged fallacy arising whenever moral terms such as 'good', 'ought' and 'right' are defined purely descriptively or factually; for example 'what I like', 'what will benefit members of the club', and 'what the law requires'.
necessary condition	An A is a necessary condition for a B if B must have A. Thus oxygen for combustion, nutrients for life, straight lines for triangles. An A is a sufficient condition for B if the presence of A is a guarantee of B. Having been blown to little pieces is a sufficient condition for a person's death. Both necessary and sufficient conditions may be either logically necessary or logically contingent.
reductionist	A claim that a complex somewhat is really only something or somethings more simple. Thus: ghosts on the moors are really merely marsh gases; love is nothing more than sexual attraction; morality is only a matter of emotion.
subjectivism	A species of reductionism where all statements of the relevant discourse are translated into autobiographical remarks: e.g. 'stealing is wrong' means nothing more than, 'stealing upsets me, goodness gracious me, it does'.
synthetic	Opposite of 'analytic', q.v.
tautology	Repeating the same thing in different words.
truth value	The two main truth values are true and false. Other values are indeterminate, indeterminable, known to be true, certainly false, probably true and the like.
utilitarianism	The ethical doctrine that morally good actions are those which produce the greatest happiness for the greatest number. It is a doctrine which is interesting principally because of the rejoinders made by its many critics.
valid	Adjective applied to the patterns or forms of arguments. An argument is valid when, if its premises are true, its conclusion must be true. If it does not satisfy this condition it is invalid. The adjective is also used of legal procedures and formalities, for example, marriage, and has even been employed by disengaged persons who speak mysteriously of certain experiences as being very valid and deeply cosmic but this is some distance from its formal and original use.

Chronological Map

This chronological map has been compiled to help readers increase their knowledge of the period in which the Political Thinkers lived and to help locate them within a series of events. Some readers may find it enriching to reflect that their own ancestors lived through these times and were thus contemporaries of the people mentioned.

Plato
(chapter 1)
427–347B.C.

Homer c850fl. Thales c636–546. Aesop c550fl. Pythagoras c582–500. Buddha 560–480. Aeschylus 525–456 Sophocles 496–406. Pericles 495–429. Zeno 490–430. Herodotus 485–425. Euripides 480–406. Socrates 469–399. Aristophanes 450–380.

Battle of Marathon 490. Thermopylae Pass, Athens sacked, Sea Battle of Salamis 480. Periclean Golden Age 460–429. Peloponnesian War 431–404. Student of Socrates c.410. Socrates judicially killed 399. Rise of Macedon; Philip conquers Greece 338.

Aristotle
(chapter 2)
382–322B.C.

Student of Plato c365–347. Tutor to Alexander of Macedon 342. Founded Lyceum in Athens 335. Alexander defeats Persia 331. Hellenistic period. Euclid c300fl. Archimedes 287–212. Growth of Roman power. Great Wall of China built 210.

Augustine
(chapter 3)
353–430A.D.

Cicero 106–43B.C. Caesar 102–44. Lucretius 99–55. Virgil 70–19. Cruxifixion of Jesus of Nazareth 30A.D. Saul-Paul c.4B.C.–65A.D. Pax Romana 30B.C.–235A.D. Christianity legalized throughout Roman Empire 313. Christian convert Emperor Constantine inaugurates Constantinople, centre of western culture 330. Roman legions begin to leave Britain 383. Decline of Western Roman Empire. Goths sack Rome 410. Growth of spiritual outlook, monastic orders. Mohammed 570–632. Growth of Islam. Early Middle Ages. Increase in power of papacy.

Feudalism well established in western Europe c900. Golden Age of Muslim learning c900–1100. Norman Conquest of England 1066. First Crusade 1096. High Middle Ages. Foundation of Universities at Bologna c1140, Paris c1160, Oxford c1180. Thomas a'Beckett canonized 1173. Gothic Cathedrals from 1194 at Chartres, Rheims. Children's Crusade, 30,000 children from France and Germany set off for Holy Lands 1212. Magna Carta 1215.

Roger Bacon 1214–92.

Aquinas
(chapter 3)
c1225–74

Dante 1265–1321. Giotto 1266–1327. Petrach 1304–74. Wycliffe 1320–80. Huss 1369–1415.

Foundation of Franciscan Order 1212. Sixth Crusaders recapture Jerusalem 1228. De Montfort's Parliament 1265. Growth of merchants of Venice: Marco Polo returns from court of Kublai Khan 1295.

Black Death ravages Europe 1348. England v France Hundred Year War 1337–1453. Wat Tyler's Peasant Rebellion 1381. Chaucer begins *The Canterbury Tales* 1387. Florentine humanism grows 1397. Joan of Arc 1412–31.

Constantinople falls to Ottoman Turks, scholars flee to the West 1453. Renaissance. Printing by movable type, Gutenburg 1454. English Wars of Roses 1455–85.

Machiavelli
(chapter 4)
1469–1527

Leonardo da Vinci 1452–1519. Michelangelo 1475–1564. Raphael 1483–1520. Cellini 1500–71.

Lorenzo the Magnificent, ruler of Florence 1469–92. Spanish Inquisition established by Ferdinand and Isabella 1478. Christopher Columbus sails west 1492, dies in poverty 1506. Magellan circumnavigates the earth 1519. Alexander VI (Roderigo Borgia) Pope 1492–1503. Bull of Demarcation apportions New World between Portugal and Spain 1493. Savonarola burned 1498.

Luther
(chapter 5)
1483–1546

Copernicus 1473–1543. Thomas More 1478–1535. Knox 1505–72. Calvin 1509–64.

Luther's *95 Theses* 1517. Diet of Worms 1521. Spanish conquest of Mexico 1521, Peru 1531. Loyola founds Society of Jesus 1534. Henry VIII and Act of Supremacy 1534. Knox brings Reformation to Scotland 1541. Council of Trent 1545. English *Book of Common Prayer* 1549. Queen 'Bloody' Mary burns Archbishop Cramner 1556. Battle of Lepanto finishes Turkish predominance in Meditteranean Sea 1571.

St Bartholemew's Day massacre of Huguenots 1572. Dutch Protestants continue fight for independence from Spain 1581. Gregorian calendar 1582.

Hobbes
(chapter 6)
1588–1679

Francis Bacon 1561–1626. Brahe 1546–1601. Galileo 1564–1642. Kepler 1571–1630. Descartes 1590–1650. Marlowe 1564–93. Shakespeare 1564–1616. Rubens 1577–1640. Velazquez 1599–1660.

Spanish Armada defeated 1588. Elizabeth I grants charter to English East India Company 1600. Guy Fawkes Conspiracy 1605. King James authorizes new translation of Bible and advocates Divine Right of Kings 1611. Czar Michael Romanov founds Romanov dynasty 1613. First negro slaves arrive in Virginia 1619. Pilgrim Fathers ex *Mayflower* reach Cape Cod 1620. James I dissolves Parliament for claiming a right to debate foreign affairs 1622. Execution of Christian missionaries in Japan reaches its height 1624. Charles I dissolves Parliament for failing to vote him money 1625. Charles I accepts Parliament's statement of civil rights in return for money 1628. William Harvey demonstrates circulation of the blood 1628. Charles I fails in attempt to arrest five members in Parliament. English Civil War. Rise of Cromwell and Parliament 1642. Charles I executed. Rise of Cromwell 1649. Serfdom completely established in Russia 1650. Charles II restored to English throne 1660. English acquire Bombay 1661. Great Plague in London 1665. Great Fire of London 1666.

Locke
(chapter 7)
1632–1704

Milton 1608–74. Molière 1622–73. Bunyan 1628–88. Racine 1639–99. Defoe 1660–1731. Rembrandt 1606–69. Boyle 1627–91. Spinoza 1632–77. Hooke 1635–1703. Leibniz 1646–1716. Newton 1642–1727.

First American parliament meets at Jamestown, Virginia 1619. Capetown founded by Dutch 1652, Convention Parliament restores Charles II 1660. Test Act aimed at depriving English Roman Catholics and Nonconformists of public office 1673. Habeas Corpus Bill passed; Bill of Exclusion blocked by Charles II who dismissed Parliament. King rejects petitions for a new Parliament 1679. Petitioners called 'Whigs', royalists 'Tories'. James II disregards Test Act 1686. England's 'Glorious and Bloodless Revolution' creates a limited and contractual monarchy 1688. Witchcraft trials in Salem New England 1692. Isaac Newton publishes *Optics* 1704.

Hume
(chapter 8)
1711–76

Defoe 1660–1731. Swift 1667–1745. Congreve 1670–1729. Handel 1685–1759. Pope 1688–1744. Richardson 1689–1761. Hogarth 1697–1764. Fielding 1707–54. Johnson 1709–84. Gray 1716–71. Reynolds 1723–92. Adam Smith 1723–90.

Peter the Great, Czar 1689–1725, modernizer of Russia. Robert Walpole first British Prime Minister 1721–42 John Wesley founds Methodism movement 1739. Britain takes Quebec from French 1759. Manchus from Manchuria oust the Mings in China; hegemony extended to Korea, Mongolia, Indo-China.

Hargreaves invents spinning jenny 1764. Mason-Dixon line separates free states from slave states 1767. James Cook begins his first Endeavour voyage 1768. Priestly isolates ammonia 1774.

Rousseau
(chapter 9)
1712–78

Vivaldi 1678–1741. Rameau 1683–1764. Watteau 1684–1721. Couperin 1688–1750. Montesquieu 1689–1755. Voltaire 1694–1778. Diderot 1713–84. Helvetius 1715–71. Kant 1724–1804. Marquis de Sade 1740–1814. Lavoisier 1743–94. Blake 1757–1827.

Growth of European, especially British, slave trade from 1713. South Sea Bubble 1720.

First family pact between the Bourbons of France and of Spain 1733. Montesquieu's *The Spirit of the Laws* published 1748. First parts of *Encylopédie* published 1751. Seven Years' War (1756–63) ends; Treaty of Paris strengthens Britain. Watt invents condensing steam engine 1765. Antoine Baume invents hydrometer 1768. Louis XVI King of France 1774.

Russia gains entry to Black Sea ports 1774. France supports colonists in American War of Independence 1778. Emperor Napoleon dissolves Holy Roman Empire 1806.

Burke
(chapter 10)
1729–97

Handel 1685–1759. Haydn 1732–1809. Mozart 1756–91. Beethoven 1770–1827. Sheridan 1751–1816. Scott 1771–1832. Jane Austen 1775–1817. Turner 1775–1851.

Catherine the Great makes Russia a major European power 1762–96. Warren Hastings, Governor of Bengal, appointed first Governor General of India 1774. American Revolution 1775–83. First convicts from Britain transported to Australia 1778. French Revolution, Bastille stormed 1789. Thomas Saint invents sewing machine 1790. Radical phase of French Revolution: rise of Jacobins Marat, Danton and Robespierre. Republic declared 1792. Louis XVI executed, Reign of Terror begins, compulsory national service introduced 1793. First free settlers arrive in Australia 1793. Robespierre executed 1794. Edward Jenner performs first vaccination 1796. End of Japanese policy of isolation 1797.

Paine
(chapter 11)
1737–1809

George Washington 1732–99. Thomas Jefferson 1743–1826. Alexander Hamilton 1757–1804. William Cobbett 1763–1835. Wordsworth 1770–1850.

Benjamin Franklin experiments with electricity in a thunderstorm 1752. Boston Tea Party 1773. British Parliament passes a series of repressive Acts against Northern American colonies 1774.

United States Declaration of Independence 1776. United States Constitution adopted 1789. Tennis Court Oath 1789. Committee of Public Safety ensures rights for revolutionaries 1793. Malthus' 'Essay on the Principle of Population' 1798. Alessandro Volta produces first electric battery 1800. Act of Union formally unites Great Britain and Ireland as United Kingdom 1801. Bonaparte crowns himself Napoleon I, Emperor of the French 1804. Slave trade abolished in British Empire 1807.

Hegel
(chapter 12)
1770–1831

Goethe 1749–1832. Schiller 1759–1805. Schubert 1797–1828. Heine 1797–1856. Pushkin 1799–1837. Wagner 1813–83. Bismarck 1815–98.

Russia conquers the Crimea 1771. Pope Clement XIV suppresses Jesuits 1773. India Act gives British control in India 1783. Napoleon sells Louisiana to the United States 1803. Argentina, Paraguay and Venezuela independent 1811.

Zulu empire founded in South Africa 1818. Zollverein (customs union) begins in Germany under influence of Prussia 1819.

Greek War of Independence 1821–29. Monroe Doctrine 1823. First passenger steam railway open 1830. Revolts in Poland crushed by Russia, revolts in Modena, Parma and Papal States put down by Austria. Leopold of Saxe-Coburg becomes Leopold I, King of the Belgians 1831.

Mill
(chapter 13)
1806–73

Jeremy Bentham 1748–1832. Turner 1775–1851. Constable 1776–1837. Darwin 1809–82. Tennyson 1809–92. Dickens 1812–70. George Eliot 1819–80. Victoria, Queen of Britain 1837–1901. G.B. Shaw 1856–1950.

Luddite riots in England against mechanization 1811. Repressive anti-workers legislation introduced in England 1812. Battle of Waterloo 1815. Peterloo massacre 1819. Singapore founded by British administrator Stanford Raffles 1819. Aspdin invents Portland cement 1824. Catholic Emancipation Act 1829. Reform extends franchise to middle class in Britain 1832. Slavery abolished in British colonies; Act forbids employment of children under nine in factories 1833. Tolpuddle Martyrs 1834. Chartist movement begins 1836. Opium War 1839–42. Potato famine reaches height in Ireland 1846. First Maori War 1847. Californian Gold Rush 1848.

Indian Mutiny 1857. *On Liberty* and *Origin of Species* published 1859. Italy unified 1861. American Civil War 1861–65. Suez Canal opened 1869. German Empire formed 1871. Queen Victoria proclaimed Empress of India 1877.

Marx
(chapter 14)
1818–83

Wagner 1813–83. Engels 1820–95. Dostoevsky 1821–81. Ibsen 1828–1906. Tolstoy 1828–1910. Borodin 1833–87. Zola 1840–1902. Nietzsche 1844–1900. Lenin 1870–1924.

Liberia, West Africa, founded as a colony for freed American slaves 1822. Blast furnace invented 1828. Harvester invented 1834. Famine Migration from Ireland begins 1845. Revolutions in Paris, Milan, Naples, Venice, Rome, Berlin, Vienna, Prague, Budapest, Tipperary 1848. *The Communist Manifesto* written by Marx and Engels 1848. Crimean War 1854–56. British and French occupy Peking 1860. Oil drilled in Pennsylvania 1859. Expedition of British, Dutch, French and Americans bombards Shimonoseki, Japan 1864. Marx founds First International in London 1864. First Vatican Council asserts Papal Infallibility 1869–70. Trade unions legalized in Britain 1871. Paris Commune 1871. Barbed wire invented 1873. Battle of Little Big Horn 1876. Telephone invented 1876. Berlin Conference agrees upon European powers' 'spheres of influence' in Africa 1885; partition completed 1895.

Twentieth Century
(chapter 15)

Freud 1856–1939. Proust 1871–1922. Weber 1864–1920. Gandhi 1869–1948. Russell 1872–1970. Einstein 1879–1955. Stravinsky 1882–1971. Kafka 1883–1924. Keynes 1883–1946. Gershwin 1898–1937. Brecht 1898–1956. Hemingway 1899–1961. Ryle 1900–76. Orwell 1903–50. Sartre 1905–80. Berlin 1909–; Koestler 1905–84. Solzhenitsyn 1918–; Sakharov 1921–; Rawls 1921–; Nozick 1938–.

Motor car engine 1887. Wireless telegraphs 1895. Boxer rebellion 1900. Radio telephone 1902. Aeroplane 1903. Japan wins Russo-Japanese war 1905. First Labour M.Ps. to House of Commons 1906. Sun Yat-sen revolution overthrows Manchu dynasty 1912. First World War 1914–18. Russian Revolution 1917. League of Nations formed 1919. Civil War in Ireland 1919. Jewish State Palestine formed 1920. Prohibition of alcoholic drinks in USA 1920 (until 1933). USSR established 1922. Egypt gains independence from Britain and France 1922. British Broadcasting Corporation founded 1922. Fascist Mussolini dictator of Italy, 1923. Death of Lenin, succession of Stalin 1924 (until 1953). Television 1925. Fleming discovers pencillin 1928. Wall Street collapse 1929.

Adolf Hitler Chancellor of Germany 1933. Stalin's purge of Communist party begins 1933. Hitler Führer of Germany 1934. Mao's Long March 1934. (until 1936). German planes bomb Guernica, Spain, 1937. Japanese capture Shanghai and Peking, 1938. Germany invades Poland 1 September 1939, beginning of Second World War. Nuremberg War Crimes Trial 1946. Ghastly extent of holocaust emerges. India gains independence, Pakistan formed, 1947. United Nations declaration asserts that all humans have rights 1947. State of Israel declared 1948. South African government adopts apartheid as official policy, 1949. Mao establishes Communist regime in China 1949. Germany divided 1949.

McCarthy inquiries into 'un-American activities' 1950. Campaign for nuclear-disarmament blasts off, 1952. Korean War 1953. Watson and Crick discover DNA's binary structure 1953. Opposition to capital punishment strengthens, Soviet Premier Khrushchev denounces former Premier Stalin 1956. Treaty of Rome forms EEC 1957. Hungarian uprising crushed by USSR 1956. Soviet Union's 'Sputnik' 1957. Castro defeats dictator Batista in Cuba, 1954. Chinese crush Tibetan revolt 1959.

Seventeen colonies in Africa gain independence 1960. Antarctica reserved for scientific research; all territorial claims waived 1960. Contraceptive pills available 1960. Women's Liberation movements gained momentum. Berlin Wall built 1961. Soviet cosmonaut Gargarin first man in space 1961. Vatican Council II 1962–65. Cultural Revolution in China begins 1966 to 1969. US military involvement in Vietnam grows 1964. Environmentalist movement escalates 1966. Military coup in Greece 1967. Student revolutions begun in Paris, lead to world wide questioning of educational procedures 1968. Soviet troops invade Czechoslovakia 1968.

Britain sends troops to Northern Ireland; USA invades Cambodia 1970. International terrorism increases. China joins United Nations. Formosa expelled 1971. South Vietnam surrenders to North Vietnam, end of war 1975, fighting continues in Cambodia. Concern for welfare of animals grows. Race riots in South Africa 1976. Death of Mao. Jimmy Carter inaugurated as US President 1977. Zimbabwe independence 1978. Oil crisis sparks economic crises 1978. Margaret Thatcher UK Conservative Prime Minister 1979. Pope John Paul II visits Poland, Ireland, USA and Latin America 1979. Ayatollah Khomeni sole leader of revolution in Iran 1979.

USSR invades Afghanistan 1980. US spacecraft 'Voyager I' takes close range photographs of Saturn 1980. Ronald Reagan inaugurated as US President 1981. Martial law in Poland, Solidarity movement grows 1981. Socialist Mitterand elected Premier of France 1981. Widespread famine in Africa 1982. Falklands war 1983. US invades Grenada, 1983. P.M. of India, Indira Gandhi, assassinated; succeeded by son, Rajiv 1984. Star Wars strategy 1984. Bishop Tutu appointed to see of Johannesburg. Gorbachev succeeds Chernenko to USSR leadership 1985–   . Microchippery continues.

Index